P9-DEO-354

Language
Development

LINCOLN CHRISTIAN COLLEGE

Language Development
Structure and Function

PHILIP S. DALE
University of Washington, Seattle

THE DRYDEN PRESS INC.
Hinsdale, Illinois

for Jonathan,
who knows more about this than I do

Copyright © 1972 by The Dryden Press Inc.
All Rights Reserved
Library of Congress Catalog Card Number: 72-79742
ISBN: 0-03-089137-X
Printed in the United States of America
6789   090   9

401.9
D13

Twinston

Preface

The past decade has been an exciting one for the study of language development. It has been a period of ferment, as major developments such as generative grammar and the revival of cognitive psychology have come together to face one of the most difficult problems in the study of human behavior; understanding language development. To be sure, the result of this ferment has been the growing realization that we do not understand the process very well; even less than we thought.

I have, in this book, attempted to indicate how recent research has sharpened many of the key questions and to give some idea of the kinds of research that offer some promise in the search for answers. Under the heading of "key questions" I would include, among others: What kind of capacities do children have for learning language? Is there an innate capacity for language? How do mothers talk to, and with, their children? What kind of changes occur in a child's language from stage to stage? Is reading essentially a process of translation from printed symbols into spoken language? What is the nature of dialect differences

54864

in our society, and how do they affect the educational process? The Appendix of this book, which contains a few examples of investigations which the reader might undertake, has as its goal the conversion of the student from a passive observer to an active investigator. More important than suggesting specific techniques, I hope that the book will encourage the reader to see language development as a fascinating puzzle, one worth the effort of exploring.

An annoying factor that has prevented better communication among the various fields interested in child language — psychology, linguistics, speech, and education, among others — is the tendency of each discipline to develop its own terminology, its own theories, and its own journals. This book grew out of a course at the University of Washington which brings together students from all these fields. I attempt to serve as an interpreter in that course by eliminating jargon where possible and by defining the necessary technical terms of each discipline. And the book is written in that spirit.

Every book is a collaboration, this one more than most. I am deeply indebted to my teachers, colleagues, and students for the opportunity to develop in the give and take of dialogue my own thinking on the difficult questions of language development. Several served above and beyond the call of duty by reading and commenting on earlier drafts of this book. I am especially grateful to Sidney Culbert, Nancy Jackson, Ken Kaye, Susan Kaye, and Wendy Shelton; it is a better book thanks to their help. But the final responsibility for the content must be laid to my own obstinacy.

Last, and perhaps most important, my thanks to Cindy Howarth for her efficiency and toleration of an erratic schedule and all but unintelligible manuscript; and to my wife, Beverly, for her support, skeptical reading of drafts, and patience.

Philip Dale
University of Washington

Seattle, Washington
February, 1972

Contents

Language
Development

The Structure of Language

Children and Language

The question "How do children learn to talk?" has fascinated men for centuries. In Reading 1.1 Herodotus (writing in the fifth century B.C.) reports on some "research" carried out by the Egyptian king Psammetichus I sometime before 610 B.C. Although the methodology of this experiment is dubious both scientifically and ethically, it illustrates the hold of this question and the belief that understanding the origin of language would illuminate the nature of man.

For many years the question of language learning was primarily a matter of philosophical speculation; empirical research did not begin until the late nineteenth century. However, as we will see, the philosophers did raise many of the important questions considered today.

In the decade 1960–1970, the study of language development, and our understanding of this achievement, changed greatly. Two fundamental insights underlie the work of the period. The first was the realization that the child does not merely speak a garbled version of the adult language around him, handicapped by limited attention and memory span and other psychological deficits. Rather, he speaks his own language, with its own characteristic patterns, about as consistently as an adult does his — which is, of course, not perfectly. Thus it became appropriate to study a child as the speaker of an exotic language, to describe its structure with a *grammar* — that is, an explicit statement of the patterns, or rules, of the language — and to observe the sequence of changes in the child's language as he brings it into closer approximation to the surrounding adult language.

This concept represents a significant contrast with earlier approaches to the study of language development in which the framework of adult language was imposed on the child's language. The earlier research focused on deviations from adult patterns (which were simply viewed as errors) and their extinction; the size of the vocabulary (often classified into adult categories) without consideration of the actual pattern of use by the child; and the set of sounds produced, as opposed to the distinctions drawn between them in the child's sound system.

The second insight was that the child himself must act as a linguist: he is faced with a finite set of utterances, many of them ungrammatical (due to slips of the tongue, false starts, memory lapses, and so on), from which he must extract the underlying rules in order to be able to use the language creatively for the remainder of his life. Therefore, it becomes fruitful to look for analogies between the child's performance on this task and the linguist's performance. Two striking analogies have been suggested. The first is that language learning, both for the child and for the linguist, is a matter of **hypothesis-formation** and **hypothesis-testing.** In other words, it is an active process. The child continually formulates hypotheses about underlying rules of the language he hears and tests them by attempting to use them to understand speech and also to construct his own utterances. Such hypothesis-formulation is shown most vividly by what appear to be grammatical mistakes, for example, a child's utterances of *comed* or *doed*. Because such utterances cannot be the result of imitation, their production demonstrates that the child has arrived at an hypothesis: past tense forms are produced by adding *ed*.

A second analogy is even more far-reaching (as well as somewhat controversial). Although the languages of the world

appear to be highly diverse on the surface, recent linguistic research has demonstrated remarkable similarities. And, in fact,
whether consciously formulated or not, such similarities are in
the mind of the linguist when he approaches a new language and
guide his analysis. For example, in analyzing a new language a
linguist knows that certain aspects of speech sound production
are likely to be important (where the tongue is, whether the
passage to the nasal cavity is open and so on); that there will be
subjects and predicates; that it will be possible to ask questions,
give commands, deny statements, and more. Similarly, the child
may "know" about certain aspects of language — in other words,
the knowledge is innate — and these aspects do not have to be
learned in the usual sense.

Linguistics thus plays a doubly important role; first, in the
empirical study of child language and, second, in the task of
constructing theoretical explanations of language acquisition.
For this reason, this first chapter is an introduction to linguistics.
The following six chapters describe child language, its regularities
and development, and some attempts to explain the process of
development. Midway in Chapter 7 the focus changes from the
structure of language and its acquisition to the functions of language and their developing competence. Reading, communication, dialect differences, and early education might be viewed as
"applied" questions; but, in fact, they all raise issues that are
essential to an understanding of the development of the child.

Language as Rule-Governed Behavior

Imagine tying a necktie, if you are a man, or brushing your
hair, if you are a woman. Now try to explain exactly how you do it.
To keep the game honest, clasp your hands together in front of
you so you cannot simply demonstrate the action. It is all but
impossible to explain the process.

Language has this elusive I-can-do-it-but-I-cannot-tell-
you-how property. As human beings, we spend a large proportion of our time engaged in speaking or listening; but the process
is usually so effortless that we are unaware of how we do it. In
this chapter we will attempt to stand back and examine this
activity that permeates our lives.

We will begin with two of the most important facts about
language. First, **a language is a productive system.** In other
words, using a language is a creative act. The overwhelming

majority of all the sentences that a person utters or hears are novel. They have not occurred in his experience. For example, there are over five thousand sentences in this book, and no two are identical. This does not mean that sentences are never repeated. Many standard formulas — such as, *How are you?* — are repeated thousands of times in a lifetime, but they are clearly exceptional.

Although the set of words of a language, its **vocabulary,** or **lexicon,** is finite, the number of possible sentences in a language is unlimited. There are just so many words, and it is possible to construct a list of them. But there is no limit to the number of sentences or to their length. From any English sentence, a new and longer sentence may be created by adding *and the moon is not made of green cheese* to the end, or adding *I think that* to the beginning. There are dictionaries of words of English, but no dictionaries of sentences. To say that a person knows a language means that he is able to understand any sentence of the language (assuming he knows the meanings of the words used). But he cannot have learned these sentences as a list; he must have mastered some set of principles which specifies how words can be combined to form sentences. Because the human mind is finite, a human being can learn only a finite amount. In other words, with a finite amount of knowledge, a speaker of a language[1] can understand or produce an unlimited number of sentences if he knows the principles of combining words meaningfully.

This may seem somewhat paradoxical, but in fact it is not unusual. For example, to know how to multiply means we know how to obtain the product of any number with any number. One way to multiply would be to refer to a table of the products of all possible pairs of numbers. Such a table would be very easy to use, but infinitely long because there is an unlimited number of numbers. It would also be impossible to learn. Instead, we multiply using a short (one hundred entry) multiplication table:

$$3 \times 4 = 12$$
$$3 \times 5 = 15$$
$$3 \times 6 = 18$$

and so on, and a relatively short set of rules for using the table:

---

[1]"Speaker of a language" is merely a shorthand term. It does not mean that speaking is the most important language function or even that speaking and understanding are completely distinct activities.

1. Multiply the rightmost digit of one number by the rightmost digit of the second.
2. Then multiply the rightmost digit of one number by the next to rightmost digit of the second and move the product one place to the right.
3. And so on until each digit of each number has been multiplied by each digit of the other, moving the product an appropriate number of places to the left.
4. Add all the resulting products.

Once the table and rules have been mastered, we are prepared for any possible multiplication problem, not just the ones that have been practiced. It is in this sense that a speaker of a language, equipped with only a finite amount of knowledge, can understand or produce any of an unlimited number of sentences.

Second, **many** (perhaps most) **of the utterances encountered in normal conversation are not perfectly grammatical.** There are slips of the tongue, changes of topic in midsentence, false starts, forgetting the subject of the sentence by the time the verb rolls around, and more. The child who is acquiring language, therefore, is not even presented with very high quality information.

These two facts imply that language consists essentially of a set of patterns, or **rules** — rules that can be applied in situations that are not identical to those in which they were learned and rules that can be violated.

The behavioral sciences, other than linguistics, have not used the concept of rule-governed behavior, and it is easily (and often) misunderstood. The business of linguistics is to *describe* language, not to *prescribe* it. Linguists tell us *how* we talk, not how we *should* talk. The rules comprising a language are not the same as the rules of grammar, like a high school teacher telling a student when to use *whom* and when to use *who*.

The phrase **grammatical sentence** occurs over and over again in this book and in the literature of linguistics. Linguists do not decide for other people whether sentences are grammatical or not. They want to know which strings of words are grammatical sentences for the speakers of a language and which are not. Grammatical sentences and ungrammatical ones are the raw data of linguistics, not the result. For example, any speaker of English can recognize that *Wash your hands* is a well-formed sentence in a sense that *Your wash hands* is not. *I play the flute* is correct in a sense that *Flute I the play* is not. There is a large (in fact unlimited) number of word strings that are well formed, or grammatical; and a large (again, unlimited) number of strings that are not. And, of course, there are the inevitable fuzzy cases in between. This is all linguists mean by "grammatical" and "ungrammatical." Their task is to determine what it is that makes some strings grammatical and some not. There must be some underlying system, because each speaker can have only a finite amount of knowledge.

If it is true, as was claimed at the beginning of this chapter, that not all sentences produced by speakers actually follow the rules, that is, that many of them are ungrammatical, what kind of reality do these rules have? It is easier to answer this question for the case of multiplication. Although a person may know the principles for multiplying two numbers, he will in fact occasionally (or often) make mistakes in multiplying, especially if the numbers are large. Suppose a person can correctly multiply any two 2-digit numbers in his head but not any two 8-digit numbers. Would we say that he knows how to multiply only 2-digit numbers and not 8-digit numbers? That would be unnatural; it would be more reasonable to say that he knows *how to multiply any two numbers*, but when the numbers are large and many steps are involved, he is likely to make mistakes. Additional support for this view is the fact that given enough time, and paper and pencil, he can probably multiply two 8-digit numbers accurately.

The same principle holds for language. People make mistakes for a variety of reasons. Perhaps a speaker is tired or distracted. Although the speaker has knowledge of the principles that define grammatical sentences, he may not use this knowledge without error. This is the foundation of the important distinction between linguistic competence and linguistic performance. **Linguistic competence** is the set of principles which a person must have in order to be a speaker of a language. **Linguistic performance** is the translation of this knowledge into action. Linguists are concerned with competence. Performance involves many factors, including competence, memory, distraction, perception, and others. These are essentially psychological in nature, and therefore performance is the subject matter of the psychologist. Multiplicative competence consists of knowledge of the rules of multiplication; multiplicative performance is the actual work of multiplying. Obviously the rules for multiplying are involved in the work, but so are many other factors, such as fatigue, distraction, and memory.

There is one very important difference between multiplicative competence and linguistic competence. Anyone who can multiply can state explicitly the rules he uses. They are part of his conscious knowledge. This is not the case with language. In general, speakers of a language cannot state the rules of their language. It is the goal of linguistics to formulate them. Linguistic competence is, then an example of *tacit knowledge*.

Grammars

A grammar is essentially a theory. Like any other scientific theory, it attempts to explain some domain of natural phenomena. In the case of a theory called "a grammar," the natural phenomena is *the knowledge of a language that is possessed by every native speaker of any language*. This includes knowledge about which utterances are grammatical sentences and which are not (*His authority persuaded John* or *John persuaded his authority*); which sentences are ambiguous (*Visiting relatives can be a nuisance);* which sentences have the same meaning as other sentences (*Silas Marner counted the gold* and *The gold was counted by Silas Marner*), and more. Furthermore, like any scientific theory, it must be *explicit:* it must clearly and unambiguously lead to testable predictions. In the case of a grammar, the predictions include, among others, statements about which strings of words are grammatical sentences and which are not. It is the requirement of explicitness that leads, in linguistics as in many other sciences, to the expression of theories in symbolic form.

Sentence Structure

CONSTITUENT STRUCTURE

What is it that makes some utterances grammatical English sentences and some ungrammatical? Before we can answer that question we must look closely at the thing called a "sentence." We can say, "a sentence is made up of smaller units, or words." For example, *I see her* is composed of three words, *I, see,* and *her.* But, many words themselves consist of two or more smaller units, each making a contribution to the meaning of the sentence. The word *walked,* for example, consists of two units; *walk,* which is a word referring to a particular kind of action, and the ending *-ed,* which indicates that the action took place in the past. Although the -*ed* ending cannot stand by itself, it is a distinct unit, or element, and can be combined with almost any verb. Similarly, *troubleshooter* consists of three distinct elements, *trouble*, *shoot*, and -*er*, and the meaning of the word is a composite of the meanings of its three basic elements. These basic elements of meaning are called **morphemes.**

Using the concept of a morpheme, we can now attempt a definition of a sentence: **A sentence is a collection of morphemes.** Some collections are acceptable (that is, they are grammatical sentences) while others are not acceptable (ungrammatical sentences). Now let us compare the sentence *John loves Mary* with *Mary loves John*. They consist of exactly the same morphemes, but their meanings are quite distinct. The difference in meaning is signaled by the difference in **order.**

So now we see that we must take order into account in the definition of a sentence: **a sentence is an ordered string of morphemes.** But, although this is an improvement, it too misses aspects that are important about sentences. Perhaps most important is the way in which sentences seem to break up into **subunits,** or **clusters.** Often a given ordered string of morphemes is **ambiguous,** that is, it corresponds to *two* meanings. For example, *They are eating apples* is ambiguous. One sentence is a statement about some apples; the other is a statement about the activity of several individuals. The two meanings appear to correspond to two ways of breaking up the sentence. In the first, *eating* and *apples* form one unit, and *are* comprises another; in the second, *are* and *eating* form one unit, and *apples* comprises another.

Let's look more closely at this process of dividing sentences. Consider the sentence *The old woman saw a small boy*. (We will return to *They are eating apples* shortly.) The sentence consists of a string of seven words, arranged in a particular order. In addition, the words of the sentence fall into groups, or clusters, which speakers of English have little difficulty in recognizing. Suppose you were asked to divide this sentence into two parts in the way that seemed most natural to you. Would you produce

The   old woman saw a small boy

or

The old woman saw a small   boy

Probably neither; instead you would undoubtedly divide the string into

the old woman   saw a small boy.

There is something in this string of words which enables you to make this division. If, instead, you were given the string

brick ham cloud girl dog water tree

which is also an ordered string of seven items, and were asked to divide it naturally, you would have no idea of how to do it. Probably everyone would do it differently. The difference between *The old woman saw a small boy* and *brick ham cloud girl dog water tree* is that the sentence has **structure:** There are natural subunits in the sentence, clusters of words that go together.

One way of indicating how words are clustered in a sentence is to diagram them:

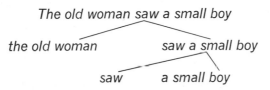

Going further, suppose you were asked to divide the string *saw a small boy* into two clusters. The most likely answer would be *saw* and *a small boy*. The diagram would then look like this:

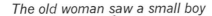

Since diagrams like this begin to look like upside-down trees, minus trunks, they are called **tree diagrams.**

The clusters of words into which a sentence can be divided in this way are called the **constituents** of the sentence. We have found four constituents so far: *the old woman, saw a small boy, saw,* and *a small boy*. The example can be continued by dividing *the old woman* into two parts; *the* and *old woman*. *Old woman* can be divided into *old* and *woman*. *A small boy* can be divided into *a* and *small boy*. Finally, *small boy* yields *small* and *boy*. Keeping track of all these divisions in a tree diagram produces:

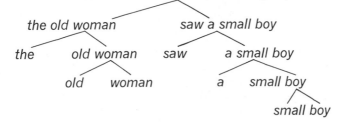

For the sake of completeness, the entire sentence is also considered to be a constituent. Counting it, we have a total of thirteen constituents. Notice that many of the constituents are made up of smaller constituents and, themselves, are part of larger constituents. *A small boy*, for example, is made up of *a* and *small boy* and is part of *saw a small boy*. This kind of structure is called **hierarchical structure.** The fact that language has hierarchical structure is one of its most important properties, for it allows unlimited elaboration of detail to be combined into a coherent structure.

Looking over the thirteen constituents of our sentence, there appear to be some similarities and some differences among them. The constituent *the old woman* seems to be similar to the constituent *a small boy* and *the* seems to be similar to *a*, in a way that is not true of *the* and *small boy*. One way to check if two constituents are of the same general type is to try substitution. To do this, replace each constituent with the other and see if the resulting string of words is a grammatical sentence. For example switching *the* and *small boy*, we have *small boy old woman saw a the* which is not a grammatical sentence. But if we switch *the old woman* and *a small boy*, we have *a small boy saw the old woman*, which is grammatical. In this way we can determine the basic types of constituents.[2]

We have just analyzed the **constituent structure,** that is, the set of constituents and how they are combined, of one sentence. Now let us consider these sentences.

1. My new radio makes an unpleasant noise.
2. The big turkey gobbled his last meal.

These sentences have the same constituent structure as *The old woman saw a small boy:*

1. *My new radio makes an unpleasant noise*

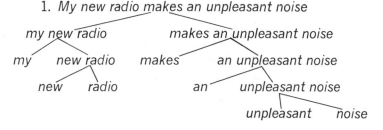

---

[2]The substitution test is not perfectly reliable, and other techniques must be used in many cases. As an example of the inadequacy of the substitution test, consider the sentences *Falstaff drank hot buttered rum* and *Falstaff drank incessantly* (from Jacobs and Rosenbaum, 1968). The constituents *hot buttered rum* and *incessantly* can be substituted for each other in these sentences, but they are not the same type of constituent and cannot be substituted in the frame *I think I'll have another mug of . . .*

2. *The big turkey gobbled his last meal*

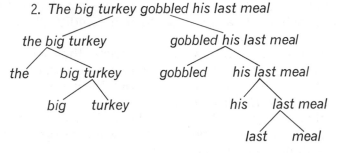

This similarity of structure suggests part of the answer to our question: What makes a string of words a grammatical sentence? The answer is, *if a string of words has a correct English constituent structure, it is a grammatical sentence.* If it violates English constituent structure, it is ungrammatical.

Knowing the constituent structure of a sentence is necessary in order to determine the meaning of the sentence as well as whether or not it is grammatical. Not only must the hearer perceive all the words of the sentence, he must determine the constituent structure to know how the meanings of the individual items are to be combined to form the meanings of the sentence. Now we should be able to understand some kinds of *ambiguity* better. Let us now consider again the sentence *They are eating apples.* The two meanings, one about apples and one about people, correspond to the two constituent structures this sentence can have:

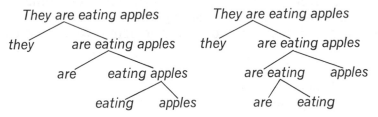

This ambiguity is not due to a difference in words or in the order of words but, rather, to a difference in constituent structure. Another example is the phrase *little girl's bike.* If it is divided (*little girl's*)(*bike*), it refers to a bike which belongs to a little girl. If it is divided (*little*)(*girl's bike*), it refers to a girl's bike that is little.

PHRASE-STRUCTURE GRAMMAR

We have been examining a few English sentences and their properties. But looking at individual sentences will not lead to a complete theory of English because there is an unlimited number of sentences in English. We want to describe the knowledge that speakers of English must have in order to create and understand these sentences.

We have just seen that one characteristic that seems to distinguish sentences from nonsentences has to do with the constituent structure of the sentence, that is, with the way the words are grouped together. How can we represent this in a grammar? Remember, that the goal is to have a theory that explicitly indicates, among other things, which strings of words are grammatical English sentences and which are not.

When we considered the constituent structure of sentences, we saw that there are characteristic ways in which the various kinds of constituents can be further divided. And this is the basic principle we will use.

Each type of constituent in a sentence has a characteristic name, which is usually represented symbolically. Constituents such as *the old woman* and *a small boy* are called **noun phrases** (NP). Constituents such as *saw a small boy* are called **verb phrases** (VP). Individual words, which are themselves constituents, are also labeled: *the* and *a* are **articles** (Art), *old* and *small* are **adjectives** (Adj), and *saw* is a **verb** (V). And we will use S to represent "sentence." We can now say that a sentence (S) consists of a noun phrase (NP), and a verb phrase (VP), and we can write this:

PS1.1[3] $S \rightarrow NP + VP$

where the arrow is read "may be written." A noun phrase is an article followed by an adjective followed by a noun. Of course, some noun phrases do not contain an adjective. We can write this:

PS1.2 $NP \rightarrow Art + (Adj) + N$

where ( ) means "optional."

A verb phrase is a verb followed by a noun phrase:

PS1.3 $VP \rightarrow V + NP$

Some possible nouns are *man, dog*, and *cat:*

PS1.4 $N \rightarrow \begin{bmatrix} man \\ dog \\ cat \end{bmatrix}$

---

[3]PS is an abbreviation for "phrase structure." When it appears in front of a rule, it designates a "phrase-structure rule." The rules are double-numbered by chapter.

where { } means "any one of these." Some possible verbs are *saw* and *heard:*

PS1.5 $V \rightarrow \begin{Bmatrix} saw \\ heard \end{Bmatrix}$

Some possible adjectives are *young* and *black:*

PS1.6 $Adj \rightarrow \begin{Bmatrix} young \\ black \end{Bmatrix}$

And some possible articles are *the* and *a:*

PS1.7 $Art \rightarrow \begin{Bmatrix} the \\ a \end{Bmatrix}$

This set of seven statements is a **phrase-structure** grammar. ("Phrase" here means about same thing as "constituent.") It indicates that certain strings of words are sentences. It does this by:

   i. starting with S (sentence)
   ii. interpreting the arrows as instructions to rewrite; that is, S may be rewritten as NP + VP
   iii. and continuing in this way until the string of symbols has been replaced by a string of words. For example:

S		
1.	NP + VP	PS1.1
2.	NP + V + NP	PS1.3
3.	Art + N + V + NP	PS1.2 (without option)
4.	Art + N + V + Art + Adj + N	PS1.2 (with option)
5.	*The* + N + V + Art + Adj + N	PS1.7
6.	*The* + *man* + V + Art + Adj + N	PS1.4
7.	*The* + *man* + *saw* + Art + Adj + N	PS1.5
8.	*The* + *man* + *saw* + *a* + Adj + N	PS1.7
9.	*The* + *man* + *saw* + *a* + *black* + N	PS1.6
10.	*The* + *man* + *saw* + *a* + *black* + *cat*	PS1.4

Keeping a record of the steps involved in this process is called a **derivation.** From the derivation, we are able to produce the proper tree diagram:

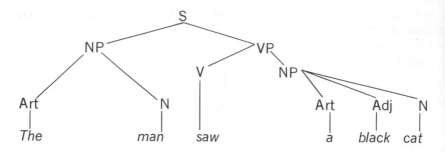

This phrase-structure grammar we have constructed is a theory of English. It indicates which strings of words are English sentences; namely, those strings which can be produced by the mechanical procedure we used to derive *The man saw a black cat*. There are in all eighty-nine sentences that can be derived using this set of seven rules, including *The dog heard the cat*, *The cat heard the young man*, and others. Notice that just seven rules generate eighty-nine sentences. Furthermore, this grammar indicates the constituent structure of these sentences.

However, this grammar is not a very complete theory of English. It only produces only a small number of quite simple sentences. But the grammar can be expanded to produce more sentences, of more varied structure, by adding rules and modifying the existing ones. The most obvious expansion would be the addition of vocabulary items. Simply adding one adjective to PS1.6 will result in the production of 267 additional sentences.

But adding new vocabulary items will not lead to the derivation of sentences in which there is no object, such as *The man fell*. A simple way to do this would be to first change PS1.3:

PS1.3   VP → V + NP
PS1.3a   VP → V + (NP)

making the inclusion of a noun phrase optional, and then to add *fell* to PS1.5.

PS1.5   V → $\begin{Bmatrix} saw \\ heard \end{Bmatrix}$

PS1.5a   V → $\begin{Bmatrix} saw \\ heard \\ fell \end{Bmatrix}$

The grammar as now modified can be used to derive the sentence *The man fell*. However, it will also produce sentences such as

The man fell a beautiful cat[4] and *The dog saw*, which are un-grammatical. What we have to do is distinguish between **transitive verbs** (VT), those that take an object, and **intransitive verbs** (VI), those that do not:

PS1.3b   VP → $\begin{Bmatrix} VT + NP \\ VI \end{Bmatrix}$

that is, only a transitive verb take a noun phrase; an intransitive verb does not. And now that V has been divided into VT and VI, PS1.5 is expanded even further:

PS1.5b   VT → $\begin{Bmatrix} saw \\ heard \end{Bmatrix}$

PS1.5c   VI → $\begin{Bmatrix} fell \\ ran \end{Bmatrix}$

Now the grammar will produce *The man fell* but not *The man fell a beautiful cat.*

In this way, by adding to the number and complexity of rules, and by carefully distinguishing classes of words that are used differently, phrase-structure grammars can be extended to account for more and more English sentences.

There is more to knowledge of a language than just knowledge of which strings are grammatical sentences. Speakers of a language can recognize when a sentence is ambiguous; and phrase-structure grammars can explain certain types of ambiguity. Remember the sentence: *They are eating apples?* Suppose we add to our grammar a few more rules:

PS1.8   NP → $\begin{Bmatrix} (Art) + (Adj) + N \\ Pro \end{Bmatrix}$

where Pro means "pronoun."

PS1.9   Pro → they
PS1.10   N   → apples
PS1.11   VP → are + NP

(for sentences such as *They are baseball players.*)

PS1.12   V → are + MV + ing

---

[4]It is a linguistic convention to place an asterisk before a sentence that is not grammatical.

where MV means "main verb" (for sentences such as *The men are watching the girl.*)

PS1.13   MV → $\begin{bmatrix} \text{eat} \\ \text{watch} \\ \text{hearing} \end{bmatrix}$

Now the sentence *They are eating apples* may be derived from this grammar in two distinct ways, which result in two distinct tree-diagrams:

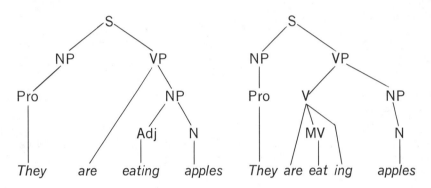

And these two structures correspond to the two meanings of the sentence.

Transformational Grammar

DEEP STRUCTURES

During most of this century, linguists have written their theories of particular languages in the form of phrase-structure grammars. Although not always formalized in quite the way illustrated in the previous section, they were essentially the same kind of grammar (Postal, 1964). Phrase-structure grammars do account for our intuitions about how the words of a sentence are grouped together, the constituent structure of a sentence, and they also account for certain kinds of ambiguity, such as that of *They are eating apples*. Despite these qualities, such grammars are now considered to be inadequate for the description of language. Instead, linguists have turned to **transformational grammar.**[5] The major claim of transformational grammar is that in addition to indicating the constituent structure of a sentence just described, which is called the **surface structure,** it shows another level of constituent structure, called the **deep structure** (or **base structure,** or **underlying structure**). **Structure** is defined as "the relationship between the morphemes of a sentence."

This claim amounts to a complication in our theories of language. Why is it necessary? For just the usual reasons leading to the rejection of one scientific theory in favor of another one: the new theory is more powerful, more efficient, captures more generalizations, and so on. In the next three sections we will examine several specific aspects of English which can be best explained by distinguishing between deep and surface structure. But first, we will look at a general motivation for this innovation.

Consider these two ambiguous sentences:

1. They are eating apples.
2. Visiting relatives can be a nuisance.

The two meanings of sentence 1 correspond to two different surface structures, which can be indicated in shorthand form with parentheses:

1a. (They) [(are) (eating apples)]
1b. (They) [(are eating) (apples)]

One cue to the intended meaning of this sentence might be the placement of pauses: *they——are——eating apples* is clearly a statement about apples; *They are eating——apples* is a statement about some individuals. The difference in meaning between 1a and 1b can also be cued by **stress** (or accent). When spoken, 1a

[5]Transformational grammar is a relatively new theory and is currently developing rapidly. The particular version presented here is certainly not the one that is most widely accepted at the present time, and the reader should be prepared for differences in the literature. However, such variations do not seem to be crucial for studies of child language at this time. A particularly important question is whether the level of deep structure, as proposed here, is "deep enough"; that is, whether deep structure should be even more distinct from surface structure. One hypothesis currently under consideration is that the deep structure is not merely closer to the meaning of the sentence than the surface structure but, rather, is identical with the meaning of the sentence. For recent research on transformational grammar, see the papers collected in Bach and Harms (1968) and Jacobs and Rosenbaum (1970).

is likely to have stress on *eating;* 1b, on *apples.* In simple constructions of this type, the stress usually falls on the first vowel of the noun phrase. Pauses and stress are aspects of the sound system of a language, its **phonology.** As the example suggests, the pronunciation of a sentence is largely determined by its surface structure.

Sentence 2 also has two meanings; one about relatives who visit (2a), the other about going to visit relatives (2b). But the two meanings cannot be distinguished using pauses, for the most natural place for a pause in either case is *visiting relatives——can be a nuisance.* Stress is placed on the first syllables of both *visiting* and *relatives* for both meanings. In fact, the surface structure is identical for the two meanings:

2a and 2b   (Visiting relatives) [(can be) (a nuisance)]

Nevertheless, the relationship between the words of the sentence is different for each interpretations. If we transform, or **paraphrase,** the sentence, attempting to preserve the meaning, we can produce for 2a, *Relatives who visit can be a nuisance;* and for 2b, *It can be a nuisance to visit relatives.* The difference between 2a and 2b corresponds to the different relationship between *relatives* and *visit* in these two paraphrases. The surface structure does not reflect this difference; the ambiguity is due to the presence of *two* deep structures corresponding to the single surface structure. As the example suggests, the meaning of a sentence is primarily determined by its deep structure.

The theory of transformational grammar claims that every sentence has a deep structure and a surface structure, and that the two are by no means identical. How the deep structure and the surface are related is specified by the **rules of transformation, or,** simply, **transformations.**

One defect of surface structure analysis of sentences is that it fails to clarify the relationship between sentences of different form. Speakers of English feel intuitively that sentences are related, even though they are of distinct surface structure. Perhaps the clearest example of this in English is the case of active and passive sentences. The sentences *The dog bites the man* and *The man is bitten by the dog* have the same meaning, even though the elements of the sentence are arranged quite differently. According to a surface structure analysis, they are simply two different sentence types with entirely distinct structures;

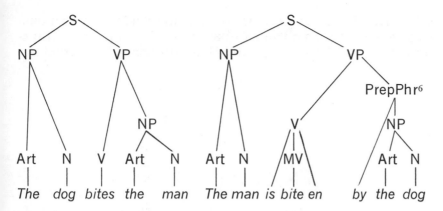

Although there is nothing essentially incorrect about such an analysis, it misses many important facts about English; that is, it does not provide generalizations that hold true for active, passive and other types of sentences. Not only can active and passive sentences have the same meaning (although they may have a different emphasis), they can also have many aspects of structure in common. Consider the following sentences:

1. John prefers steak.
2. Steak is preferred by John.
3. *Steak prefers John.
4. *John is preferred by steak.

Sentences 1 and 2 are grammatical while 3 and 4 are ungrammatical. What is needed is a rule, or **restriction,** on possible combinations of words to prevent the occurrence of ungrammatical sentences. In this case, verbs, such as *prefer, admire,* and so on, must be used with a human noun as "actor," that is, with an **animate subject.** Sentences 3 and 4 violate this restriction and are therefore ungrammatical. Now, if we limit ourselves to surface structure, we find that we have to state the restriction twice: once for the relationship between the subject and the verb of active sentences (*animate/noun prefers X*) and again for the verb and the so-called agent in passive sentences (*X is preferred by animate/noun*). This explantion is much too complicated, because in a passive sentence the agent is really the subject. The simplest solution would seem to be that *actives and passives are essentially the same at the level of deep structure*, and that a transformation

[6]Prepositional phrase.

will convert the deep structure of an active sentence into a passive sentence. Such a transformation is called a **passive transformation.** Thus sentences 1 and 2 have the same deep structure:

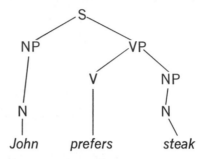

This deep structure may be converted into the sentence *Steak is preferred by John* by the passive transformation, which inverts the two noun phrases *steak* and *John*, changes the form of the verb, and supplies *by*. Or it may be left essentially as is; this results in the sentence *John prefers steak.*

Similarly, sentences 3 and 4 have the same deep structure:

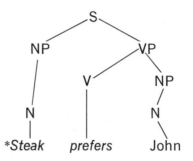

Depending on whether or not the passive transformation applies, this deep structure corresponds to the sentence *John is preferred by steak* or *Steak is preferred by John.*

Now we can state the restriction just once: *prefer* must have an animate subject *in the deep structure* (we will consider the first NP in a sentence to be the subject for the present). This rules out the deep structure for 3 and 4 and, therefore, the sentences themselves. But the deep structure for 1 and 2 is admissible, and the passive transformation can apply to produce the passive sentence (2).

In this way, we can use the distinction between deep and surface structure to make an important linguistic generalization (here a statement about a class of English verbs, but there are many other similar restrictions), ignoring the distinction between active and passive sentences, which is irrelevant *to this generaliza-tion*. The fact that sentences 1 and 2 have the same meaning follows from the claim that *it is the deep structure that determines the meaning of a sentence*.

With this framework, many other related facts about English can be explained. For example,

5. Does John prefer steak?

is a grammatical sentence, while

6. *Does steak prefer John?

is ungrammatical. We can postulate another transformation, the question transformation, which applies to deep structure and converts them into questions. The fact that sentence 5 is gram-matical, while 6 is not, follows from the restriction stated earlier; no modification or addition to the theory is necessary.

Is steak preferred by John? and **Is John preferred by steak* illustrate the application of both the passive and question trans-formations. Assuming the deep structure postulated earlier, the restriction already stated explains why the first sentence, but not the second, is grammatical. And now it should be obvious how negative sentences — *John does not prefer steak* and *Steak does not prefer John* — may be described.

In this way, many important generalizations that are in-dependent of the surface form of the sentences can be made. This is probably what underlies our intuitive feeling that actives, passives, questions, and negatives are related forms.

It is important to realize that it is not the active sentences themselves that are transformed into passive sentences, ques-tions, and so on, but, rather, the deep structures. Is the introduc-tion of such an abstract entity as deep structure an unnecessary complication? Perhaps we could simply postulate that active sentences are directly transformed into passive ones. The passive transformation could be stated quite simply: invert the first and second noun phrases, place *is* before the verb and *-en* after it[7], and supply *by* before the (new) second noun phrase. Or symbolically,

$$T_{\text{passive}}: NP_1 + V + s + NP_2 \Rightarrow NP_2 + is + V + en + by + NP_1$$

[7]Some verbs add an *-en* in the passive (*eat, is eaten by*), while others add *-ed* (*prefer, is preferred by*). The transformation is stated here with *-en* to emphasize that it is *not the past tense ending that is used* (*eat* has the past tense *ate*, not *eaten*, and so on).

This transformation will convert *John prefers steak* into *Steak is preferred by John*. However, the active sentence *The boy drops the cookies* would be converted by this transformation into *The cookies is dropped by the boy*, which is ungrammatical. The correct version of the sentence is *The cookies are dropped by the boy*. The number on the verb has changed; that is, *boy* is singular and takes one form of the verb and *cookies* is plural and takes another form. The number on the verb is determined by the first noun phrase in the sentence, and this is not determined until *after* the passive transformation has or has not applied. It is not possible to state a *single* passive transformation that applies to active sentences directly and produces correct passives, although separate transformations for the singular and plural cases are possible. However, a single passive transformation that correctly produces passives can be stated, if it applies to a deep structure that does not have the verb marked for number. This is one difference between the structure to which the passive transformation applies and the active sentence itself; there are many others.

FORM OF A TRANSFORMATIONAL GRAMMAR

Considerations such as those just discussed lead to the construction of a transformational grammar consisting of three parts: (1) a deep (or underlying or base) structure component, which produces the set of deep structures (and this is essentially a phrase-structure grammar); (2) a set of transformations which operates on the deep structures; and (3) the set of surface structures which are the result of the transformations. Diagrammed it looks like this:

Transformational Grammar

Semantic System	Deep structure component	Trans-formations	Set of surface structures	Phonological System

Each sentence has a deep structure, which is produced by the deep structure component, and each also has a surface structure, which is the result of the transformation acting on the deep structure. The deep structure of the sentence is one essential factor in determining the meaning of the sentence. The other essential factor is the set of meanings for the individual words in the sentence. The diagram indicates that the deep structure component is attached to the **semantic system** of the language: The specific rules whereby individual word meanings are combined to form the meaning of the sentence. Similarly, the surface structure of the sentence is an essential factor in determining the actual sound of the sentence, along with the sound of the individual words. The diagram indicates that it is the surface structures that are important for the **phonological system:** The specific rules whereby the pronunciation of the sentence, including stress and intonation, is determined.

The difference, then, between a phrase-structure grammar and a transformational grammar is that a phrase-structure grammar *directly* generates the surface structure of sentences:

Phrase-Structure Grammar

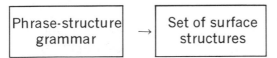

whereas the transformational grammar generates surface structures in more than one step.

The Auxiliary Verb and the Affix Transformation

One of the more complicated aspects of English is its system of auxiliary verbs. When Chomsky (1957) showed how simply it could be handled in a transformational framework, it was a compelling argument for transformational grammar. Auxiliaries are also important because they occupy a central position in the grammar of English.

First we have to look at the facts to be explained. (This is something you already know, since you all use auxiliary verbs in your speech.) Consider the verbs in the following sentences[8]:

7a. He walks.   (present singular)
7b. They walk.   (present plural)
7c. He walked.   (past singular)
7d. They walked.   (past plural)

---

[8]This example is adapted from Miller and McNeill (1968), which is in turn based on Chomsky (1957).

Two distinctions are being made: number and tense. And the verb uses three different endings to make the distinctions: -s for the present singular; ϕ (no ending) for the present plural; and -ed for the past tense regardless of the number. We can let C represent this entire set of endings; that is, let C be our **marker** for number and tense, and write a phrase-structure grammar for these sentences:

PS1.14   S → NP + VP

where NP is either singular or plural.

PS1.15   VP → MV + C
PS1.15a   C → $\left[\begin{array}{l} \text{-}s \text{ after singular NP} \\ \phi \text{ after plural NP} \\ \text{-}ed \text{ after either singular or plural NP} \end{array} \right]$

Now consider a slightly more complicated set of constructions:

8a. He is walking.   (present singular)
8b. They are walking.   (present plural)
8c. He was walking.   (past singular)
8d. They were walking.   (past plural)

The first thing to notice is that using any form of be as an **auxiliary verb** adds -ing to the main verb. But C, our marker for number and tense, which *was attached to the verb* in sentences 7a–7d, is attached to the auxiliary verb in 8a–8d. And these forms follow the pattern:

VP → be + C + MV + ing

PS1.15a fills in the ending C; be + s is pronounced *is*; be + ϕ is pronounced *are*, and be + ed is pronounced *was* or *were*.

Now if we try a different auxiliary, *have*, something fairly similar happens:

9a. He has walked.   (present singular)
9b. They have walked.   (present plural)
9c. He had walked.   (past singular)
9d. They had walked.   (past plural)

Here the main verb has the suffix -ed, rather than -ing, added to it, and C is again moved forward to the auxiliary. Actually, this is not the past tense -ed but, rather, the past participle -en, as can be seen from consideration of *he bites, he is biting, he has bitten.*

These forms follow the pattern:

$$VP \rightarrow have + C + MV + en$$

with the appropriate pronouncing rules, including one to the effect that -en is pronounced -ed for some verbs.

We can combine the use of have and be:

10a. He has been walking.   (present singular)
10b. They have been walking. (present plural)
10c. He had been walking.   (past singular)
10d. They had been walking. (past plural)

Here the auxiliary have has done its usual work — it has added a past participle ending, -en, to the verb that follows, in this case the auxiliary be. And be, as expected, has added an -ing to the following verb, the main verb to produce walking. And C has moved forward all the way to the first auxiliary, have. These forms follow the pattern:

$$VP \rightarrow have + C + be + en + MV + ing$$

Finally, we can add one more auxiliary, a so-called **modal verb,** along with have and be. (Although there is more than one modal, we will use will as our example.)

11a. He will have been walking.   (present singular)
11b. They will have been walking. (present plural)
11c. He would have been walking.   (past singular)
11d. They would have been walking. (past plural)

C has moved forward again to the first auxiliary, the modal (M), will; have still adds a past participle to the following verb, be; and be still adds -ing to the following main verb. These forms follow the pattern:

$$VP \rightarrow M + C + have + be + en + MV + ing$$

We have now considered five sets of sentences. Actually, there are eight possibilities of this type: have can be present or not, be can be present or not, and a modal can be present or not, independently. You can easily work out the three cases not displayed as they are entirely analogous.

We have arrived at three general principles:

1. C, the marker for number and tense, always operates on the first part of the verb construction, whatever it is.

All speakers of English recognize that *He had been walking* is an acceptable sentence, but **He have was walking* (where C is attached to *be*) is not. Furthermore, C is present in every sentence, whether attached to an auxiliary or to the main verb.

2. There is a contingency between *have* as an auxilliary and a past participle suffix on the verb following it. Whenever one is present, so is the other.

3. There is also a contingency between *be* as an auxiliary and an *-ing* suffix on the verb following it. Whenever one is present, so is the other.

These general principles are all part of the competence, the knowledge, of a native speaker of English. This can be demonstrated by constructing sentences that violate one or more of these principles. These sentences, such as **They are walk* (which violates principle 3), will be rejected as ungrammatical.

These are the facts of English auxiliary verbs. How can we account for them? First, let's ask a specific question: How could all these sentences be generated with phrase-structure rules? We would need eight different and independent rules, one for each possible combination of auxiliary verbs:

PS1.15	VP → MV + C
PS1.16	VP → be + C + MV + ing
PS1.17	VP → have + C + MV + en
PS1.18	VP → have + C + be + en + MV + ing
PS1.19	VP → M + C + MV
PS1.20	VP → M + C + be + MV + ing
PS1.21	VP → M + C + have + MV + en
PS1.22	VP → M + C + have + be + en + MV + ing

These rules cannot be further simplified or combined, even by the use of the parenthesis notation for optional elements, because the position of certain elements, in particular C, depends on the particular construction. For example, PS1.18 and PS1.22 do not differ simply in the presence or absence of the modal (if they did, we could combine the two in a rule which had M in parenthesis) — the relative position of *have* and C change.

This formulation also overlooks the important linguistic generalizations that we mentioned earlier — the C always appears first in the auxiliary: *-ing* depends on *be*; *-en* depends on *have*. It is also a rather clumsy set of rules. Is there another way to represent these facts about competence? We could call the entire construction **auxiliary** abbreviated Aux, and assume there is a rule in the grammar for the form:

PS1.23   V → Aux + MV

C is the only obligatory element in the auxiliary; everything else is optional and may be written in parentheses. The general order of the auxiliary is: modal, followed by *have* plus *-en*, followed by *be* plus *-ing*. So PS1.23 must be expanded to:

PS1.23a   Aux → C + (M) + (*have* + *en*) + (*be* + *ing*).

What kind of strings would be produced by such a rule? Let's try to derive the sentence *They would have been walking*. This sentence contains a modal, *have*, and *be*, so all three optional elements are selected. Here is the deep structure that would be produced by a rule of the form we have just constructed, along with other rules:

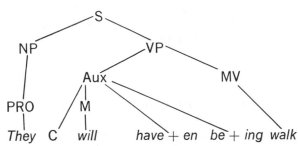

We have produced the deep structure: *they* + C + *will* + *have* + *en* + *be* + *ing* + *walk*. But what we really want is the surface structure: *they* + *will* + C + *have* + *be* + *en* + *walk* + *ing*.

The first string was produced by taking into account the three linguistic generalizations. This deep structure contains all the necessary information for determining the meaning of the sentence. However, the second string indicates the actual order of pronunciation of the elements of the sentence. The deep structure is abstract — that is, it is not directly manifested in actual speech — but it does represent real linguistic information. Somehow it must be transformed into the surface structure. In this case, the transformation is simple. Call *-en*, *-ing*, and C **affixes**. Whenever the sequence *affix* + *verb* appears in the deep structure, change the order to *verb* + *affix*. If you do this, the correct surface structure will be produced automatically. We can write the transformation:

$$T_{\text{affix}}: \quad \text{Af} + \text{V} \Rightarrow \text{V} + \text{Af}$$

where Af means "affix." Now the *one* phrase-structure rule we constructed, and this *one* affix transformation, will produce all *thirty-two* auxiliary constructions and no ungrammatical constructions. (Try some!)

There is an important distinction between the phrase-structure rules and the transformation. The phrase-structure rules indicate what the basic elements of a construction are — *have* + *en* is such a basic element — and they give the basic order — C is first, and so on. This is the essential information for determining the meaning of the sentence. The transformation, in contrast, makes no contribution to meaning. It exists only because in English as in all other languages, sound and meaning are not identical. The transformation relates the two.

We have seen that the transformational solution to this problem, which requires only one phrase-structure rule and one transformation, is much simpler than the cumbersome set of eight distinct phrase-structure rules. Thus, two of the most powerful arguments for transformational grammar are: first, *it is more economical;* second, *it permits important generalizations to be made.*

The Passive Transformation Revisited

Now that we have looked at English auxiliary verbs, we can return to the passive voice and try to formulate the passive transformation precisely. We could not do this earlier because sentences with auxiliary verbs can be transformed into passives, and the auxiliary system and the passive transformation interact.

Lets compare some active and passive sentences:

12.   The man bites the dog.
12a. The dog is bitten by the man.
13.   The man is biting the dog.
13a. The dog is being bitten by the man.
14.   The man has bitten the dog.
14a. The dog has been bitten by the man.

The situation looks complicated, and it might seem that we need a distinct passive transformation for each sentence type (and in fact, if we tried to construct a passive transformation that applied directly to the active sentences, this *would* be necessary). But because transformations apply to deep structures, we can handle all these sentence types quite easily.

Notice that in addition to the flipping of the first and second noun phrases in the passive and the insertion of *by*, there are always two more elements in the passive than were in the active — *be* and *-en*. Notice also that the *be* ends up just before the main verb, and the *-en* ends up just after the main verb. Suppose we formulate the transformation symbolically in this way:

$T_{passive}$: $NP_1 + Aux + MV_t + NP_2 \Rightarrow$
$$NP_2 + Aux + be + en + MV + by + NP_1$$

Then the affix transformation:

$$T_{affix}: \quad Af + V \Rightarrow V + Af$$

applies to the intermediate structure produced by the passive transformation. In addition to the changes it produces in the auxiliary, it inverts the *-en* introduced by the passive transformation and the main verb.

This pair of transformations will account for all the various forms of passive sentences. As an example, we will derive the sentence *The dog has been bitten by the man*. When we use the auxiliary phrase-structure rule, PS1.23a:

$$Aux \rightarrow C + (M) + (have + en) + (be + ing)$$

we will select only C + *have* + *en*. Thus we will have a deep structure of the form:

$$the + man + C + have + en + bite + the + dog$$

Now the passive transformation will apply to produce:

$$the + dog + C + have + en + be + en + bite + by + the + man$$

and the affix transformation applies to produce:

$$the + dog + have + C + be + en + bite + en + by + the + man$$

which is exactly the surface structure of *The dog has been bitten by the man*.

It is rare for only a single transformation to change a deep structure into a surface structure. It is more common for several transformations to apply. When a number of transformations are required, the structures formed between the deep structure and the surface structure are called **intermediate structures.**

A passive question, such as *Is steak preferred by John?* is an example of multiple transformations in a single sentence. Here the deep structure is essentially the same one as for the active declarative sentence *John prefers steak*, but at least two transformations apply, the passive transformation and the question transformation. Which one of these two transformations applies first? Or does it matter?

Let's look at the two transformations in a little more detail. The declarative sentence *John can swim* has as its corresponding question *Can John swim?* The sentence *Mary will peel the potatoes* has as its corresponding question *Will Mary peel the potatoes?* In general, the question transformation changes the order of (*inverts*) the subject of the sentence and the auxiliary verb. But what if there is no auxiliary verb in the sentence? The sentence *Columbus discovered America* has a corresponding question *Did Columbus discover America?* When there is no auxiliary verb, the dummy auxiliary *do* is inserted and inverted with the subject.

The passive transformation also inserts an auxiliary verb, namely, *is*. *The man bites the dog* has as its passive counterpart *The dog is bitten by the man*.

Now look what happens in passive questions. *The man bites the dog* has as its passive question counterpart *Is the dog bitten by the man?* Suppose the question transformation is applied first to the deep structure (*the* + *man* + *bites* + *the* + *dog*)[9], and this is followed by the passive transformation. The question transformation converts the deep structure of the sentence into the intermediate structure underlying *Does the man bite the dog?* And then the passive transformation applies, producing **Does the dog is bitten by the man?* which is incorrect.

But if the order is the reverse, first the passive transformation and then the question transformation, the sentence is successfully generated. The passive transformation converts the deep structure for *The man bites the dog* into the structure underlying *The dog is bitten by the man*. Then the question transformation does not have to insert *do*; it merely inverts the subject and auxiliary verb producing *Is the dog bitten by the man?* This example illustrates a very general point for English and for other languages: *transformations may be ordered*. The affix transformation applies after both the passive and question transformations.

---

[9]Although a deep structure can be represented fully only with a tree diagram, to save space we will often use only the bottom line of the tree, which indicates the elements of the deep structure and their order. The example is further simplified by omitting the analysis of *bites* into C + *bite*.

Complex Sentences

The creativity and flexibility of any language, such as English, is largely due to the fact that we are not limited to simple sentences, such as the ones discussed above, but can combine them into complex sentences to express complex meanings. Two important processes of combination are **conjunction** and **embedding.**

When two simple sentences are **conjoined,** they are simply combined as equals. *Tom plays the flute* and *Alice plays the piano* may be conjoined to produce *Tom plays the flute, and Alice plays the piano.* Conjunction is most useful when the two simple sentences share part of their content. When *I went to the store* and *I bought some milk* are combined, the resulting sentence is *I went to the store and I bought some milk.* But it is possible to abbreviate it to *I went to the store and bought some milk* using a transformation. Similarly, the conjoined sentence *Tom can drive and John can drive* may be abbreviated to *Tom and John can drive.* Whenever two **conjuncts,** corresponding elements of the two conjoined simple sentences, are identical, one may be deleted. Actually, the two conjuncts must be not only identical in form but also in reference. *John ate and John drank* can be transformed into *John ate and drank* only if the two occurrences of *John* refer to the same individual. If John Smith ate and John Jones drank, this deletion cannot occur.

The complex sentence *The man whom you met yesterday is outside* is a combination of two simple sentences, *You met the man yesterday* and *The man is outside.* However, these two simple sentences are not simply conjoined. Instead, the first is inserted, or **embedded,** in the second as a *relative clause* in order to identify more precisely the man referred to in the second sentence. The embedding occurs through a rule of the form:

PS1.24   NP → NP + S,

where S is now the origin of a derivation of a new sentence, *You met the man yesterday.* The deep structure of the complex sentence is, approximately:

[the man (you met the man yesterday)] (is outside)

A sentence may be embedded as a relative clause only if it contains an NP identical to the NP it modifies. Several transformations (called **relativization transformations**) then move the second occurrence of the NP to the beginning of the embedded sentence and replace it by a *relative pronoun* (*that* or *which*, for nonhuman entities; *who* or *whom* for humans and pets), producing *The man whom you met yesterday is outside*. There is another optional transformation that deletes the relative pronoun, producing *The man you met yesterday is outside*. However, this transformation cannot apply in every case. *The man who called yesterday* cannot be transformed into **The man called yesterday is outside*.

Relative clauses, like free-standing simple sentences, can be transformed by the passive transformation. *The dog chased the cat* may be embedded in *The cat caught the rat* to produce [*the cat* (*the dog chased the cat*)](*caught the rat*). If the embedded sentence is made passsive, *The cat was chased by the dog*, before the relativization transformations apply, the sentence *The cat who was chased by the dog caught the rat* will be produced.

Conjunction and relative-clause embedding are only two of the mechanisms in English for combining simple sentences. There are many other types of embedding; that is, means whereby one sentence may serve as part of another "framework" sentence. Two examples are **complementation** (*He knew that I wanted the book*) and **nominalization** (*His wanting to go home complicated the situation*). Many of these structures are discussed in Jacobs and Rosenbaum (1968). They are all powerful tools for the precise expression of complex messages.

Summary

In this chapter we have examined the end product of language acquisition, namely, adult linguistic competence.[10] Language acquisition is, in a sense, just the opposite of linguistic performance in the usual sense. Speaking and listening consist of converting knowledge into action, whereas, in language acquisition, action — the sentences the child hears and produces — must be converted into knowledge.

The description of language provided by linguistics demonstrates just how impressive the achievement of language learning is. Language is extremely complex. We have looked at three transformations of English; they are part of a large and interlocking network of hundreds of transformations. Language is also highly abstract in the sense that many of the entities which

---

[10]Actually this chapter focused almost entirely on syntax, with very little consideration of either the meaningful aspect of language or its sound system. This is deferred until Chapters 6 and 7, respectively.

exist in language are never directly presented in speech. NP's and VP's do not occur in the stream of speech. They are at least one step removed from what the hearer perceives. Deep structures are even more abstract, yet knowledge of the deep structure is necessary in order to understand a sentence. How can children learn about these structures that he cannot directly perceive?

1.1 The Natural Language of Man*

The Egyptians before the reign of Psammetichus used to think that of all races in the world they were the most ancient; Psammetichus, however when he came to the throne, took it into his head to settle this question of priority, and ever since his time the Egyptians have believed that the Phrygians surpass them in antiquity and that they themselves come second. Psammetichus, finding that mere inquiry failed to reveal which was the original race of mankind, devised an ingenious method of determining the matter. He took at random, from an ordinary family, two newly born infants and gave them to a shepherd to be brought up amongst his flocks, under strict orders that no one should utter a word in their presence. They were to be kept by themselves in a lonely cottage, and the shepherd was to bring in goats from time to time, to see that the babies had enough milk to drink, and to look after them in any other way that was necessary. All these arrangements were made by Psammetichus because he wished to find out what word the children would first utter, once they had grown out of their meaningless babytalk. The plan succeeded; two years later the shepherd, who during that time had done everything he had been told to do, happened one day to open the door of the cottage and go in, when both children running up to him with hands outstretched, pronounced the word "becos." The first time this occurred the shepherd made no mention of it; but later, when he found that every time he visited the children to attend to their needs the same

*From *Herodotus, The Histories*, tr. Aubrey de Selincourt. London: Penguin Books Ltd. Copyright 1964. Pp. 102-103. Reprinted by permission.

word was constantly repeated by them, he informed his master. Psammetichus ordered the children to be brought to him, and when he himself heard them say "becos" he determined to find out to what language the word belonged. His inquires revealed that it was the Phrygian for "bread," and in consideration of this the Egyptians yielded their claims and admitted the superior antiquity of the Phrygians.

SELECTED REFERENCES

Bach, E., & Harms, R. T. (Eds.) *Universals in linguistic theory.* New York: Holt, Rinehart and Winston, 1968.

Chomsky, N. *Syntactic structures.* The Hague: Mouton, 1957.

Chomsky, N. *Aspects of the theory of syntax.* Cambridge, Mass.: M.I.T. Press, 1965.

Herodotus. *The histories.* Translated by A. de Selincourt. Baltimore: Penguin Books, 1954.

Jacobs, R. A., & Rosenbaum, P. S. *English transformational grammar.* Waltham, Mass.: Blaisdell, 1968.

Jacobs, R. A., & Rosenbaum, P. S. *Readings in English transformational grammar.* Waltham, Mass.: Blaisdell, 1970.

Miller, G. A., & McNeill, D. Psycholinguistics. In G. Lindzey & E. Aaronson (Eds.), *Handbook of social psychology.* Vol. 3. Reading, Mass.: Addison-Wesley, 1968. Pp. 666–794.

Postal, P. *Constituent structure: A study of contemporary models of syntactic description.* Publication 30, Indiana University Research Center in Anthropology, Folklore, and Linguistics. Bloomington: Indiana University Press, 1964.

FURTHER READING

Bolinger, D. *Aspects of language.* New York: Harcourt Brace Jovanovich, 1968.

Langacker, R. W. *Language and its structure.* New York: Harcourt Brace Jovanovich, 1967.

Lyons, John (Ed.) *New horizons in linguistics.* Baltimore: Penguin Books, 1970.

2

The Course
of Syntactic
Development, I

The fundamental technique of most recent studies of the acquisition of language has been to write grammars, or parts of grammars, for the language of individual children at successive points in development, and then to observe how these grammars change. Obviously these grammars are not explanations of language acquisition in any sense. Rather, they are the data that any theory of language acquisition must attempt to explain if it is to account for the development of language from the child's first words to his fully developed adult language. This chapter, then is primarily descriptive.

Studying Child Language

The best way to begin studying child language is to find a young child and listen. All his utterances in a given period of time should be recorded (and as much of the context, verbal and non-verbal, as possible) in order for the sample to be analyzed for the underlying patterns. The next few chapters describe some of the results of this "grammar-writing" approach. But here we will consider some of the serious methodological difficulties.

This grammar-writing procedure amounts to viewing a child in exactly the same way a linguist views a speaker of an unknown language. Such a linguist has several techniques available to him. First, he can learn the language himself. Once he is a fluent speaker, he is better able to understand and analyze the language. This, of course, cannot be done with a child. It is not possible to unlearn all you know of your language. Further, the child's language is changing too rapidly for an adult learner to keep up with him.

Once the linguist has acquired some knowledge of an unknown language, he can ask native speakers of the language such as questions *Does x mean the same thing as y?* Or *Can I say x?* This is often called "appealing directly to the linguistic intuition of the speaker." It does not work so well with the typical two year old:

> INTERVIEWER: Adam, which is right, 'two shoes' or 'two shoe'?
> ADAM: Pop goes the weasel [Brown & Bellugi, 1964, p. 135].

For these reasons we are limited, for the most part, to observed speech, that is, to *performance*. There also are sampling problems: does the absence of an item from a child's speech mean that he cannot produce it or merely that he has not found it necessary to produce it? In addition, we know that the speech of adults, that is, their **performance,** does not reflect their knowledge, that is, their **competence,** perfectly. There are mistakes, slips of the tongue, memory lapses, and the like. Presumably similar processes occur in children's speech also. Young children have a very restricted short-term memory capacity, which in turn probably constrains sentence production. "Unimportant" words — auxiliaries, prepositions, conjunctions, and so on — may simply be left out, although the child understands their use. More than simple memory span for distinct items is relevant here; often a child will expand a complete sentence into a longer but simpler one. There is a complex interaction between memory and linguistic structure. Because of this possibility, it is difficult to decide if an observed difference between a child's speech and adult language is due to different *competence* or to *performance* factors.

Even the production by a child of a construction identical to the adult form is not always easy to interpret. For a period of time, Adam, a boy studied by Roger Brown and his co-workers (Brown & Bellugi, 1964), often used the expression "just checking." In adult grammar, the word *checking* is a combination of two morphemes, *check* and *-ing*. The morpheme *-ing* may be added to almost any verb. However, Adam never used *-ing* except in the compound *checking*, and it would be entirely unjustified to claim that he had acquired the *-ing* morpheme. This particular case is not difficult to interpret: Adam undoubtedly picked up "checking' (and probably the entire phrase "just checking") from his parents as a single unit, through imitation. But how often must a child use a morpheme or construction, and in how many different contexts, before it is safe to assume he that has acquired a new rule? The problem is aggravated by the fact that we have only a modest amount of data to work with. We cannot return for more data as required, as the linguist does when analyzing an unknown language, because a child's language is constantly changing, often with surprising rapidity.

Because the major source of data is the child's own productions, we often do not know what a word or grammatical construction *means* to the child when he uses it. This is important to consider because of the very general belief that children understand, or comprehend, more than they can produce at any point in development. Does the child really understand the sentence, including its structure, or is he simply reacting to a few salient words? If a parent at home says *Would you like some ice cream?* the child may walk, or run, to the refrigerator that contains the ice cream. And a proud parent might point to the child's understanding. But the child might have done the same thing if the parent had said *I don't want any ice cream* or *There isn't any ice cream in the refrigerator* or even *Colorless green ice cream sleeps furiously.* "Ice cream" is, of course, the salient phrase. In natural settings we do not produce these sentences that would test the child's comprehension, but there are some obvious experiments that can be done. This problem also suggests that such experiments may play a more important role in the study of children's language than they would for that of adults.

A final difficulty: Given all these problems, how do we evaluate a proposed grammar or compare several alternative grammars? Linguists distinguish between the **observational adequacy** and the **descriptive adequacy** of a grammar (Chomsky, 1965). A grammar is observationally adequate if it accounts for, that is, **generates,** the sentences that have been observed. This is the weakest requirement that can be placed on a grammar. As we have seen in the previous chapter, speakers of a language can analyze a sentence into its constituent structure, make judgments of ambiguity, distinguish between well-formed and deviant sentences, and so forth. They do this using their linguistic competence, the knowledge that allows them to use their language creatively. A descriptively adequate grammar is capable of these accomplishments in a way that agrees with the competence of native speakers. As such, it goes beyond the actual set of sentences that have been observed and makes predictions about the correctness or deviance of other strings of morphemes, their ambiguity, and so on. Descriptive adequacy will be difficult, if not impossible, to achieve in studies of child language. For descriptive adequacy requires evidence of just the type we have seen to be difficult to obtain from children. We are essentially limited to observational adequacy. This is still an unresolved problem for which the only possible solution is to devise means to obtain more information about a child's linguistic competence than can be obtained from merely observing his productions.

The Holophrastic Stage

At about a child's first birthday, his first truly linguistic utterances, the first words, appear. Just when the child achieves this milestone is not easy to determine. It is an event so eagerly anticipated by parents that they often read meaning into the child's babbling. It is difficult to set up firm criteria for true linguistic usage of a word, but some that have been proposed are: consistent usage of the word by the child; spontaneity of usage (not merely imitated from adult speech); evidence of understanding; and occasionally the more stringent requirement that the word be a word of the adult language. Depending on the criteria established, different ages will be obtained for the appearance of the first word. But the range between ten and twelve months includes most of the observations recorded (McCarthy, 1954).

The first single-word utterances are among the most difficult to interpret and to study. They seem to be attempts to express complex ideas, and are called **holophrastic speech.** For instance, when a child says, "Milk" he may not mean simply to indicate a white liquid but that he wants milk or that the listener is supposed to look at the milk. The very first words are most often nouns, adjectives, or self-invented words (McNeill, 1970b). However, the nouns are seldom used simply as names, although this does occur when the object being named evokes strong feelings, for example when the child sees a familiar ball and says "Ball!" More typical is the child who sees his father's slippers and says "Daddy." He is making a comment about the slippers, that they are daddy's. In many ways, the first nouns and adjectives are used as comments, or predicates, on some aspect of the nonlinguistic setting. This is one reason why it is so difficult to understand such utterances; De Laguna (1963) suggested that "In order to understand what the baby is saying you must see what the baby is doing [p. 91]."

Holophrastic utterances are strongly linked to action, particularly the child's own action and the desired action of others. Werner Leopold's daughter Hildegard, at twenty months, said "Walk" as she got out of a cart, "Away" as she pushed something aside, and "Blow" as she blew her nose (Leopold, 1949a). Leopold labeled these utterances **self-imperatives,** to distinguish them from **true imperatives,** which are directed toward someone else and which are also common. Holophrastic speech is often highly expressive of the child's emotional state. Hildegard used "nenene" to scold and "dididi" in a loud voice to indicate disapproval. Disentangling emotional expression from denotative meaning is a major achievement in language learning. "Mama" originally meant "food" or "delicious" or "hungry" to Hildegard; undoubtedly all were said to her mother, who was either feeding her or was desired to do so. For Hildegard, the meaning of *mama* was a combination of emotion, desire, and name. Only after several months did "mama" come to refer to a person.

Often a transitional stage occurs between the holophrastic stage and the first appearance of multiword utterances. Sequences of two or three words are produced, but with distinct utterances, that is, with a pause between them. Bloom's daughter Allison (Bloom, 1970b) said "Door, open" as she passed a door being opened; "Daddy, door" when daddy came home; and both "Daddy, car" and "Car, daddy" when daddy left to get the car. As the examples demonstrate, there are no constraints on the order of combination of words. This contrasts with the next stage of development, and is one justification for not viewing these utterances as single sentences.

The Beginning of Syntax

At about eighteen or twenty months, the child's first two-word utterances appear (however, there is great variation in this onset). In the sense that language is essentially a means for expressing an unlimited number of ideas with a limited system, this is the true beginning of language.[1]

When two-word utterances appear, there is at first a gradual increase in frequency and then a very rapid acceleration. For example, Braine's (1963) data for one child show the following number of *new distinct* two-word utterances recorded in successive months:

> 14, 10, 30, 35, 261, 1050, 1100+ (count terminated during month)

This explosive growth reflects the child's creative use of language from the very earliest stages of syntactic development.

These utterances are very definitely not random or unstructured combinations of words, as one might expect if the child were simply imitating a few words from parental utterances. In the most common type of language at this stage, two classes of words can be distinguished (Braine, 1963; McNeill, 1970b; Slobin, in press). The terminology varies from author to author but we will call them **pivot class** and **open class**. The pivot class is small, and each word in it is used with many different words from the much larger open class. For example, a child might say "bandage on," "blanket on," "fix on" and other similar utterances. For this child, *on* is a pivot word. It is always used in the second position, and many other words can occur with it. Or a child might say "allgone shoe," allgone lettuce," allgone outside," and others. Here *allgone* is a pivot that always occurs in the first position. A pivot word may be the first or the second element in two-word utterances, but *each pivot word has its own fixed position.*

---

[1] Our major source of data for American children learning English comes from the studies carried out by Roger Brown's group at Harvard (which originally included Ursula Bellugi, Courtney Cazden, Colin Fraser, Jean Berko Gleason, David McNeill, and Dan Slobin); by Susan Ervin-Tripp and Wick Miller at Berkeley; by Martin Braine at Walter Reed Army Institute of Research; and by Louis Bloom at Columbia. Brown's research on American children learning English is extremely extensive; it is based on samples of several children's speech obtained regularly over a period of several years which has been intensively analyzed. Many papers resulting from this research are collected in Brown (1970). Despite what may seem to be a good deal of data from these and other investigators, the outline of syntactic development presented here is based on an embarassingly small number of children. Most of the work of Brown's group, for example, is based on data from three children (named, appropriately, Adam, Eve, and Sarah). Although many aspects of development observed first with this small sample have been replicated with other children, several have not (see, especially, Bloom, 1970a). Bloom's book is especially valuable because it presents a large body of evidence useful to later investigations. Caution in generalizing is essential, especially with respect to ages at which developments occur. The *sequence* of development appears to be relatively, though not totally uniform, whereas the *rate* of development is highly variable.

The pivot class is generally small and contains words of high frequency in the child's speech. The words are called pivots because the child seems to be attaching other words to them. The membership of the pivot class expands slowly; only a few new words enter it each month. In contrast, the open class is large and contains all the words in the child's vocabulary that are not in the pivot class. Most of the early growth in vocabulary occurs in the open class. All of the open class words can occur as single-word utterances, but pivot words seldom, if ever, do.

We can summarize these facts about a child's language at this stage with a very simple phrase-structure grammar:

PS2.1 $S \rightarrow \begin{cases} (P_1) + 0 \\ 0 + (P_2) \end{cases}$

PS2.2 $P_1 \rightarrow$ allgone, byebye, and so on
PS2.3 $P_2 \rightarrow$ off, on, fall, and so on
PS2.4 $0 \rightarrow$ boy, sock, mommy, and so on

where P stands for "pivot" word, O for "open" word

(Some children at the very earliest stage of two-word utterances may have only one class of pivot words. Shortly thereafter, such children develop the second pivot class.)

This grammar will produce all combinations of pivot class words with open class words. Since there may be hundreds of open class words, the grammar will produce a very large number of sentences. Most of these will not be acceptable adult English sentences or even simplified versions of them. But this cannot be considered an objection to the grammar because many of the utterances that the child actually produces are not acceptable adult English sentences or simplified versions of them. Some examples from Braine (1963) are "allgone sticky," said after washing hands; "more page," a request to continue reading; and "allgone outside," after the door was closed. It is highly unlikely that the child ever heard sentences quite like these. They must represent attempts by the child to express himself in his own way, through his own linguistic system.

Although children's sentences at this stage are all of the same general, rather primitive, structure, they are used to express a wide variety of meanings. *More* is often used as a pivot to indicate a demand or desire — *more milk*. *There* is often used as a pivot to locate or name an object — *there book*. *No* and *allgone* are common pivots that serve a negative function — *no wash*, *allgone milk.* Possession is a common function — *mama dress* — as is modification — *pretty dress*. And there are other functions. It would seem that the child is aware of more types of relationships than he can express by means of purely syntactic devices. Because the child cannot always unambiguously indicate the relationship he has in mind, it is not always possible to interpret them on linguistic grounds alone. *Daddy hat* may mean "daddy's hat" it or may mean "daddy is wearing a hat"; the only way to know which one is intended is to be there where the child utters the sentence to see if there is a hat or a daddy or both present.

Stress, that is, *accent*, probably plays an important role here. Miller and Ervin-Tripp (1964) reported that one of the children they studied used the expression *Christy room* sometimes as a possessive construction meaning "Christy's room" and sometimes as a locative construction, meaning "Christy is in the room." The difference was that the first was pronounced with the stress on the first word, "*Christy* room," and the second, "Christy *room*." Unfortunately, we know very little about the development of stress in children's language.

This earliest stage of syntax, two-word utterances with a pivot-open grammar, appears in the acquisition of other languages, as well as English.[2] Of course, in different languages, different words will be in the pivot and open classes. Even within the English-speaking community, different children will have different words in the two classes, but the similarity of children's earliest language is remarkable. Just as *there* is a common English pivot, so is German *da*, Russian *tam*, Finnish *tuossa*, and Samoan *lea*, all of which have approximately the meaning of "there." Corresponding to English *more* are German *mehr* and Russian *yesche*. Corresponding to English *allgone* are Russian *tyu-tyu* and Samoan *uma*. And so on down the list. As Slobin wrote:

> If you ignore word order, and read through transcriptions of two-word utterances in the various languages we have studied, the utterances read like direct translations of one another [1970, p. 177]."

[2]Dan Slobin (in press) has surveyed research on children learning other languages, especially Russian. Much of the literature on languages other than English is in the form of diary studies by parents who may or may not have been linguistically trained. Such diary studies are, of course, of very uneven quality, and Slobin discusses some of the difficulties in using such material. There are, however, at least two excellent diary studies, according to Slobin — Gvozdev's study of his son Zhenya learning Russian (discussed in Slobin, 1966a) and Leopold's study of his German-English bilingual daughter Hildegard (Leopold, 1949a). In addition, Slobin's students have conducted several field studies of children acquiring non–Indo-European languages (discussed below).

And he has compiled an impressive table showing the similarities of form and function in the two-word sentences of children acquiring a variety of languages (see Table 2.1).

Either simultaneously with the emergence of pivot constructions or slightly later, children begin to produce sentences made of two words from the open class. These can be accommodated in the grammar easily, by expanding the first rule to:

PS2.1a. $S \rightarrow \begin{bmatrix} (P_1) + 0 \\ 0 + (P_2) \\ 0 + 0 \end{bmatrix}$

This rule does not specify the positions of the two open class words. And indeed we can find utterances such as *man car*, with *car* in the second position, and *car bridge*, with *car* in the first position.

STRUCTURAL MEANINGS AND PIVOT-OPEN GRAMMARS

Pivot-open grammars have been used widely to describe the earliest stages of syntactic development. However, these grammars are inadequate as descriptions of early child language because they have two defects. First, the speech of some children cannot be described by a pivot-open grammar; second, even when such a grammar is appropriate, it fails to capture the richness of the linguistic system. Table 2-1 displays a remarkable variety of functions, all of which are described with a single rule by a pivot-open grammar.

The core of a pivot-open grammar is the pivot class: a small class of words which is used with high frequency and in a fixed position. That is, either the pivot word is first or it is second each time the child uses it. Some children, such as Kathryn in Bloom's study (1970a), use a small stock of words frequently, each in combination with many different words but not in a fixed position. Kathryn produced many utterances with *make*; sometimes it occurred in first position, "make house"; sometimes in second position, "Kathryn make house." According to a pivot-open analysis, pivot words do not occur alone. But there are many exceptions to this generalization; *no* often occurs as a pivot word in two-word combinations, and it also occurs alone.

Even when a pivot-open grammar does describe child language, it says very little about the relationship between the words in the sentence. Bloom kept very complete records of the context of each utterance of Kathryn and was able to identify the

TABLE 2-1 *Functions of Two-Word Sentences in Child Speech, with Examples from Several Languages*[a]

Function of Utterance	English	German	Russian	Finnish	Luo	Samoan
Locate, name	there book that car see doggie	buch da (book there) gukuk wauwau (see doggie)	Tasya tam (Tasya there)	tuossa Rina (there Rina) vetta siina (water there)	en saa (it clock) ma wendo (this visitor)	Keith lea (Keith there)
Demand, desire	more milk give candy want gum	mehr milch (more milk) bitte apfel (please apple)	yesche moloko (more milk) day chasy (give watch)	anna Rina (give Rina)	miya tamtam (give-me candy) adway cham (I want food)	mai pepe (give doll) fia moe (want sleep)
Negate[b]	no wet no wash not hungry allgone milk	nicht blasen (not blow) kaffe nein (coffee no)	vody net (water no) gus'tyu-tyu (goose allgone)	ei susi (not wolf) enaa pipi (anymore sore)	beda onge (my slasher absent)	le 'ai (not eat) uma mea (allgone thing)
Describe event or situation[c]	Bambi go mail come hit ball block fall baby highchair	puppe kommt (doll comes) tiktak bungt (clock bangs) sofa sitzen (sofa sit) messer schneiden (cut knife)	mama prua (mama walk) papa bay-bay (papa sleep) korka upala (crust fell) nasbla yaechko (found egg)	takki pois (cat away) Seppo putoo (Seppo fall) balli 'ban ban' (garage 'car')	chungu biro (European comes) odhi skul (he-went school) omoyo oduma (she-dries maize)	pa'u pepe (fall doll) tapale 'oe (hit you) tu'u lalo (put down)

Indicate possession	my shoe mama dress	mein ball (my ball) mamas hut (mama's hat)	mami chashka (mama's cup) pup moya (navel my)	tati auto (aunt car)	kom baba (chair father)	lole a'u (candy my) polo 'oe (ball your) paluni mama (baloon mama)
Modify, qualify	pretty dress big boat	milch heiss (milk hot) armer wauwau (poor doggie)	mama khoroshaya (mama good) papa bol'shoy (papa big)	rikki auto (broken car) torni iso (tower big)	piypiy kech (pepper hot) gwen madichol (chicken black)	fa'ali'i pepe (headstrong baby)
Question[d]	where ball	wo ball (where ball)	gdu papa (where papa)	missu palle (where ball)		fea pupafu (where Punafu)

SOURCE: Reprinted from Slobin, D. L. Universals of grammatical development in children. In G. B. Flores d'Arcais and W. J. M. Levelt (Eds.), Advances in psycholinguistics, Amsterdam: North Holland-Publishing Company, 1970. Table 1, pp 178–179. Reprinted with permission of the publisher.

[a]The examples come from a variety of studies, published and unpublished. Data from the three non–Indo-European languages are drawn from the recent doctoral dissertations of Melissa Bowerman (Harvard, in progress: Finnish), Ben Blount (Berkeley, 1969: Luo), Keith Kerman (Berkeley, 1969: Samoan). The examples given here are representative of many more utterances of the same type in each language. The order of the two words in the utterance is generally fixed in all of the languages except Finnish, where both orders can be used freely for some utterance types by some children.

[b]Bloom (Columbia dissert., 1968) has noted three different sorts of negation: (1) non-existence (e.g., "no wet," meaning "dry"), (2) rejection (e.g., "no wash", meaning "don't wash me"), and (3) denial (e.g., "no girl," denying a preceding assertation that a boy was a girl).

[c]Descriptions are of several types: (1) agent + action (e.g., "Bambi go"), (2) action + object (e.g., "hit ball"), (3) agent + object (e.g., "mama bread," meaning "mama is cutting bread"), (4) locative (e.g., "baby highchair," meaning "throw it to daddy"). (The use of the terminology of grammatical case is suggestive here; cf. Fillmore's discussion of deep cases as underlying linguistic universals.)

[d]In addition to wh-questions, yes-no questions can be made by pronouncing any two-word utterance with rising intonation, with the exception of Finnish. (Melissa Bowerman reports that the emergence of yes-no questions is, accordingly, exceptionally late in Finnish child language.)

meaning of the utterance quite precisely in many cases. Kathryn said "Mommy sock" twice in one day; once when she picked up her mother's sock and again when her mother put Kathryn's own sock on her. In the first case, *mommy* is a possessive modifier of *sock*; in the second, *mommy* is an agent of an action upon the *sock*. A pivot-open grammar assigns both sentences identical structures. The word *mommy* also presents a difficulty. It occurs frequently and almost always in initial position, which would appear to classify it as a pivot word. However, it is a *content* word, and content words are usually classified as open class words. Such a classification is supported by the observation of sentences such as *No mommy* (P + O). Classifying *mommy* as an open class word and, therefore, *Mommy sock* as an **open-open** construction (O + O) fails to represent the fact that *mommy* is almost always in initial position. PS2.1a, S → O + O, allows combinations of words from the open class in either order; but *Sock mommy* never occurs.

An alternative framework for analyzing early child language was developed by Bloom (1970a) and independently by Schlesinger (in press). The basic idea of their approach is to describe sentences, not only in terms of word classes and their combinations, but also in terms of the functions that the words serve in the sentence. The first *Mommy sock* is a possessive, consisting of a possessor followed by an object. The second *Mommy sock* is an instance of an **agent-object** construction. In the sentence *Sweater chair*, the second word indicates the location of the object named first; it is a **object-location** construction. When Kathryn picked up a hat for a party, she said "party hat," an instance of an **attribute-object** construction. And finally, when Kathryn's mother walked in to the room carrying an umbrella and boots, Kathryn said "Umbrella boot," an instance of a **conjunction**, or object-object, construction.

Nearly all of Kathryn's N + N constructions, which would be analyzed as open-open in a pivot-open grammar, could be classified as one of the above constructions. Agent-object constructions were the most common, whereas object-location and conjunction constructions were least common.

Kathryn also produced true pivot-open constructions. These too included a variety of relationships. For instance, *hi* was a pivot that served to indicate notice, or attention — *Hi spoon*. And *more* was a pivot that called for the recurrence of the event or object which followed — *More cereal, More hair curl. This* and *that* served to point to an immediately present object — *This necklace.*

Thus a variety of relationships, or **structural meanings,** can be expressed with very primitive formal means. Brown (1970) has analyzed the speech of a number of children acquiring a wide variety of languages, and he has found a small stock of structural meanings which recur in the speech of every child (see Table 2-2).

TABLE 2-2   *The First Sentences in Child Speech*

Structural meaning	Form	Example
1. Nomination	that + N it + N	that book
2. Notice	hi + N	hi belt
3. Recurrence	more + N, 'nother + N	more milk
4. Nonexistence	allgone + N no more + N	allgone rattle
5. Attributive	Adj + N	big train
6. Possessive	N + N	mommy lunch
7. Locative	N + N	sweater chair
8. Locative	V + N	walk street
9. Agent-Action	N + V	Eve read
10. Agent-Object	N + N	mommy sock
11. Action-Object	V + N	put book
12. Conjunction	N + N	umbrella boot

SOURCE: Adapted from Brown, R. *Psycholinguistics.* New York: Free Press, 1970. P. 220.

The first four structural relationships are often expressed with pivot words, while the remaining eight are often expressed with open-open constructions. The child has more relationship to express than he has distinct syntactic devices for their expression. The distinction between **structural relationship** and **syntactic form** (pivot-open or otherwise) might be thought of as the forerunner of the distinction between deep and surface structure, although at this stage there is no purely syntactic motivation for drawing such a distinction.

THE DEVELOPMENT OF NOUN PHRASES

After this first stage of syntactic development, the complexity of the child's language increases rapidly. Sentences become longer with the appearance of three-word combinations.

They are often combinations of the two-word structural meanings of the first stage (see Table 2-1 for list), such as **agent-action-object** and **agent-action-location.** Furthermore, one element of structural meanings, the object, begins to be elaborated into a noun phrase. Table 2-3 illustrates how longer phrases that include nouns now come to stand in the same positions as single nouns did at the early stage.

TABLE 2-3   *Some Privileges of the Noun Phrase*

Noun positions	*Noun phrase positions*
That (flower)	That (a blue flower)
Where (ball) go?	Where (the puzzle) go?
Adam write (penguin)	Doggie eat (the breakfast)
(Horsie) stop	(A horsie) crying
Put (hat) on	Put (the red hat) on

SOURCE: Brown, R., & Bellugi, U., "Three Processes in the Child's Acquisition of Syntax" *Harvard Educational Review*, 34:2, 1964, 133–151. Copyright © 1964 by President and Fellows of Harvard College. Reprinted with permission.

The noun phrases continue to be expressions of possession, recurrence, and attribution.

The process of developing noun phrases is largely one of **differentiating** (or splitting) the class of modifying words in the child's vocabulary. The child's language begins with a few relatively large word classes, whereas adult language requires many word classes, each with distinct patterns of use. Brown and Bellugi (1964) have traced the development of various classes of modifiers in the speech of Adam. When Adam was first observed, at two years, he already had three classes of words, which were roughly nouns, verbs, and modifiers.

At first, Adam's sentences were short, and only a single modifier could proceed a noun (this period is called Stage I). But this could be any modifier (M_1) in his vocabulary, whether it was adjective, possessive pronoun, or article in adult language:

Stage I: $S \rightarrow (M_1) + N$ (my, that, a big, green, . . .) $+ N$

At this stage, Adam's language has only a single, undifferentiated class of modifiers, although they are used to express a variety of structural meanings, including possession, attribution, and others.

At the second stage, it is possible to infer a separation of some parts of the original class. Adam produced sentences such

as *That's a your car*, but not **That's your a car; A mine pencil* but not
*Mine a pencil; That a blue flower but not **That blue a flower.* Articles now form a separate class, because they have a special
privilege of occurrence in Adam's speech. They occur before
other modifiers. Another class can be distinguished, because
Adam produced *That's a horse* but not **A that's horse; That a blue
flower* but not **Blue a that flower.* Demonstrative pronouns
(Dem) also have a special privilege of occurrence; they can occur
before modifiers and even before articles. All the other modifiers,
however, remain in a class together (M_2) because they all occur
in the same context — before nouns but after articles. The situation can be summarized by the statement that the modifier class
has split into three classes with a specified order of combination.

Stage 2: $S \rightarrow (Dem) + (Art) + (M_2) + N$

The process of differentiation continues. Possessive pronouns (Poss) eventually form a separate class because, unlike
other modifiers, they do not occur after articles. This separation
has occurred when constructions such as *a my car* disappear
from Adam's speech. At this point, adjectives form their own
distinct class because they still occur after articles, in phrases
such as *a blue flower.*

Stage 3: $S \rightarrow \left\{ \begin{array}{l} (Dem) + (Art) + (Adj) \\ M_3 \\ Poss \end{array} \right\} + N$

M_3 comprises a miscellaneous class of modifiers, including *other,
more, one*, and a few others.

In Adam's case, one class of modifiers split into five
classes over a period of about five months. The process of differentiation is coupled with the development of more complex syntactic rules for the combination of the increasing number of
classes. Adam is well on the way to having a variety of syntactic
forms to express his structural meanings unambiguously. The
process is not complete yet; full development of the noun phrase
will require the emergence of *inflections* such as the possessive
and the plural. (These will be discussed in the next two sections.)

Differentiation is not the only process of development. It
would be a sufficient mechanism if each word class of adult language were contained entirely in one or the other of the original
word classes. Nouns are typically found in the open class and not

in the pivot class, so it is theoretically possible to develop the adult class of nouns through differentiation. However, there are cases in which members of an adult class are found in both the pivot and open class. This is most common with adjectives. Differentiation alone can lead only to the development of *two* classes of adjectives. Children must do more than differentiate, they must *reclassify* as they elaborate their language. **Reclassification** is a mysterious process; little is known beyond the fact that it must occur. One hypothesis will be discussed in the next chapter.

In the analysis above, all noun phrases were considered equivalent through development. Bloom (1970a) has observed that this is not entirely correct; there is a strong tendency for sentence elaboration to proceed right-to-left. In the earliest sentences of children, nouns frequently occur as objects of actions but seldom as the agents who perform the action. Agents appear later. Similarly, during the development of noun phrases, elaboration occurs first for noun phrases that are objects and only later for noun phrases that occur earlier in the sentence. Sentences like *I see the old man who sells ice cream* occur before sentences like *The little old man who sells ice cream is down the block.* The second sentence seems more complex, more difficult to comprehend and remember, even for adults. Perhaps the same mechanism underlies the difference between the two sentences for both children and adults.

Word Order in Child Language

Two of the major devices used by languages to indicate the syntactic structure of sentences are **word order** and **inflections.** Languages differ in the extent to which they rely on these devices. Some languages rely almost entirely on inflections. Latin and Russian are examples; the words of a Latin sentence may be placed in almost any order. *Vir mordet canem, Mordet canem vir, Canem mordet vir, Vir canem mordet, Canem vir mordet,* and *Mordet vir canem* all mean, approximately, "Man bites dog." What makes the sentences intelligible are the *inflections,* in this case, *suffixes* at the ends of words. The subject is unambiguously marked regardless of its position by the nominative case ending (in the example, no suffix at all); while the object is unambiguously marked regardless of its position by the accusative case ending (in the example, *-em*). The verb is marked by tense, number, and other suffixes. English is closer to the other extreme; *Man bites dog* is not the same as *Dog bites man*. English has very few inflections (among them are the pronoun inflections: nominative *he* versus accusative *him*), and order is extremely important for determining the meaning of a sentence.

In the preceding descriptions of child language, order has played the most important role. Virtually all studies of child language report that the child begins his language development by stringing words together without inflections. Only later are the inflections added. Children's imitations of adult speech share this property. Typically the inflections, and also the "little words," the so-called function words, are omitted in the imitation. For example, when two of the children studied by Brown's group were asked to imitate the sentence *I showed you the book*, both Eve and Adam produced *I show book*. Adam imitated *I am drawing a dog* with *I draw dog* (Brown and Fraser, 1964).

To the extent that the child's language does indicate syntactic structure, it does so by use of word order, as the previous sections have illustrated. At least some of the rules of the grammar specify a fixed order for members of the various word classes. This reliance on word order is apparent in imitation and comprehension, as well as in spontaneous speech. The imitations above, like most children's imitations, preserve the order of the elements that are successfully produced. There is a period in development when American children are likely to interpret passive sentences such as *The dog is chased by the cat* to mean that the first noun, *dog*, is the subject, and the second noun, *cat*, is the object. They do so because that is the order in active sentences, which are the most common, even though it is exactly the wrong interpretation in this instance (Fraser, Bellugi, & Brown, 1963; Bever, 1970). The reliance on word order as the primary grammatical device is not limited to English. And this fact has considerable theoretical importance. Martin Braine (1963) has formulated a theory of language acquisition which he calls "contextual generalization." This theory can be summarized by his assertion that "What is learned are primarily the proper locations of words." The child focuses his attention on a particular position and classifies together all the words that occur in that position. With increasing development, more refined positions are utilized. Braine's theory, which will be discussed more fully in Chapter 5, does have a certain plausibility for the acquisition of English, in which word order plays such an important role. The crucial evidence, however, must come from observations of the acquisition of highly inflected languages such as Russian.

Russian has a rich noun-inflectional system and no articles. For simple sentences, all six orderings of subject(s), verb(v), and object(o) — SOV, SVO, OSV, OVS, VSO, VOS — are grammatical and all are stylistic variants. What can be learned from Russian by a child learning language by means of contextual generalization? There is a great variety of orders of words, but combinations of words with inflections are rigidly fixed and ordered. The child should first learn the inflections and attach them to members of the appropriate word classes and then combine the resulting words in relatively free order. In fact, child grammar in Russian begins with uninflected forms combined in a relatively inflexible order. The flexibility of adult Russian does not appear until the inflectional system has been mastered, a feat which occurs considerably later. Gvozdev reports that his son Zhenya's first sentences of this type were in the order subject-object-verb (SOV). Later Zhenya changed to SVO (Slobin, in press). But during each stage, his language was highly consistent. Another Russian child produced sentences in both the SVO and SOV orders.

Studies of German and Finnish children, reviewed in Slobin (in press), show similar orders. The four remaining orders — OSV, OVS, VSO, and VOS — are extremely rare. In summary, children's early grammar is quite rigid in order, although it is occasionally not quite as rigid that of children learning English.

An objection to any conclusion drawn from the fact that children learning flexibly ordered languages begin with an ordered language is that mothers may restrict themselves in speaking to young children to one or two orders. A similar claim is often advanced in an attempt to explain how young children can use data that are as complex and irregular as normal adult speech. In fact, we have very little evidence of this question. This lack of knowledge concerning how mothers talk to their young children is one of the most serious problems in attempting to understand the learning process. The small body of evidence available (to be discussed in Chapter 5) suggests that some simplification does occur, but it is not of the magnitude which would invalidate the arguments above.

A more serious problem is raised by the fact that reliance on word order is not completely universal. The two best-documented examples are a Finnish child studied by Bowerman (1969, cited in McNeill, 1970b) and one of the English-speaking children studied by Miller and Ervin (1964). These children joined words together without inflections but also without fixed word order. Since Finnish is a language with flexible word order, whereas English is not, this phenomenon does not appear to be determined entirely by the language the child hears. Perhaps, as McNeill suggests, "English-learning children who use juxtaposition without inflections or rigid word order may be following the erroneous hypothesis that they are learning an inflected language. The converse can be said of children learning inflected languages who use rigid word order [McNeill, 1970, P. 67]." Nevertheless, it does not appear that children simply select from two alternative, equally likely possibilities. No child attempts to use inflections from the beginning, and most children begin with rigid word order.

The Development of Inflections

Although word order seems to be the dominant feature of early child language, inflections appear not too long after the beginning of grammatically structured speech. We do not have enough information to be able to say just when this is likely to happen, but Slobin (1970) has offered the tentative generalization that it seems to occur when the child passes from the two-word stage to the three-word stage; in other words, at about the same time hierarchical structure appears. And perhaps there is some connection here. Once inflections are introduced, they develop more or less rapidly. The child seems to have no difficulty with the general notion of suffixing, only with some particular inflectional systems.

In general, the inflectional classes whose reference is most concrete are developed first (Cazden, 1968; Slobin, in press). The plural inflection on nouns appears to be the first developed for both English and Russian children. Classes based on relational criteria such as case and persons of the verb, as well as tense, are next (followed in Russian by the conditional marking of verbs). Suffixes indicating rather abstract categories of quality and action, such as the possessive and the progressive tense, are developed later. Grammatical gender has virtually no systematic semantic reference in Russian: *stol* ("table") is masculine, *kniga* ("book") is feminine, and *piero* ("pen") is neuter. The classification is on the basis of the final sound of the word, in the nominative case. Mastering this system — adjectives and other modifiers must be marked to agree with the noun in gender — is the most difficult and drawn-out learning process for the Russian child.

The plural suffix on nouns is always one of the first inflections to be produced, and usually is *the* first. There are two general contexts in which pluralization is necessary. The first is **number agreement** between subject and verb, illustrated in the sentence *The chickens walk.* Both *chickens* and *walk* must be pluralized, if either one is. The second type of context where pluralization is called for is illustrated in *Those chickens* (*crossed the road*). Here both the demonstrative pronoun and the noun must be pluralized, if either is. This is **agreement between modifier and noun** in a noun phrase. The difference between this type of agreement and that between subject and verb is that in the latter, the agreement is entirely within a single noun phrase, while in the former, the agreement extends across the noun phrase boundary to the verb. Children are more consistent in providing the plural form when it is required on words within a noun phrase, that is, in the latter case, than they are in the former case, where pluralization is required by agreement across a phrase boundary (Cazden, 1968). This is another indication of the unity of the noun phrase in the language of children.

The learning of the present progressive tense illustrates an important characteristic of early child language. You recall that a transformational grammar of adult English introduces (*be* + *ing*) in the auxiliary position in the deep structure, and then the affix transformation moves the *-ing* to the following verb, producing sentences such as *The boy is running.* In development, however, the attachment of *-ing* to the following verb and the introduction of *be* appear to be independent accomplishments, mastered in that order. Children consistently use *-ing* on the main verb before they use a form of *be*, producing sentences such as *The boy running.* Later the auxiliary verb will be introduced. Sentences of this kind can be produced without transformations, which are necessary to account for the adult forms. Presumably, for children at this stage, *-ing* is introduced as an optional element by a phrase structure rule of the form:

PS2.4.   V → MV + (ing)

This is further evidence for the conclusion that child language in its early stages is basically phrase-structure in nature, not transformational. In the next chapter we will consider some implications of this generalization.

The learning of inflections illustrates one of the most interesting phenomena of children's language learning — their

overregularization of inflections. Children learning English use *comed, goed, breaked*, and similar forms. The irregular, or strong, verbs of English are inflected for the past tense in the same manner as the regular, or weak, verbs. This is true even of first-born children from middle-class homes who do not hear these incorrect overgeneralizations in their linguistic environment. We might expect that children would begin by using some regular forms correctly, such as *walked* or *helped*, and then extend this rule to the irregular verbs, producing the incorrect forms *comed, goed*, and so on. But this is not what happens. The first past tense forms used are the *correct* forms of the irregular verbs — *came, went, broke*, and so on. After a few weeks or months, the regular past tense morpheme *-ed* suddenly appears on all verbs, regular and irregular alike: *comed, breaked, walked*. The correct irregular past tense forms are simply abandoned. Ervin (1964), who first reported this sequence of development, actually observed the incorrect overregularization (*comed*) before she observed a correct regular form (*walked*), although this is probably due to the fact that the irregular verbs are more frequent in the speech of children and adults.

The crucial point here is that the irregular verbs, even though they are the most frequent verbs in English, do not follow a pattern; we can only conclude that the child is fundamentally a pattern learner. Once a pattern is acquired, it will be applied as broadly as possible, even if this results in the production of words that he has never heard before. Ervin (1964) observed a similar process in the development of English plurals.

Linguists, and many alert language learners, have noticed that it is usually the most common words of a language that are irregular. In English, for example, the irregular verbs *be, come, go*, and *do* are among the most frequent verbs. The phenomenon of overregularization suggests an explanation for this fact. Children have a strong tendency to regularize all verbs. In the case of infrequent verbs, they hear the correct form very few times or not at all, and there is little to prevent them from regularization. But they have heard the common irregular verbs often and are thus reminded of their irregularity. Furthermore, adults are more likely to correct children when they produce forms such as *doed* than they are when children produce regularized forms of infrequent verbs. Even adults are unsure about the few infrequent irregular verbs of English, such as *thrive* — is the past tense *thrived* or *throve*? This hypothesis might be tested by examining linguistic change.

Overregularizations are common in the acquisition of Russian. Russian case endings are almost as difficult for the child as for the second-language learner. One of the Russian cases in the *instrumental*. In the Russian equivalent of the sentence *He hit the block with a hammer*, the word for "hammer" has an *instrumental case ending* because "hammer" is the instrument of hitting. The exact form of the instrumental case suffix depends on the gender of the noun and on its number, singular or plural. Masculine and neuter singular nouns require -*om*, while feminine singular nouns require -*oy*. Zhenya first used the suffix -*om* for all instrumental singular nouns, even though it was correct only for masculine and neuter singular nouns (Slobin, 1966a). This is surprising, since feminine nouns are more frequent in Russian child speech. However, the suffix -*om* has only one other function — as the masculine and neuter prepositional case ending for adjectives. In contrast, the suffix -*oy* serves a variety of other functions, being an adjectival suffix for four cases in the feminine and one in the masculine. Zhenya selected the suffix with fewer meanings for use in all instances of the singular instrumental case.

This -*om* ending was dominant in Zhenya's language from age two years and one month to two years and four months. (Ages of this type are usually abbreviated to read 2;1 and 2;4. And that system will be used throughout this book.) But as soon as he began using the feminine singular instrumental ending -*oy*, he completely abandoned -*om* and used -*oy* universally. This lasted from 2;5 to 3;0, after which he mastered the conventional usage. Table 2-4 summarizes this development and compares it with the development of the past tense by English-speaking children.

TABLE 2-4   *The Development of Two Inflections*

Stage	English	Russian
I	came, went, etc.	-*om* for masc., neut., fem.
II	comed, goed, helped, etc.	-*oy* for masc., neut., fem.
III	came, went, helped, etc.	-*om* for masc., neut.; -*oy* for fem.

Here again, a well-practiced form, which was in many cases correct, is abandoned and an overregularization made. In one sense, this is an even more striking phenomenon than that observed in the development of the past tense in English. In that case, a pattern drove out the use of certain special cases. In Zhenya's case, one pattern replaces another pattern. This development appears to be quite general in Russian children.

The singular accusative case for nouns also is overregularized. There are actually four forms in adult Russian: the zero ending (no suffix at all), *-u*, *-a*, and *-o*. As we would expect, Zhenya used one form for all nouns; but which form was it? The zero ending is the most frequent form in adult speech, followed by *-u*. But it is *-u* which enters child language first, and it is used for all singular accusative nouns. This example suggests that children prefer marked forms to unmarked forms, probably for reasons of distinctiveness; unmarked forms are highly ambiguous.

Notice that the dominant inflections, which Slobin (in press) has called "imperialistic inflections," are not simply chosen from one particular paradigm. The predominant instrumental singular suffix *-om* is masculine and neuter, while the predominant accusative singular suffix *-u* is feminine. The choice is made separately in each case, presumably on the basis of distinctiveness and lack of ambiguity.

Like English, Russian has both **count nouns** and **mass nouns.** Count nouns can be pluralized and counted: *brick, two bricks.* Mass nouns cannot: *some sugar* but not **two sugars.* It is quite common in Russian that when noun plurals first appear, any noun may be pluralized or counted. Children count mass nouns, for example, *odna sakhara* ("one sugar"), and pluralize them, *bumagi* ("papers"). They also invent singulars for plural nouns which have no singular form in Russian: *lyut,* a singular for *lyudi* ("people"). Only later is the class of nouns divided into count and mass nouns. At first, the children treat all nouns the same, capable of having singular and plural forms; this is an overgeneralization from the count nouns.

In this chapter we have been concerned with a primarily descriptive account of early child language. Instead of proceeding directly to later developments, such as the emergence of questions, we will make two digressions. Both are concerned with general views of the nature of language and the process of language acquisition. The first, discussed below, concerns Russian views of language acquisition. The second, the subject of Chapter 3, concerns the nature of man's biological endowment for language development.

Russian Views of Language Acquisition

Despite the fact that American behaviorism looked to Pavlov as its intellectual father, and despite the great veneration Soviet psychologists have for Pavlov, Soviet psychology has never adopted the mechanistic, rather passive models of learning and experience characteristic of the behavioristic tradition of psychological theorizing. Late in his life Pavlov himself came to the conclusion that although fundamental reflex principles of the kind he had studied in dogs and other species apply to all species, the presence in humans of a complex and organized system of linguistic signals lead to a new dimension of behavior. He carefully distinguished "first signals" — all the individual physical stimuli to which animals and humans alike can respond — from "second signals" — primarily words. Although some second-order signals are observable in other animals, in man the second signal system is a large and organized *system*, with its own structures and functions. Slobin quotes Pavlov:

> The word created a second system of signals of reality which is peculiarly ours, being signal of signals. On the one hand, numerous speech stimuli have removed us from reality . . . On the other hand, it is precisely speech which has made us human [1966c, p. 112].

There are many reasons for this conclusion on the part of Soviet psychologists. Pavlov himself felt that virtually all the laws he discovered concerning classical conditioning did not hold for the second signal system. For example, words can affect behavior immediately, without the gradual process of conditioning. But one of the most important reasons, especially for Soviet theories of language and language behavior, comes from the extensive and productive **morphology** — the means of constructing words out of morphemes — of the Russian language, which children use so creatively. Slobin quotes Gvozdev:

> The child makes wide use of the means of word-formation provided by his native language. He makes an especially vast use of suffixes — and this is distinguished by exceptional precision and consistency of both meaning and sound [in press].

The most charming and enlightening record of such creactivity is Kornei Chukovsky's *From Two to Five* (1968). Chukovsky was a famous Soviet writer and translator of children's stories who, over many years, collected hundreds of child language anecdotes and analyzed them. A few examples from the first chapter of the book, "A Linguistic Genius," are a fitting close to this chapter.

Some of the examples tell us about the child's conceptual powers and imagination:

> Can't you see? I'm barefoot all over!

I'll get up so early that it will still be late.

Isn't there something to eat in the cupboard? There's only a small piece of cake, but it's middle-aged."

But many of the examples illustrate the child's manipulation of Russian morphology and syntax:

> Another child, whose exact age I did not know, created the words shoe-ware' (*obutki*) and clothesware' (*odetki*) . . . (these were formulated by a small child from the household words for footwear and clothes heard from adults.

Interestingly enough, Chukovsky discovered that in another section of Russia, far from the area in which this child lived, these words had been part of the Russian language, in precisely the same form and with the same meaning, several centuries ago.

> A two-year-old girl was taking a bath and making her doll "dive" into the water and "dive out" of it, commenting: "There, she drowns-in — now, she drowns-out!" *Vot pritonula, vot vytonula* . . . "Drowns-in" is not the same thing as drowns — it is to drown only temporarily with a definite expectation implied that the doll would be "drowing-out" again . . .

In another example, a child refers to the husband of a grass-hopper as a daddy-hopper. Chukovsky writes:

> It seems to me that, beginning with the age of two, every child becomes for a short period of time a linguistic genius. Later, beginning with the age of five or six, this talent begins to fade.

Chukovsky also illustrates children's activity as critics of adult speech. Despite their highly creative use of language, children are essentially nonmetaphorical and almost completely literal. Here are two examples:

> "Why do you say penknife? It should be pencilknife," a little boy objected.

> A woman . . . asked her four-year-old Natasha: "Tell me, what does it mean to say that a person is trying to drown another in a spoonful of water (a Russian expression)?"

> "What did you say? In what kind of spoon? Say that again."

> The mother repeated the adage.

> "That's impossible" Natasha said categorically. "It can never happen!"

> Right then and there she [Natasha] demonstrated the physical impossibility of such an act; she grabbed a spoon and quickly placed it on the floor.

"Look, here am I," and she stood on the spoon. "All right, drown me. There isn't enough room for a whole person — all of him will remain on top . . . Look for yourself . . . the foot is much larger than spoon!"

And Natasha expressed scorn for such an absurd idea conceived by grownups, saying: "Let's not talk about it any more — it's such nonsense."

Summary

It is striking how little difficulty a child has with any of the general mechanisms of language: the notion of a sentence, the establishment of word classes and rules for combining them, the concept of inflections, the expression of a wide variety of meanings, and more. All are present from a very early age. Particular word classes, rules, inflections, or meanings may, however, require time for mastery.

As impressive as the complexity of child language is, it appears to be outstripped by the uses to which the child wants to put it. The basic syntactic structures, pivot-open or otherwise, are put to a wide variety of uses, even at the cost of considerable ambiguity.

The child's establishment and differentiation of word classes and the overregularization of inflections show a search for patterns on the part of the child. He is divided between his tendency to extend patterns as widely as possible and his desire to match the patterns of the language about him.

The widespread, though not universal, reliance on word order as the primary grammatical device is evidence that language learning is more than a purely formal process of position learning. The early appearance of many structural meanings, together with the striking differences between many child utterances, for example, *allgone outside* being said when the front door is closed, and the adult speech around the child strongly suggests that the child is above all attempting to express his own ideas, emotions, and actions through whatever system he has thus far constructed.

SELECTED REFERENCES

Bloom, L. *Language development: Form and function in emerging grammars.* Cambridge, Mass.: M.I.T. Press, 1970. (a)

Bloom, L. Semantic features in language acquisition. Paper presented at the Conference on Research in the Language of the Mentally Retarded, University of Kansas, February, 1970. (b)

Bowerman, M. F. The pivot-open class distinction. Unpublished paper, Harvard University, 1969.

Braine, M. D. S. The ontogeny of English phrase structure: The first phrase. *Language*, 1963, **39**, 1–13.

Brown, R. The first sentences of child and chimpanzee. In *Psycholinguistics: Selected papers of Roger Brown*. New York: Free Press, 1970. Pp. 208–231.

Brown, R., & Bellugi, U. Three Processes in the child's acquisition of syntax. *Harvard Educational Review*, 1964, **34**, 133–151.

Brown, R., & Fraser, C. The acquisition of syntax. In U. Bellugi & R. Brown (Eds.), *The acquisition of language*. Monographs of the Society for Research in Child Development, 1964, **29** (Serial No. 92), 43–79.

Cazden, C. The acquisition of noun and verb inflections. *Child Development*, 1968, **39**, 433–438.

Chomsky, N. *Aspects of the theory of syntax*. Cambridge, Mass.: M.I.T. Press, 1965.

Chukovsky, K. *From two to five*. Translated by M. Morton. Berkeley: University of California Press, 1968.

DeLaguna, G. *Speech: Its function and development*. Bloomington, Ind.: Indiana University Press, 1963.

Ervin, S. Imitation and structural change in children's language. In E. H. Lenneberg (Ed.), *New directions in the study of language*. Cambridge, Mass.: M.I.T. Press, 1964, Pp. 163–189.

Fraser, C., Bellugi, U., & Brown, R. Control of grammar in imitation, comprehension, and production. *Journal of Verbal Learning and Verbal Behavior*, 1963, **2**, 121–135.

Leopold, W. F. *Speech development of a bilingual child: A linguist's record*. Vol. 1. *Vocabulary growth in the first two years*. Vol. 2 *Sound learning in the first two years*. Vol. 3 *Grammar and general problems in the first two years*. Vol. 4. *Diary from age 2*. Evanston, Ill.: Northwestern University Press, 1939, 1947, 1949 (a), 1949 (b).

McCarthy, D. Language development in children. In L. Carmichael (Ed.), *Manual of child psychology*. New York: Wiley, 1954. Pp. 492–630.

McNeill, D. The development of language. In P. H. Mussen (Ed.), *Carmichael's manual of child psychology*. Vol. 1. (3rd. ed.) New York: Wiley, 1970. Pp. 1061–1161. (a)

McNeill, D. *The acquisition of language: The study of developmental psycholinguistics*. New York: Harper & Row, 1970. (b)

Miller, W., & Ervin-Tripp, S. The development of grammar in child language. In R. Brown & U. Bellugi (Eds.), *The acquisition of language*. Monographs of the Society for Research in Child Development, 1964, **29** (Serial No. 92), 9–34.

Schlesinger, I. M. Production of utterances and language acquisition. In D. I. Slobin (Ed.), *The ontogenesis of grammar*. New York: Academic Press, in press.

Slobin, D. I. The acquisition of Russian as a native language. In F. Smith & G. A. Miller (Eds.), *The genesis of language: A psycholinguistic approach*. Cambridge, Mass.: M.I.T. Press, 1966. Pp. 129–248. (a)

Slobin, D. I. Grammatical transformations and sentence comprehension in childhood and adulthood. *Journal of Verbal Learning and Verbal Behavior*, 1966, **5,** 219–227. (b)

Slobin, D. I. Soviet psycholinguistics. In N. O'Connor (Ed.), *Present-day Soviet psychology*. Oxford: Pergamon Press, 1966. (c)

Slobin, D. I. Universals of grammatical development in children. In G. B. Flores d'Arcais & W. J. M. Levelt (Eds.), *Advances in psycholinguistics*. New York: American Elsevier, 1970. Pp. 174–184.

Slobin, D. I. Early grammatical development in several languages, with special attention to Soviet research. In T. G. Bever & W. Weksel (Eds.), *The structure and psychology of language*. New York: Holt, Rinehart and Winston, in press.

FURTHER READING

Bloom, L. *Language development: Form and function in emerging grammars*. Cambridge, Mass.: M.I.T. Press, 1970.

Brown, R. *Psycholinguistics*. New York: Free Press, 1970.

Chukovsky, K. *From two to five*. M. Morton (Trans. and Ed.) Berkeley: University of California Press, 1968.

Slobin, D. I. The acquisition of Russian as a native language. In F. Smith & G. A. Miller (Eds.), *The genesis of language: A psycholinguistic approach*. Cambridge, Mass.: M.I.T. Press, 1966, Pp. 128–152.

3

An Innate Capacity for Language?

Language is often viewed as the characteristic that defines human beings. Is language transmitted entirely culturally from one generation to the next, or do children possess an innate biological capacity for language? If the latter, how may this capacity be described? The very earliest stages of language development, as described in Chapter 2, are especially important with respect to these questions, because here we can see most clearly the strategies children use in their initial organization of language, when they have the least information on the particular language of the adult community.

The Innateness Hypothesis

The hypothesis that human beings are endowed with a biological capacity for language — the **innateness hypothesis** — is not a statement about how children learn language. Rather, it is an hypothesis about aspects of language which need *not* be learned in the usual sense. If it is correct, however, it does have implications for our understanding of the learning process. To formulate the problem faced by a child beginning his language learning, we must have a clear idea of what the child must learn — adult grammar, as described in Chapter 1— *and* an equally explicit understanding of where he begins. The distance between these two points is the gap that must be bridged by any theory of language learning.

Traditionally there have been two divergent positions on the question of man's language ability. At one extreme it has been claimed that no linguistic structure is innate; language is learned entirely through experience. In Locke's vivid phrase, children begin as *tabula rasa* ("blank slates"). They learn language through general learning principles, which are usually assumed to be the same in many species of organisms. This is the **empiricist** position.

At the opposite extreme is the **rationalist** (or **nativist**) position. The structure of language is to a considerable degree specified biologically. The function of experience is not so much to teach directly, but to activate the innate capacity, to turn it into linguistic competence (Chomsky, 1968).

There are two important differences between these positions. The empiricist view holds that very little psychological structure is innately specified, while the rationalist view claims that a great deal is. This is a difference of degree, but of a very large degree. The empiricist position admits that there are certain innate abilities but insists that these are relatively simple, such as the ability to form associations. The rationalist position does not deny that experience has a function, since children must hear language in order to learn to speak and, indeed, eventually speak the language spoken in their community.

The second difference between these positions is absolute. In the empiricist view, the human child has no special ability for language, only general abilities to learn. Language is induced from experience by means of the same processes that are responsible for other aspects of mental development. In the rationalist view, there is a specific, and strong, capacity for language.

Undoubtedly the original stimulus for the formulation of the rationalist position was the observation that man is alone in possessing language. But equally important is the observation that language is the common possession of nearly all humans. That is, language is **species specific** and **species uniform**. Descartes was aware of both these points in the seventeenth century when he wrote:

> . . . it is a very remarkable fact that there are none so depraved and stupid, without even excepting idiots, that they cannot arrange different words together, forming of them a statement by which they make known their thoughts; while, on the other hand, there is no other animal, however perfect and fortunately circumstanced it may be, which can do the same [Descartes, 1955, p. 116].

Both species specificity and species uniformity are suggestive or the innateness hypothesis. First, species specificity: Chimpanzees are intelligent animals; they can learn to use tools and solve problems that are not trivial for humans. Several chimpanzees have been raised like children, in a home, but despite this experience and direct instruction in language, they have not made any significant progress toward the kind of linguistic system that human children develop naturally (Hayes, 1951).[1]

Species uniformity is also consistent with the innateness hypothesis. If language is the result of general learning abilities, as the empiricist position holds, linguistic competence should be a function of learning ability, that is, intelligence. Intelligence is highly variable, so some children should do far better in language than others and some should fail altogether, just as some children fail to learn how to take square roots or play the piano. But this is not the case. Over a wide range of intelligence, down to IQ levels of about 50 (Lenneberg, 1967), bright, average, and less intelligent children learn how to talk. They differ greatly in their inclination to talk, in their vocabulary, and in what they have to say; but the mastery of the linguistic system does not vary greatly. The variation which does occur is far less than the mastery of, for example, arithmetic, which is much less complex than language. This is consistent with the rationalist position, which claims that language specifically is part of the biological endowment of man.

The nature of child language should provide evidence on this question. In Reading 3.1, McNeill (1966) argues for the essential identity of the task faced by a child, a linguist in the field, a computer, or any "language acquisition device." He hypothe-

---

[1]The recent success of Gardner and Gardner (1969) in teaching a form of the American Sign Language (the deaf sign language) to Washoe, a chimpanzee, may modify this conclusion, but not totally falsify it. Washoe has acquired a productive communicative system, but one which appears to contrast with human natural languages in several ways. For comparisons of Washoe and human children, see Bronowski and Bellugi (1970) and Brown (1970).

sizes that in each case an important role is played by knowledge of linguistic universals, the features common to all the languages of the world. These universal properties are the subject of **linguistic theory,** the science of human language, in contrast to the study of individual languages. Language universals exist because all languages are acquired by children. Each generation creates language anew; and in the process, children impose features corresponding to their innate capacity.

This emphasis on similarities among languages seems surprising. When we first compare languages — in learning a foreign language, for example — we are usually struck by the differences. Languages do differ greatly in their superficial details. But the underlying principles are far more uniform. Two types of universal properties of language are possible (Chomsky, 1965). A particular element, or rule, (a shared element) may appear in all languages. It appears that nouns and verbs are found in all languages, although the concepts encoded by them vary. The deep structure rule for negative sentences may be universal. These are examples of **substantive universals.** In addition to actual shared elements, languages may have strong similarities in form, that is, constraints on the possible form of a language. Such constraints are **formal universals.** A grammar is a system for combining morphemes to express meanings. Similarities among languages imply that the existing language systems are a highly restricted subset of the systems which are logically possible. The general form of a transformational grammar is universal; it is necessary to draw a distinction between the surface structure and a more abstract deep structure for every language. Even if there were no other similarities among languages, this would be one formal universal. Furthermore, the deep structure is hierarchical in nature and generated by phrase-structure rules, although the precise nature of the rules may vary.

The study of language universals is in its infancy, but the research that has been done indicates that most universal features are properties of the deep structure: the existence of a hierarchical deep structure; grammatical relations between subject and predicate and other elements; the possibility of posing questions, giving commands, and expressing negations; and more. Whether or not the entire deep structure is universal is still a controversial question. In Reading 3.2, Chomsky (1968) argues that the existence of abstract (in the sense of underlying, not directly observable) universal properties of language is itself an argument for a rationalist theory of language. The particular transformations that appear in any language are unique. The affix transformation discussed in Chapter 1 is unique to English (although a very similar one is found in French), as is the passive transformation. However, the operations performed by transformations — the ways in which transformations change deep structures by adding, deleting, substituting, or permuting constituents — are remarkably similar from language to language.

If the argument in the preceding paragraphs is correct, the innateness hypothesis can be rephrased more precisely: *The features of language that children must acquire from the speech around them are the unique features of their language, and these include the actual transformations of that language. They do not have to learn those features of the deep structure which are universal, nor do they have to eliminate those possibilities that are ruled out by the formal universals.*

Two major predictions follow from the hypothesis just stated. Because the child has not yet had time to learn much about the unique features of the language about him, early child language should be free of transformations. The structure of the child's sentences should be similar to the deep structure of adult sentences, and not necessarily similar to the surface structure that he actually hears.[2]

The second prediction is a corollary of the first. The early speech of all children should be very similar, regardless of the form of linguistic input. The universals of child language should be even more apparent than the universals of adult language, which are more abstract. The language of children exposed to English or Russian or Japanese should be essentially the same even though the adult languages around them are highly diverse in surface structure.

To evaluate this sweeping hypothesis by testing the two predictions requires a substantial amount of evidence from children acquiring a wide variety of languages. There is not nearly enough information of this kind available, although an increasing amount of cross-linguistic research is in progress.

The descriptions of child language in the previous chapter provide some evidence directly. The earliest grammars of children learning diverse languages are remarkably similar. Syntactic development begins with a two-word stage in which there are at

---

[2]This is an enormous oversimplification. What the child actually hears is a continuous acoustic signal. He must first segment the signal, then identify the words, and then determine the surface structure. Even this ordering is an oversimplification (see Neisser, 1967).

least two distinct classes of words. If the language is analyzed as a pivot-open grammar, there is a small number of function words (the pivots) and a larger class of content words (the open class). Words from the two are combined to express a wide variety of thoughts. If the language is analyzed as a set of structural meanings, there are substantial similarities in the set of structural meanings utilized by children acquiring different languages. Only about a dozen combination types occur in early child language; many other possibilities which occur in adult speech do not, such as indirect-object–direct-object (*doggy ball* meaning "give the doggy the ball").

In addition, word order is usually the dominant grammatical mechanism, whether the adult language is highly dependent on word order (English) or whether it is an inflected language with flexible word order (Russian). The exceptions to this generalization are difficult to evaluate. Is it enough to consider only a statistical universal? However, it is probable that order plays a role at a deeper level for the apparent exceptions. A child who says "Mommy pigtail" and "See mommy" is not using *mommy* in a specified order, but the functions which the words serve are constrained by order. All the child's subject-object constructions occur in just that order, and the same is true for verb-object constructions. Preference for fixed order extends to comprehension, as well as production. The fact that young children interpret the passive as if it were the active, as reported in the last chapter, is one example of this.

These observations are consistent with the second prediction: the similarity of child language. Evidence bearing on the first prediction, child language as deep structure, is scanty at this time. Like many languages, English has a number of contraction transformations that combine distinct morphemes in the deep structure into single words. Despite the fact that children are likely to hear contracted forms — *I'll*, *isn't*, and so on — their first productions with these morphemes are always in the full, uncontracted form — *I will*, *is not* — even when directly imitating an adult contracted form (Bellugi, 1967). What appear to be counterexamples, such as the early appearance of *can't* and *don't* in the negatives of some children (Klima and Bellugi, 1966) do not represent mastery of both morphemes but, rather, the adoption of the adult form as a single morpheme approximately synonymous with *no*. These children do not use *can* and *do* in their nonnegated form.

McNeill has called attention to three additional pieces of evidence that provide some confirmation for the prediction of child language as deep structure; they are the first appearances of negative sentences, questions, and the basic grammatical relations. In each case there is a difference between deep and surface structure in the adult language surrounding the child; the child resolves the conflict by structuring his own early language according to the deep structure.

Negation

Negative sentences appear in the very first grammatically structured sentences. They are predictably simple (Klima and Bellugi, 1966): *No fall; No drop mitten; No want soup; Get car no.* Affirmative sentences are negated by simply attaching a special negative operator, in this case the word "no."

This is exactly the form posited for the deep structure of English negative sentences by the linguist Klima (1964) on the basis of consideration of adult language alone. The deep structure has a morpheme that stands outside the rest of the sentence and is used specifically for negation. It is called the Neg morpheme. There is a system of transformations which permute the elements of the deep structure to produce the surface structure; the principle effect of these transformations is to attach the Neg morpheme to the auxiliary verb (compare *He can swim* with *He can't swim*). The children have not yet acquired these transformations, which are unique to English.

Russian children show identical forms in early negation, according to Slobin. This is particularly interesting, because the adult forms often include double negatives: *Nyet ni kavo* ("Not no one"); *Nyet ni dam* ("No, not I will give"). But Zhenya's early negations are identical in form to those of English speaking children: *Nyet kavo* ("no one"); *Nyet dam* ("no I will give"). In fact, Zhenya always used the same negative word, *nyet* even when another form, *ni*, was appropriate and presumably provided in the adult speech about him. He appears to be voicing the Neg morpheme directly, through a rule Neg → *nyet*.

Similarly, the first negatives in French are of the form *non* + S or *pas* + S; and those of Japanese children, S + *nai*

(McNeill & McNeill, 1968). (The placement of the Neg morpheme at the beginning or end of the sentence is not universally fixed.)

Questions

Like negations, questions appear at the very beginning of language acquisition (Bellugi, 1965): *Fraser water? See hole? Mommy eggnog? Who dat? What doing? Why not?* The first three questions are recognizable as questions only by the rising intonation at the end of the sentence. This intonation can be applied to any sentence to produce a question The questions with *wh* words appear to be single units, with very little internal structure. The basic scheme for all these questions is S + Q, where Q stands for the question intonation. This is very much like the form of the first negations, Neg + S or S + Neg. Again, this is very much like the deep structure of questions in adult English formulated by linguists (Katz and Postal, 1964). There is a special Q morpheme that stands outside the remainder of the sentence. In adult English, there is a set of transformations that apply to this deep structure and make considerable changes in the sentence, and these will be discussed in the next chapter. But the child begins with the deep structure alone.

The fact that Q is *always* manifested as rising intonation, just as the Neg in Zhenya's speech was always manifested as *nyet*, is interesting because in adult English it is not really necessary for all questions to end with a rising intonation. In fact, questions with *wh* words are usually pronounced with normal sentence intonation, for example, *What did he do?* This aspect of surface structure is not copied by children. They use a simpler rule: pronounce Q as rising intonation.

Basic Grammatical Relations

In Chapter 1 no mention was made of the traditional grammatical notions of subject, predicate, and object. These concepts, usually drummed into us in junior high school, are essential to the description of English. But they are very different concepts from those introduced in Chapter 1, such as noun phrase and verb phrase. Consider simple sentence *The dog bit the timid mailman*, which has the surface structure:

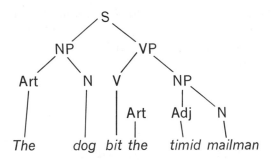

The dog is an NP. It is also the subject of the sentence. But being the subject of a sentence is not the same thing as being an NP. *The timid mailman* is also an NP, but it is the object of the verb and is not the subject. Saying that a constituent is an NP is a statement about how the constituent is constructed, that it has a certain kind of **internal structure** — Art + N or Art + Adj + N, and so on. In contrast, being a subject or an object is a statement about the **function** of the constituent in the sentence; that is, it is a statement about how it relates to the other parts of the sentence.

The sentence *The dog bit the timid mailman* suggests that the subject of a sentence might be defined as the first NP. Such a definition is adequate only for very simple sentences. In the passive sentence *A timid mailman was bitten by the dog*, it is the second NP, *the dog*, which is the true subject of the verb, although the first NP is sometimes called the "grammatical subject." Recall the argument in Chapter 1 about *John prefers steak and *John is preferred by steak;* the subject of a sentence is the constituent that has a special relationship with the verb. Consistent definitions can be stated and applied only if they refer to the deep structures of sentences, not to the surface structures. The subject of a sentence is the first NP in the deep structure; the predicate of a sentence is the following VP. Transformations, such as the passive, may then move constituents of the sentence.

Consider the pair of sentences:

1. John is easy to please.
2. John is eager to please.

Any definition of subject and object, if it applies to the surface structure, will imply that the relation between *John* and *please* is the same for the two sentences because the surface structures of these sentences are identical. But this relation is not the same for the two cases. *John* is the object of *please* in sentence 1, which might be paraphrased *It is easy to please John*. In sentence 2, *John* is the subject of *please*, which might be paraphrased *John is eager that he please*. This distinction is reflected in the deep structures. Sentences 1 and 2 each contain two simple sentences in their deep structures:

1. (It is easy.) (Someone pleases John.)
2. (John is eager.) (John pleases someone.)

The definitions of subject and object given above correctly identify the role of *John* in these deep structures.

There are six basic grammatical relations in all. Their definitions all apply to the deep structure of sentences:

1. If a sentence consists of a NP and a VP, the NP is the *subject of the sentence* and the VP is the *predicate*.
2. If a VP consists of a V and a NP, the V is the *main verb of the verb phrase* and the NP is the *object*.
3. If a NP consists of a N and something else, the N is the *head of a noun phrase* (or the *head noun*), and the "something else" (usually called a *determiner*) is the *modifier*.

These concepts appear to be universal among languages. The innateness hypothesis predicts that they are part of children's capacity for language. If this prediction is correct, children's earliest efforts to produce multiword utterances should be structured by these basic grammatical relations. Notice that the relations come in pairs: subject-predicate (which make up a sentence); main verb–object (which make up a verb phrase); and modifier–head noun (which make up a noun phrase). The prediction, then, is that early speech should be structured in terms of subject-predicate, or main verb–object, and modifier–head noun pairs.

In his survey of research on the acquisition of several languages, Slobin has pointed out that even at the two-word stage, subject-verb, verb-object, and modifier-noun constructions are common. And at the three-word stage, the structuring is even more apparent:

> Another linguistic universal, which manifests itself in the earliest three-word utterances, is the arrangement of sentences in hierarchically organized constituents. A simple subject-verb-object sentence can already be analyzed into subject and predicate, with further differentation of the predicate into verbal and nominal elements. In all of the children we have studied there was rapid development of the constituents of noun phrases and verb phrases, with early emergence of such categories as modifier, determiner, auxiliary, and the like [1970, pp. 178–179].

McNeill (1966) has offered a more rigorous test of the presence of the basic grammatical relations in early child language. It is based on an analysis of Adam's speech. When Adam's speech was first recorded, he appeared to have three grammatical classes — nouns, verbs, and modifiers. These three classes can be combined to give nine distinct two-word sentence types and twenty-seven distinct three-word sentence types. If Adam combined words at random, we would expect to find all, or nearly all, of these different combinations. However, not all of them can be analyzed as having structures corresponding to some, or all, of the basic grammatical relations.

In fact, only four of the nine possible two-word sentence types are so structured. For example, N + V (*Adam run*) corresponds to the subject-predicate relation; M + M (*My that*) corresponds to none of the relations. Only eight of the twenty-seven three-word combinations are structured appropriately. For example, V + N + N (*Change Adam diaper*) is a main verb–object construction, and the object is itself a modifier–head noun construction. V + V + N (*Come eat pablum*) cannot be structured by the relations. The V + N may be viewed as a main verb–object construction, but this is preceded by a verb.

The first three samples of Adam's speech contained examples of every combination that was structured by the basic grammatical relations; twelve combinations in all. This is not surprising, since nearly 400 utterances were recorded. However, *all* of Adam's utterances were of this type. There were no others. Although sentences similar to *Change Adam diaper* (V + N + N) occurred, there were no V + V + N sentences, such as *Come eat pablum*.

This result cannot be explained simply on the basis of what the child hears. *Come and eat your pablum* is not an unusual sentence type, but Adam does not produce a reduced version of it. The surface structure of the sentence *Come and eat your pablum* is not structured by the basic grammatical relations. Adults can produce sentences like this because their language includes transformations which allow the basic grammatical relations to structure the deep structure, but not the surface structure. The deep structure of this sentence consists of two sentences: (*You come*) (*You eat your pablum.*) Here the basic grammatical relations are apparent; the first sentence is a subject-predicate construction; and the second is also a subject-predicate, where the predicate itself is a verb phrase with a main verb and object, and the object itself is a noun phrase with a modifier and head noun.

Adult grammar includes transformations that join the two sentences and delete the *you* of both. Adam does not have these transformations and cannot produce such sentences. They will appear later.

In this example a child is exposed to certain patterns and yet does not pick them up. He cannot, because he is attempting to express the basic grammatical relations; not having transformations, he can only do this directly.

This ingenious analysis has been performed only on the speech of one child and therefore can only be considered suggestive. Nevertheless, it illustrates how the microscopic examination of children's speech can illuminate major questions concerning language and human mental capacity.

Bloom (1970a) found many two-word combinations that appeared to be subject-object combinations, such as the utterance of *Mommy pigtail* in a context indicating that mommy was supposed to make a pigtail. A subject and an object do not by themselves form a unit; the verb is missing from the predicate which should accompany the subject. The appearance of these sentences is difficult to square with the universality of the basic grammatical relations. The analysis of sentences into structural meanings in the last chapter suggests that a wider range of grammatical relationships play a role in early child language than McNeill's (1966) six basic ones.

McNeill (1970) has used the hypothesis that the basic grammatical relations are part of children's capacity for language in order to explain the emergence of the first grammatical classes and some of the more puzzling aspects of their development. Suppose the relations not only structure the child's first productions but also serve as the fundamental framework for understanding the sentences he hears. If he hears, and correctly understands, the sentence *I see Rover*, he recognizes *I* as the subject, *see Rover* as the predicate, *see* as the main verb, and *Rover* as the object. How can the child use information in the set of sentences he hears to develop his own grammatical system? The simplest assumption is that he stores certain information about how words are used, that is, he "makes a mental note" of the grammatical function words serve. In this example, *I* is a subject, *see* a main verb, and *Rover* an object.

The process of development must start with a primitive version of this learning scheme. One possibility is for the child to begin with a single relation-pair, for example, modifier–head noun. Hearing the phrase *red ball*, he marks *red* as a modifier, and ball as a *head noun*. All the words marked "modifier" in the child's vocabulary are then used as pivots; other words are used as open class words. Zhenya, Adam, and many other children have pivot classes consisting of modifiers, which might have been developed in this way.

A more complex possibility, which the child might begin with or develop after a stage similar to that just described, is to use more than a single relation-pair. Suppose that the child marks words that he observes to serve as modifiers or predicates. When he hears *the red ball*, he marks *red* as a modifier; when he hears *the ball is round*, he marks *round* as a modifier. Because adjectives can occur either as modifiers or as predicates, adjectives will appear in both early grammatical classes, as has been observed in several cases. This situation will last as long as each word is only marked once; a situation which could be due to lack of sufficient data or to a temporary memory limitation.

Eventually the child will hear *red* as a predicate and *round* as a modifier. Then he has a new class of words, words that are marked both as modifier and predicate, in other words, the adjectives. The transition between the stage discussed in the previous paragraph and this stage is not merely a matter of differentiation. Adjectives are separated from both the pivot and open classes and then are combined into a new class.

Summary

Although there is hardly enough evidence to decide on the question of the innateness hypothesis, strong opinions are held on both sides. A strong genetic component to knowledge is a departure from much of recent psychological theorizing, which is basically empiricist in orientation. Even though ethological research on the interplay between instinct and environment is becoming better known, language will be difficult to integrate in this framework. Nearly all examples of biologically determined behavior require a very limited, but highly specific, input from the environment. Language is extremely complicated and requires a rich yet loosely structured input.

Three kinds of evidence can be offered to support the innateness hypothesis, although far more of each kind will be necessary: the existence of language universals, the similarity of early child language, and the appearance of relatively abstract features of language at the earliest stage of syntactic development.

If there are innate properties of language, there remains the question of whether they are the consequence of general abilities to learn, or whether they are due to a specifically linguistic endowment. This question is the second half of the rationalist-empiricist debate discussed at the beginning of this chapter. No answer can be given at the present time; much more must be learned about man's learning abilities and their development, especially any innate component.[3]

3.1 Acquiring a Universal Grammar*

Let us think, not about children for the moment, but about an abstract "Language Acquisition Device", which we shall call LAD for short (alternatively, a "Language Acquisition System", or LAS — the feminine form). LAD receives a *corpus* of speech, which is a set of utterances, some grammatical, some not. The corpus may be large but it is not unlimited in size. It contains, let us say, the numbers of utterances ordinarily overheard by a two-year old child. Upon receipt of this corpus, LAD creates a *grammatical system*. This, in turn, may be regarded as LAD's theory about the regularities that appear in the corpus of speech. As with any theory, LAD's grammatical system will allow predictions of future observations — predictions of which utterances will be grammatical sentences. It will also allow LAD to distinguish the aspects of utterances that are unimportant from the aspects that are grammatically significant.

LAD creates a grammar by passing the evidence contained in the corpus through some kind of internal structure. The sequence can be represented by a simple flow diagram:

Corpus of speech→| LAD |→Grammatical system

If we understand LAD's internal structure, we would understand how LAD invents a grammar. The problem is not unlike those exercises

[3]Bever (1970) has some interesting suggestions concerning this question.

*Reprinted from McNeill, D. The creation of language. *Discovery*, 1966, **27**, 34–35.

given to engineering students in which they must infer the internal wiring of a "black box" froms its various input-output relations. LAD is our "black box." Its input is a corpus of speech: its output is a grammatical system. Just as an engineering student, we need a theory of its internal structure.

One hint about LAD's internal structure arises from the fact that it must be able to acquire any natural language. We do not want LAD to find Bantu easier than, say, English, or Russian, or Japanese. Whatever is contained in LAD, therefore, must be universally applicable, so our theory of LAD will be (in part) a theory of linguistic universals. One way to portray some of the internal structure of LAD is to portray the structure common to all languages. This conclusion yields an important insight into the acquisition of language.

For notice that the problem of understanding LAD is exactly like the problem of understanding real children. Like LAD, children are exposed to a corpus of speech, and like LAD, they develop grammatical competence on the basis of this corpus. Morever, in the case of both LAD and children some kind of internal structure converts a corpus of speech into a grammatical system. Since the same corpus is input and the same grammatical system is output, LAD and children must have the same internal structure. LAD's internal structure therefore corresponds to the fundamental human capacity for language.

3.2 Chomsky on Language Acquisition*

Assuming the rough accuracy of conclusions that seem tenable today, it is reasonable to suppose that a generative grammar is a system of many hundreds of rules of several different types organized in accordance with certain fixed principles of ordering and applicability and containing a certain fixed substructure, which, along with the general principles of organization, is common to all languages. There

*From *Language and Mind* by Noam Chomsky, © 1968 by Harcourt Brace Jovanovich, Inc., and reprinted with their permission. Pp. 75–77.

is no a priori "naturalness" to such a system, any more than there is to the detailed structure of the visual cortex . . .

Suppose that we assign to the mind, as an innate property, the general theory of language that we have called "universal grammar" [language universals, both substantive and formal] . . . The theory of universal grammar . . . provides a schema to which any particular grammar must conform. Suppose, furthermore, that we can make this schema sufficiently restrictive so that very few possible grammars conforming to the schema will be consistent with the meager and degenerate data actually available to the language learner. His task, then, is to search among the possible grammars and select one that is not definitely rejected by the data available to him. What faces the language learner, under these assumptions, is not the impossible task of inventing a highly abstract and intricately structured theory on the basis of degenerate data, but rather the much more manageable task of determing whether these data belong to one or another of a fairly restricted set of potential languages.

The tasks of the psychologists, then, divide into several sub-tasks. The first is to discover the innate schema that characterizes the class of potential languages — that defines the "essence" of human language. This subtask falls to that branch of human psychology known as linguistics; it is the problem of traditional universal grammar, of contemporary linguistic theory. The second subtask is the detailed study of the actual character of the stimulation and the organism-environment interaction that sets the innate cognitive mechanisms into operation. This is a study now being undertaken by a few psychologists . . . It has already led to interesting and suggestive conclusions. One might hope that such study will reveal a succession of maturational stages leading finally to a full generative grammar.

A third task is that of determining just what it means for a hypothesis about the generative grammar of a language to be "consistent" with the data of sense. Notice that it is a great oversimplication to suppose that a child must discover a generative grammar that accounts for all the linguistic data that has been presented to him and that "projects" such data to an infinite range of potential sound-meaning relations. In addition to achieving this, he must also differentiate the data of sense into those utterances that give direct evidence as to the character of the underlying grammar and those that must be rejected by the hypothesis he selects as ill-formed, deviant, fragmentary, and so on. Clearly, everyone succeeds in carrying out this task of differentiation — we all know, within tolerable limits of consistency, which sentences are well-formed and literally interpretable, and which must be interpreted as metaphorical, fragmentary, and deviant along many possible dimensions. I doubt that it has been fully appreciated to what extent this complicates the problem of accounting for language acquisition. Formally speaking, the learner must select a hypothesis regarding the language to which he is exposed that rejects a good part of the data on which this hypothesis must rest. Again, it is reasonable to suppose this is possible only if the range of tenable hypotheses is quite limited — if the innate schema of universal grammar is highly restrictive. The third subtask, then is to study what we might think of as the problem of "confirmation" — in this context, the problem of what relation must hold between a potential grammar and a set of data for this grammar to be confirmed as the actual theory of the language in question.

I have been describing the problem of acquisition of knowledge of language in terms that are more familiar in an epistemological than a psychological context, but I think that this is quite appropriate. Formally speaking, acquisition of "common sense knowledge" — knowledge of a language, for example — is not unlike theory construction of the most abstract sort. Speculating about the future development of the subject, it seems to me not unlikely, for the reasons I have mentioned, that learning theory will progress by establishing the innately determined set of possible hypotheses, determining the conditions of interaction that lead the mind to put forth hypotheses from this set, and fixing the conditions under which such a hypothesis is confirmed — and perhaps, under which much of the data is rejected as irrelevant for one reason or another.

SELECTED REFERENCES

Bellugi, U. The development of interrogative structures in children's speech. In K. Riegel (Ed.), *The development of language functions.* University of Michigan Language Development Program, Report No. 8, 1965. Pp. 103–138.

Bellugi, U. The acquisition of negation. Unpublished doctoral dissertation, Graduate School of Education, Harvard University, 1967.

Bever, T. G. The cognitive basis for linguistic structures. In J. R. Hayes (Ed.), *Cognition and the development of language.* New York: Wiley, 1970. Pp. 279–362.

Bloom, L. *Language development: Form and function in emerging grammars.* Cambridge, Mass.: M.I.T. Press, 1970.

Bronowski, J., & Bellugi, U. Language, name, and concept. *Science*, 1970. **168,** 669-673.

Brown, R. The first sentences of child and chimpanzee. In *Psycholinguistics: Selected papers of Roger Brown.* New York: Free Press, 1970. Pp. 208-231.

Chomsky, N. *Aspects of the theory of syntax.* Cambridge, Mass.: M.I.T. Press, 1965.

Chomsky, N. *Language and mind.* New York: Harcourt Brace Jovanovich, 1968.

Descartes, R. Discourse on method, part V. In E. S. Haldane & G. R. T. Ross (Eds.), *The philosophical works of Descartes.* New York: Dover, 1955.

Gardner, R. A., & Gardner, B. T. Teaching sign language to a chimpanzee. *Science*, 1969, **165,** 664-672.

Hayes, C. *The ape in our house.* New York: Harper & Row, 1951.

Katz, J. J., & Postal, P. M. *An integrated theory of linguistic descriptions.* Cambridge, Mass.: M.I.T. Press, 1964.

Klima, E. S. Negation in English. In J. J. Fodor & J. A. Katz (Eds.), *The structure of language.* Englewood Cliffs, N.J.: Prentice-Hall, 1964. Pp. 246-323.

Klima, E. S., & Bellugi-Klima, U. Syntactic regularities in the speech of children. In J. Lyons & R. J. Wales (Eds.), *Psycholinguistics papers.* Edinburgh: Edinburgh University Press, 1966. Pp. 183-208.

Lenneberg, E. H. *Biological foundations of language.* New York: Wiley 1967.

McNeill, D. The creation of language. *Discovery*, 1966, **27,** 34-38.

McNeill, D. *The acquisition of language: The study of developmental psycholinguistics.* New York: Harper & Row, 1970.

McNeill, D., & McNeill, N. B. What does a child mean when he says "no"? In E. M. Zale (Ed.), *Language and language behavior.* New York: Appleton-Century-Crofts, 1968. Pp. 51-62.

Neisser, U. *Cognitive psychology.* New York: Appleton-Century-Crofts, 1967.

Slobin, D. I. Universals of grammatical development in children. In G. B. Flores d'Arcais & W. J. M. Levelt (Eds.), *Advances in psycholinguistics.* New York: American Elsevier, 1970. Pp. 174-184.

FURTHER READING

Chomsky, N. *Language and mind.* New York: Harcourt Brace Jovanovich, 1968.

Katz, J. J. *The Philosophy of language.* New York: Harper & Row, 1966. Pp. 240-282.

McNeill, D. *The acquisition of language: The study of developmental psycholinguistics.* New York: Harper & Row, 1970.

4

The Course
of Syntactic
Development, II

The child language described in the previous chapters is still quite different from adult English. But progress is rapid in the next two years, between the ages of three and five. Much of this progress is in the development of transformations. Two sets of transformations have been studied in considerable detail: those of negative sentences (Klima & Bellugi-Klima, 1966; Bellugi, 1967; Bloom, 1970; McNeill, 1970b) and of questions (Bellugi, 1965; Brown, Cazden, & Bellugi, 1969). And Menyuk (1969) has investigated a variety of other constructions.

Development of Questions

English has two types of questions. One is the **yes/no question,** which calls for a *yes* or a *no* as an answer, such as *Did Columbus discover America? Can the disease be cured?*
The other type of question is the **wh-question,** so called because such questions almost always have a word that begins

with a *wh-* in them: *Who is running upstairs? What did John make? Where is he from? Wh-*questions call for a specific piece of information rather than a yes or no, which is usually in the form of a noun phrase. For examples, the answers to the last three questions might be *The cat; A pumpkin pie; Peoria.*

YES/NO QUESTIONS

In Chapter 1 we saw that there is good reason to assume that the deep structure of yes/no questions, such as *Does John prefer steak?*, is similar to that of corresponding declarative sentences, such as *John prefers steak.* For several reasons, it is necessary to assume that there is one additional constituent in the deep structure of any question. This constituent is called Q, for question. The deep structures for *He can drive* and *Can he drive?*, therefore, are (recall that C indicates the marking for number and tense):

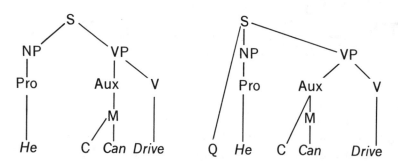

One advantage of adding the constituent Q is that it allows us to maintain the general claim that everything relevant to the meaning of a sentence is in the deep structure; obviously, questions and declaratives have different meanings.

Now what does the question transformation do? In a simple sentence such as this one, which has a single auxiliary verb in the deep structure, the transformation is quite simple. It simply flips, or **inverts,** the auxiliary and the subject, that is, the first noun phrase. More precisely:

$$T_{question} \; Q + NP + Aux + X \Rightarrow Aux + NP + X$$

where *X* means "anything" and ⇒ indicates a transformation. This transformation will change the deep structure for the question *Can he drive?* into the correct surface structure:

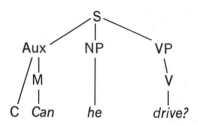

Suppose there is more than one auxiliary verb in the declarative sentence and the corresponding question:

He will be driving.	Will he be driving?
He had been drinking.	Had he been drinking?
I shall have been swimming.	Shall I have been swimming?

Only C and the first auxiliary verb (which must be either a modal or *have* or *be*) is moved to the front of the sentence. It is easy to change the transformation we just described to handle these cases:

$$T_{\text{question}}: Q + NP + C + \begin{Bmatrix} M \\ \text{have} \\ \text{be} \end{Bmatrix} + X \Rightarrow C + \begin{Bmatrix} M \\ \text{have} \\ \text{be} \end{Bmatrix} + NP + X$$

The affix transformation stated in Chapter 1 then applies, and C and the first auxiliary are inverted.

What if there is no auxiliary at all, as is the case for *John walked?* The corresponding question is *Did John walk?* Do is provided, and C, the marker for number and tense, is attached to it. This is another transformation, the **do-transformation:**

$$T_{\text{do}}: Af + X \Rightarrow do + Af + X$$

where X is anything other than a verb. Thus, the question *Did John walk?* is produced in two steps:

Q + John + C + *walk*	deep structure
C + John + *walk*	question transformation produces intermediate structure
do + C + John + *walk*	*do*-transformation supplies *do*

This *do*-transformation actually serves a number of functions. Negative sentences are similar to questions. The negative corresponding to *He can swim* is *He can't swim.* There is a negative constituent at the beginning of the deep structure, and it is moved into the sentence and attached to the auxiliary. But if there is not an auxiliary, as in *Mary sews, do* is provided to produce

Mary doesn't sew. In both cases, questions and negatives, there is an element, either C, the marker for number and tense, or the negative morpheme, which must be attached to an auxiliary verb; when there is none, a dummy auxiliary, *do*, which has no meaning, is provided.

WH-QUESTIONS

The second category of questions is the *wh*-type. A *wh*-question is similar to a "fill in the blank" test item. *What did she bake?* is very much like asking *Did she bake* _____? The structure of the question indicates just what is being asked for. This can be seen by considering a nonsense question *What can the wug sporn?* Anyone who hears or reads this question will understand it. And this understanding involves several factors. First, it is a question, calling for an answer. This is signalled by the fact that the auxiliary is before the subject *wug*. So the question transformation we just formulated applies to *wh*-questions too. In addition, *do* is supplied whenever there is no other auxiliary verb. Second, the answer that is desired is not simply a yes or no, but a noun phrase. This is signalled by the presence of a *wh*-word. And third, the answer will be the object of the verb *sporn*, despite the fact that the *wh*-word occurs at the beginning of the question and not after the verb. How do we know this? The basic order in the question differs from the common subject-verb-object order only in that the object is not present; instead there is a *wh*-word at the beginning of the question. There is a transformation that moves such *wh*-words to the beginning of the question, the **wh-transformation:**

$$T_{wh}: X + wh + Y \Rightarrow wh + X + Y$$

where *X* and *Y* refer to "anything." As usual, order matters; and the proper order for applying the four transformations is:

$$T_{question}, T_{wh}, T_{do}, \text{ and } T_{affix}.$$

In the question *What did I say?*, the first three transformations are involved:

Q + I + C + *say* + *what*	deep structure
Q + C + I + *say* + *what*	question transformation
Q + *what* + C + I + *say*	*wh*-transformation
Q + *what* + do + C + I + *say*	*do*-transformation produces surface structure

In these *wh*-questions, it is the *object of the verb* that is questioned. However, any noun phrase may be so questioned, by replacing the item of interest with a *wh*-word and moving it to the front of the question. For example, *The wug is from Oz* has a corresponding question *Where is the wug from?* The transformations just stated will handle all these cases.

There is only one other type of *wh*-question: *What can reach that limb?* corresponds to *Something can reach that limb; What hit me?* corresponds to *Something hit me.* These are questions in which it is the subject that is required for an answer. At first it appears that neither the question nor the *do* transformation apply in this type of question; however, it is not an exception. The question transformation inverts the auxiliary and the subject (which is the *wh*-word here), and then the *wh*-transformation inverts them back again. The two transformations cancel each other out for this type of question. What about the *do*-transformation? It does not apply to the first question because there is an auxiliary. What about the second question? The transformation inserts a *do* if there is no verb following the affix. But C is followed by *hit* in the second question, so no *do* is required.

In other words, questions of the type *What can reach that limb?* or *Who put the pants in Mrs. Murphy's chowder?* have the same structure as other questions, such as *What did the wug sporn?* This is a common result of linguistic research: when the rules are properly formulated, many seeming exceptions do follow the rules.

QUESTIONS IN CHILD LAGNUAGE

Bellugi (1965) has traced the development of questions, using the samples of speech collected by Roger Brown's group from Adam, Eve, and Sarah. It does not make sense to collect the questions produced by each child at a particular age, because children vary in their exact rate of development. Instead, the stages are based on an estimate of the children's overall language development, using their **mean (average) length of utterance** (MLU) as a measure. This grouping is justified because the children were producing similar structures when their mean length of utterance was the same, even though the ages at which a given MLU was attained differed considerably. Table 4.1 summarizes the development.

TABLE 4-1 *Stages in the Development of Questions*

Stage	Mean length of utterance	Ages (months)	Examples	Structures
I	1.8–2.0 morphemes	Adam 28 Eve 18 Sarah 27	a. No ear? See hole? Mommy eggnog?	S^a + Q
			b. What's that? Where Daddy going?	What NP (doing)[b] Where NP (going)[b]
II	2.3–2.9 morphemes	Adam 32 Eve 22 Sarah 32	a. You can't fix it? See my doggie? Mom pinch finger?	S + Q
			b. Who is it? What book name? Why not he eat? Why you smiling? Why not cracker can't talk?	Wh + S
III	3.4–3.6 morphemes	Adam 38 Eve 25 Sarah 38	a. Do I look like a little baby? Can't you get it? Can't it be a bigger truck? Am I silly? Does turtles crawl? Did you broke that part? Does the kitty stands up?	Aux + (n't) + NP + VP (result of question and *do* transformations)
			b. Why you caught it? What we saw? What did you doed? What he can ride in? What you have in you mouth? Why the kitty can't stand up?	Wh + NP + VP (result of *wh*-transformation; question and *do* transformations usually omitted)
			c. Who took this off? What lives in that house?	Wh + VP (*wh* subject question)

[a]S is the origin of a derivation of a new sentence (see Chapter 1).
[b]Optional; may be omitted.

The first stage is the one mentioned in the last chapter. Any utterance may be changed into a yes/no question by using the question intonation, that is, a rising intonation at the end of the sentence. The *wh*-questions have very little internal structure; they are basically frames, such as *Where . . . going?* into which almost any NP may be inserted. At this point in development, the children are also producing the very simple negatives examined in the last chapter, such as *No want soup.* Negative questions are produced by simply adding the question intonation to negative sentence. *No ear?* and *No more milk?* may be described as Q + Neg + S.

At this age, children not only fail to pronounce *wh*-questions: they also appear to fail to understand them:

Mother	Child
What did you hit?	Hit.
What did you do?	Head.
What are you writing?	Arm.

This stage is clearly pretransformational.

By Stage II, the children's grammars have become considerably more advanced. Articles and modifiers are used, some inflections appear, and occasionally a prepositional phrase may be observed. However, there are still no auxiliary verbs. The yes/no question forms are essentially the same as those of Stage I. Since there are no auxiliaries, there is no inversion of auxiliary or subject.

In addition to this simple form, one of the children (Adam) also produced a number of yes/no questions that began with *D'you want: D'you want its turn? D'you want me get it?* The introductory phrase always appears in just that form, and was pronounced as if it were a single word. Certainly it was not the result of the *do* transformation and the question transformation, since these operations were not observed anywhere else in his language. It might have been an effort to produce adult forms such as *do you want . . .* by means of phrase-structure rules. Adam may have enriched his grammar by adding a rule of the form Q → *d'you want* which operated after the rule S → Q + NP + VP.

The words *can't* and *don't* present a similar phenomenon. *Can* and *do* are never used without the negative element, and they are used in only one position: just before the verb. They are, it appears, single negative elements. In adult English, *can't* is the result of the attachment of the negative element to the auxiliary by the negative transformation. But here, as in the *d'you want* questions above, the child may be trying to find a phrase-structure solution to what is actually a transformational problem.

The *wh*-words are always sentence-initial at this stage. In adult questions, this is the result of a transformation. But there is little evidence for this in the children's questions. It is hard to distinguish subject and object questions in cases such as: *What getting? Why need him more? Where put him on a chair?* The *wh*-words merely serve as question introducers.

Another piece of evidence for this analysis is the structure of *why not* questions. The child simply adds *why not* to the beginning of a sentence, even if the sentence already contains a negative, thus producing a double negative such as *Why not cracker can't talk?* There is still no evidence for auxiliary inversion, and if the *d'you want* questions and *wh*-questions are indeed the result of phrase-structure rules, this stage is still pretransformational.

The children can answer many questions appropriately:

Mother	Child
What d'you hear?	Hear a duck
What do yu need?	Need some chocolate
Who do you love?	Mommy, you. I love fishie, too.

Adult *wh*-question forms are not being produced yet but these are understood and answered. However, the converse also occurs. Although children produce many, many *why* and *why not* questions, they are not able to answer such questions appropriately. This is an example of the ability to produce a construction before the ability to comprehend it, a counter example to the general belief that comprehension precedes production. Table 4-2 shows that these questions are closely related to the immediately preceding sentence of the mother:

TABLE 4-2 *"Why and "Why Not" Questions*

Mother	Child
I see a seal.	Why you see seal?
You bent that game.	Why me bent that game?
I guess I'm not looking in the right place.	Why not you looking right place?
You can't dance.	Why not me can't dance?

SOURCE: Brown, Roger, & Courtney Cazden, & Ursula Bellugi, "The Child's Grammar from I to III," in *Minnesota Symposium on Child Psychology*, *Volume II*, edited by J.P. Hill, University of Minnesota Press, Minneapolis, © 1969, University of Minnesota. P. 49.

As generally occurs when young children imitate an adult utterance, it is reduced: elements such as *ing*, *a*, and auxiliary verbs are dropped. Aside from these minor differences, these questions are a simple function of his mother's declaratives: *why* is placed at the beginning of affirmative declaratives, *why not* at the beginning of negative declaratives.

Major advances in syntax have occurred by Stage III. In particular, the auxiliary system has developed, including the affix transformation. These auxiliaries are used in declaratives, negatives, and questions. More complex sentences forms have appeared, including relative clauses and conjunction: *You have two things that turn around; Let's go upstairs and take it from him because it's mine.*

In the yes/no questions, the auxiliary is placed correctly before the NP, and *do* is provided if necessary. Two of the transformations of adult English, then, are present. Sometimes overextensions occur, and tense number is marked on both the auxiliary and the main verb, as in *Did you broke that part?* and *Does the kitty stands up?* Negative yes/no questions have the negative element properly attached to the auxiliary verb.

The *wh*-questions are rather different. When there are auxiliary verbs present, they are not usually inverted with the subject, as they should be. There are questions without auxiliaries, where *do* should be supplied. Questions such as *What you have in you mouth?* are missing both *do* and inversion. If inversion had been performed, the question would be *What have you in you mouth?* If both the *do* and question transformations had been performed, the question would be *What do you have in you mouth?* Two transformations that are present in yes/no questions at Stage III are frequently not performed in *wh*-questions.

What about the third transformation, which moves the *wh*-word to the initial position? At Stage II, the *wh*-questions appeared to be of the form *wh* + S; that is, if the *wh* was removed, the remainder was very much like any other sentence of the child's language at that stage. At Stage III, this is not so. If we remove the *wh*-word from some of the questions we have: *We saw,* which is obviously missing the object of *saw*; *He can ride in,* which is obviously missing the object of *in*; *Lost it,* which is obviously missing the subject of *lost.* At this stage, the *wh*-words do stand for particular constituents, and they are moved to the beginning of the question by the *wh*-transformation.

Negative questions show the same principles: negative yes/no questions, such as *Can't it be a bigger truck,* are inverted, while negative wh-questions, such as *Why the kitty can't stand up?* are not.

At Stage III, then, children appear to have developed all the transformations, but there is a limit to how many of them can be applied to a single sentence. Inversion (the question transformation) and the *do* transformation are found in yes/no questions but not in wh-questions. Perhaps transformations of this type really are some kind of mental operations. Young children have severely limited cognitive capacities, which are easily overloaded. As a result, operations that are in the child's competence may be omitted for performance reasons. Both Bellugi (1967) and Bloom (1970) have observed a tendency for the presence of a negative element in a sentence at early stages of development to be accompanied by decreased complexity of the remainder of the sentence, relative to the child's competence as manifested in affirmative sentences.

However, such an explanation has at least one important difficulty. Children always eliminate the same transformation. They do not produce questions such as *Can he ride in what?* or *We saw what?* — questions in which subject and auxiliary are inverted but *wh* is not moved. It is the question transformation that is always eliminated. At this stage the question transformation is fully mastered; perhaps the *wh*-transformation is the focus of the child's attention because it is now at the boundary of the child's competence.

At Stage III, children understand and respond correctly to even more complex questions than at Stage II:

Mother	*Child*
What d'you need a rifle for?	I wanna shoot.
Then what will you do for milk?	I gonna buy some more cows.
What d'you think we should do?	I know what I should do;
	play with some more toys.

Imitation and Comprehension

The descriptions of child language presented in the preceeding three chapters have been based almost entirely on analyses of children's productions. Productions may underestimate the child's competence, or they may overestimate it. Stage II in the development of questions contains errors of both kinds: many *wh*- questions are answered appropriately, but they are not formulated correctly. *Why* questions, on the other hand, are asked but apparently not comprehended. In order to estimate competence, other kinds of performance are needed, especially performance in **imitation** and **comprehension.**

IMITATION

There are two types of imitation: **spontaneous imitation** of the speech of another person, usually a parent, and **elicited imitation,** in which an adult in some way asks the child to imitate him. Spontaneous imitation is of interest because of the role it might play in language acquisition. Children do imitate their parents, and this might be a major process of change in child language. Elicited imitations are valuable as a research tool for the developmental psycholinguist. Suppose a child does not produce any sentences that contain auxiliary verbs. It is possible that this is the result of sampling error; that the child has the ability to use auxiliary verbs, but no occasion calling for them has arisen during the interval in which he was observed. Perhaps he could be prompted to produce auxiliaries by giving him sentences to imitate that contain auxiliaries. We will examine these two types of imitation in turn.

When children spontaneously imitate, they usually reformulate the sentence to fit their own grammar of the moment. If the progressive aspect — *is . . . ing* — has not yet been mastered, a child is likely to imitate *Adam's nose is dripping this morning* with *Nose drip.* Table 4-3 contains several examples of spontaneous imitation. In general, content words, such as nouns, verbs and adjectives, are retained in their proper order, while function words, such as articles, prepositions, and conjunctions, and, also, inflections are omitted. The resulting speech has been called "telegraphic" because it resembles the language used in telegrams. Reading 4.1 describes, and attempts to explain, this speech.

Susan Ervin (1964) studied the spontaneous imitations of five young children (between 1;10 and 2;10) and compared them with the free speech of the same children. In every case but one, she found that the spontaneous imitations were of essentially the same structure as the free speech. In the one exceptional case, she concluded that the imitations were, if anything, *less* advanced than the free speech of the child. Thus, her general conclusion was that spontaneous imitations were no more advanced than free speech.

TABLE 4-3 *Some Imitations Produced by Adam and Eve*

Model utterance	Child's imitation
Tank car.	Tank car.
Wait a minute.	Wait a minute.
Daddy's brief case.	Daddy brief case.
Fraser will be unhappy.	Fraser unhappy.
He's going out.	He go out.
That's an old time train.	Old time train.
It's not the same dog as Pepper.	Dog Pepper.
No, you can't write on Mr. Cromer's shoe.	Write Cromer shoe.

SOURCE: Brown, R., & Bellugi, U., "Three Processes in the Child's Acquisition of Syntax," *Harvard Educational Review*, 34:2, 1964, 133–151. Copyright © 1964 by President and Fellows of Harvard College. Reprinted with permission.

If the finding that the child produces in imitation only what he produces in his spontaneous speech holds for elicited imitations as well as for spontaneous ones, imitation can be used to study children's productive capacities. In general, this is the case, as long as the sentence is not too short and is not bizarre in any way, that is, does not contain unfamiliar words or violate major principles of English. This procedure can often give evidence concerning the acquisition of fairly subtle aspects of English. For example, a child studied by Slobin and Welsh (1968) whom they called "Echo" imitated *The pussy eats bread and the pussy runs fast* with *Pussy eat bread and he run fast*, demonstrating mastery of the transformation which pronominalizes a repeated noun phrase in a sentence. Even if the repeated noun phrase were deleted in the sentence offered for imitation, Echo would introduce a pronoun for the noun phrase (which is present in the deep structure), thus imitating *The owl eats candy and runs fast* with *Owl eat candy . . . owl eat candy and . . . he run fast.*

COMPREHENSION

Elicited imitations are a useful research tool for solving the sampling problem. But interpreting the observations is not always so easy. Suppose a child does not produce auxiliary verbs in either his free speech or his imitations. Does this necessarily imply that the auxiliary is not part of his language, that is, his competence, or does it merely mean that auxiliaries are omitted because the child can only produce very short sentences due to a small memory span? A question such as this can only be answered by examining the child's comprehension ability.

Studies of comprehension also provide evidence for the common belief that understanding precedes production. Children do seem to comprehend speech somewhat before they produce any true language. However, the interesting hypothesis is that specific grammatical features are understood before they are produced. A widely used technique for investigating this hypothesis, called the ICP (Imitation, Comprehension, Production) test, was developed by Fraser, Bellugi, and Brown (1963). For each of ten contrasts, such as singular–plural subject, a pair of sentences were constructed which differed only in that particular feature. For the example of singular vs. plural subject, Fraser, Bellugi, and Brown (1963, p. 127) used the sentences *The boy draws* and *The boys draw*. Then an appropriate picture was prepared for each of the sentences. In this example, one picture showed one boy drawing, and the other showed two boys drawing. Another contrast was subject-object in the active voice. The sentences were: *The train bumps the car* and *The car bumps the train* (1963, p. 127). The corresponding pictures showed the train doing the bumping, and the car doing the bumping.

There were three tasks: imitation, comprehension, and production. In the imitation task, the experimenter simply recited the two sentences and asked the children to repeat them, one by one. In the comprehension task, the experimenter first showed the two pictures and recited the two sentences, without revealing which sentence belonged to which picture. Then the experimenter recited one of the sentences and asked the child to point to the picture he had named. Then the other sentence was recited and the child asked to point to the appropriate picture. In the production task, the pictures were again used. First the child heard the sentences, but was not told which sentence went with which picture. Then the experimenter pointed to one picture at a time and asked the child to name it. In scoring the children's responses in the imitation and production tasks, only the relevant aspect of the sentences was considered. The subjects for this experiment were between thirty-seven and forty-three months old.

The findings were remarkably clear-cut (see Table 4-4). For all ten contrasts, comprehension scores exceeded production scores; on all but one, imitation scores exceeded comprehension scores. Furthermore, this pattern occurred with nearly all the children considered individually. This experiment has been repeated by Lovell and Dixon (1967) with children over a wider age range — two years to six years — and with retarded six and seven year olds. They found the expected differences due to age

TABLE 4-4 *Example Sentences and Results from the ICP Test*

Contrasts in order of increasing difficulty	No. correct (out of 24 each)			
	I	C	P	Total
I. Affirmative-Negative The girl is cooking. The girl is not cooking.	18	17	12	47
II. Singular-Plural of third person possesive pronoun His wagon. Their wagon.	23	15	8	46
III. Subject-Object in the active voice The train bumps the car. The car bumps the train.	19	16	11	46
IV. Present progressive-Future tense The girl is drinking. The girl will drink.	20	16	6	42
V. Singular-Plural marked by *is* and *are* The deer is running. The deer are running.	20	12	7	39
VI. Present progressive-Past tense The paint is spilling. The paint spilled.	17	13	6	36
VII. Mass noun-Count noun Some mog. A dap.	12	13	1	26
VIII. Singular/Plural marked by inflections The boy draws The boys draw.	14	7	1	22
IX. Subject-Object in the passive voice The car is bumped by the train. The train is bumped by the car.	12	7	2	21
X. Indirect object-Direct object The girl shows the cat the dog. The girl shows the dog the cat.	11	5	3	19

SOURCE: Adapted from Fraser, C., Bellugi, U., & Brown, R. Control of grammar in imitation, comprehension, and production. *Journal of Verbal Learning and Verbal Behavior*, 1963, **2**, 121–135.

(older children do better overall than younger ones) and due to I.Q. (normal children do better overall than retarded ones). And they also found the same highly consistent ordering of imitation, comprehension, and production scores for each group of children.

In addition to their quantitative findings Fraser, Bellugi, and Brown (1963) observed several interesting errors. Some children when presented with the pair of sentences *The girl is pushed by the boy* and *The boy is pushed by the girl* in the production task, made precisely the opposite responses to the pictures; that is, when they were shown the picture in which the girl was doing the pushing, the child said *The girl is pushed by the boy;* for the picture in which the boy was doing the pushing, *The boy is pushed by the girl*. Five children responded in this way, and they seemed to be doing so with confidence. This suggests that passive sentences are being processed in this experiment as if they were active. Thus *the girl is pushed by the boy* is not handled as object passive verb–subject, but rather as subject–"funny" verb–object.

Another process was shown by five children in the production task with the direct object–indirect object contrast in *The woman gives the bunny the teddy* and *The woman gives the teddy the bunny*. These children changed the original sentence to express the indirect object with a prepositional phrase. Instead of saying *The woman gives the bunny the teddy*, they produced *The woman gives the teddy to the bunny*, which preserves the meaning, though not the exact form. This new form is probably the more familiar one for the children. It is also closer to the deep structure for indirect object constructions, at least according to one formulation of the grammar. These same children pointed correctly on the comprehension task. However, they did not change the sentences this way in the imitation task. They simply repeated back the sentences as presented for imitation.

The fact that imitation performance was superior to production ability apparently contradicts the findings of Ervin, discussed above. There may be two distinct imitative processes; the crucial difference between them is whether or not the sentence passes through the meaning system. In imitation$_1$, the child decodes the sentence and recodes it in accordance with his current syntactic system. Spontaneous imitations, such as those observed by Ervin, are examples of imitation$_1$. There is, after all, no apparent motivation for the child to attempt perfect accuracy. Elicited imitations as well as spontaneous ones are examples of imitation$_1$, as long as the sentence to be imitated exceeds the span of immediate memory. In contrast, if the sentence is within the span of immediate memory, it can be imitated perfectly, in taperecorder fashion; this is imitation$_2$. In imitation$_2$ the meaning of the sentence is not processed. It follows from the recording in imitation$_1$, and the lack of this recoding in imitation$_2$, that

Imitation$_1$ = Production (Ervin, 1964)
Imitation$_2$ > Production (Fraser, Bellugi, & Brown, 1963)

Unfortunately, the ICP technique suffers from the limitation that only those grammatical contrasts that have a simple picturable correlate can be investigated. Many aspects of syntax either do not have such a correlate or have one that is difficult to arrange. The problem of devising methods of investigating comrehension is one of the most challenging problems in the study of children's language today.

An ingeniously simple technique, using elicited imitations, has been developed by Slobin and Welsh (1968). If the model sentences are longer than the immediate memory span of the child, they will be imitated with imitation$_1$, which combines understanding and reformulation. The reformulation is not always identical to the sentence being imitated, but the meaning is approximately the same. This requires the child to have understood the model. If the child fails to comprehend, then the imitation is most likely to express a different meaning or no meaning at all. So comprehension may be tested by noting whether the reformulated imitation preserves the meaning of the original:

ADULT: John who cried came to my party.
CHILD: John cried and he came to my party.
ADULT: The boy the book hit was crying.
CHILD: Boy the book was crying.

The child's imitation successfully preserves the meaning of the first model, indicating comprehension of the embedded clause, in particular, that John is the subject of both *cried* and *came*. But the second imitation has hardly any meaning at all, showing failure to comprehend embedded clauses of this more complicated type (note that *boy* is the subject of *was crying* and the object of *hit*). Here is another example of a successful imitation:

ADULT: The man who I saw yesterday got wet.
CHILD: I saw the man and he got wet.

The major difficulty of this method is determining whether a particular imitation preserves the meaning of the original. Some cases are clear, but others are not. If the method can be demonstrated to work reliably, it will have several important advantages over other means of assessing comprehension. First, it can be used with quite young children, especially if they are familiar with the investigator. And second, since the investigator can choose any type of sentence to be imitated, it is a very general technique. Of course, the sentence must not be too short, or it will be processed with imitation$_2$. Echo, for example, at age 2;3 could repeat all possible orders of the three words *John loves company.*

A different kind of comprehension has been explored by Roger Brown (1957). It is generally recognized that adult English parts of speech, that is, syntactic categories, are not semantically consistent. The junior high school definition of a noun is "the name of a person, place, or thing." But if the word *thing* must be extended to cover *lightning, honor,* and *democracy,* it has very little meaning. *To own* is a verb, but it is hardly an "action or state of being." For this reason, linguists define syntactic categories on the basis of **distributional properties,** that is, on the contexts in which they are used, rather than on the basis of semantic notions. Brown noticed, however, that the words used by four- and five-year-old nursery school children form more consistent categories. They tend to use only concrete nouns, verbs of action, and so on. So he devised an ingenious experiment to determine if the children were aware of the semantic correlates of the syntactic classes. He designed a set of pictures, each of which contained three things: (1) an unfamiliar, well-defined object (such as a strange container); (2) an amorphous mass (such as a confettilike mass); (3) an action (such as kneading dough). These are the kind of entities that would normally be called a count noun, a mass noun, and a verb, respectively. For each such picture, he prepared another set of three pictures. Each of these three pictures contained *one* of the three aspects of the original picture plus new entities of the other two types. For example, one of the three corresponding pictures contained the same confettilike mass but a different container and a different action. Another contained the same action, kneading, but a different mass in a different container. The third showed the same container, but with a different mass and action.

He then presented nonsense words to four- and five-year-old children in sentences that clearly marked the words as a count noun, mass noun, or verb, as they looked at the first picture of each set. The sentences were of the form: *Here is a picture of a wug* (count noun); *Here is a picture of some wug* (mass noun);

Here is a picture of someone wugging (verb). Then he showed each child the other three pictures, and asked him to point out *another wug, some more wug,* and *some more wugging* as was appropriate. He found that the children were in general able to do this, showing that they could determine something of the meaning of a nonsense word from its syntactic class, its part of speech, as indicated by its use in a sentence.

Knowledge of this correspondence between syntactic class and semantic properties could be of considerable assistance to a child, in both directions. On the one hand, if the child was presented with a "thing" and its name, from the nature of the "thing" he could determine the likely syntactic class of the name and, hence, how to use it properly in sentences, how to form the plural, and so on. In the other direction, if the child was presented with a name and was not sure to what it referred, he could determine something about the entity referred to from its syntactic markings in the sentence.

Later Syntactic Development

Past the age of five or six, differences between the child's grammar and adult grammar are not obvious from spontaneous observation of free speech. There are a few characteristic difficulties that remain, including mastery of subject-verb agreement and case endings on personal pronouns (*Him and her went*), elimination of the double negative (*nobody don't like him*) and *ain't,* and a few others. However, these are relatively minor features. The basic syntactic structure of most of the child's sentences appears to be that of adult grammar. Carol Chomsky (1969) has shown how some major syntactic differences may be observed in studies of comprehension. She reasoned that recent studies of the structure of English have increased our awareness of the complexity of a natural language such as English and that the more complex aspects should be the last to be mastered.

What does a listener do when he attempts to understand a sentence? It is necessary, of course, for him to understand the basic elements in the sentence; that is, the morphemes. But the meanings of these elements must be combined in a way that is determined by the structure of the sentence — *John hits Mary* versus *Mary hits John.* In other words, the listener must determine the structure of the sentence. And, in fact, it is the deep structure that he must determine, because it is the deep structure that indicates the basic grammatical relations between the elements of the sentence.

C. Chomsky (1969) studied several conditions under which this might be particularly difficult. We will consider two. It should be more difficult to determine the true grammatical relations that hold among words in a sentence if they are not expressed directly in the surface structure. In *John saw Mary*, the surface structure indicates that *John* is the subject and *Mary* the object, although that is not the order in surface structure. And, in fact, both children and adults find it harder to understand passive sentences than active ones. (All page references in this discussion refer to C. Chomsky, 1969.)

Now consider these sentences:

1. John is eager to see.
2. John is easy to see.

In the first sentence *John* is the subject of *see*; whereas in the second sentence *John* is the object of *see*. In both cases *John* occurs before *see*. In the deep structure of English, subjects are placed between verbs; and objects, after verbs. The surface structure of the first sentence indicates the relationship among the elements of the sentence more clearly than the surface structure of the second. Sentences of the first type should be easier to understand; perhaps they are the first to be acquired. In addition, there may be a period in which a child might interpret sentences of the second type in the same way they do sentences of the first type.

How can such comprehension (or miscomprehension) be observed? Notice that some sentences can be understood without using full knowledge of structure: *The book is hard to read; These steps are hard to climb.* Books do not read, and stairs do not climb. The correct interpretation can be determined on the basis of the words alone. To investigate the child's understanding of the syntactic structures, it is necessary to have sentences that do not provide semantic clues. The one selected was *The doll is easy to see.* This can be interpreted correctly to mean that someone else sees the doll or, incorrectly, to mean that the doll is doing the seeing.

A blindfolded doll was placed in front of the child, who was asked "Is the doll easy to see or hard to see?" Based on the child's answer, a few additional questions were asked.

The children in general answered without hesitation and with confidence, but in many cases they were wrong. Mastery of this construction is quite late; before attaining such mastery, children assign the incorrect interpretation. Here are the data on the first question:

Age	Correct
5	22%
6	42
7	86
8	75
9	100

A sample protocol follows [p. 30]:

> Lisa V., 6;5
> Q. Is this doll easy to see or hard to see?
> A. Hard to see.
> Q. Will you make her easy to see?
> A. If I can get this untied.
> Q. Will you explain why she was hard to see?
> A. (To doll) Because you had a blindfold over your eyes.
> Q. And what did you do?
> A. I took it off.

A second condition that might lead to difficulty in comprehension is if a particular structure is an exception to a general principle describing the relation between deep and surface structure. Consider the following sentences:

3. John persuaded Bill to leave.
4. John advised Bill to leave.
5. John permitted Bill to leave.
6. John selected Bill to leave.

There are many other verbs that fit this pattern — *allow, urge, cause*, and so on. Notice that the subject of the second verb, "leave," is always the second NP, "Bill." There are other verbs that may or may not have a second NP:

7. John wanted (Bill) to leave.
8. John expected (Bill) to leave.
9. John asked (Bill) to leave.

If there is a second NP, it is the subject of "leave." If not, the first NP, *John*, is the subject. The general rule in English is the **Minimal Distance Principle** (MDP): the subject of a complement verb (a verb with *to*) is the NP closest to it. This principle describes all the cases considered. However, there are some exceptions to it.

548 64

Ask is an exception, although *tell* is not; for example: *I asked him what to do* means *I asked him what I should do; I told him what to do* means *I told him what he should do.*

C. Chomsky's hypothesis was that a child would first learn the MDP and then any exceptions. At first the child interprets *I asked him what to do* as if it were *I asked him what he should do.* She started by asking informally a few five and six year olds to carry out instructions such as *Ask Laura what to feed the doll* and *Tell Laura what to feed the doll.* The children were seated at a table on which was placed a doll and some play foods. C. Chomsky found out immediately that this distinction was too difficult. The protocols looked like this:

Q. Ask Joe what to feed the doll.
A. The cucumber.
Q. Now tell Joe what to feed the doll.
A. The tomato.
Q. Now ask Joe which food to put back in the box.
A. The hot dog.
Q. And ask Joe which piece of food to pick up.
A. The watermelon [p. 45].

In a wide variety of cases, the five and six year olds were apparently interpreting *ask* as if it were *tell.*

Exploring this structure with a further experiment, she discovered a regular sequence of development. The experiment was performed with the experimentor and child seated at a table with several toys. There were essentially four constructions used in the experiment. The first was *ask* in the sense of *request: Bozo asks to go first in line*, or *Bozo asks/tells Michie to go first in line.* This is the simplest use of *ask.* The more important use of *ask* is in the sense of *question.* Here there are three cases.

Case 1: *Ask/Tell Laura what color this is* and *Ask/Tell Laura how many pencils there are here.* In case 1 sentences, the subject of the *wh*-clause is supplied. This means that the child merely has to move the words around:

Q. Ask Laura what color this is.
A. What color is that?

Case 2: *Ask/Tell Laura her/your last name* and *Ask/Tell Laura the color of this book.* Here the complement clause is abbreviated, and the question word and verb must be supplied by the child.

Q. Ask Laura her last name.
A. What's your last name?

LINCOLN CHRISTIAN COLLEGE

Case 3: *Ask/Tell Laura what to feed the doll* and *Ask/Tell Laura which food to put back in the box.* Here the subject of the verb is not supplied; the child must do this:

Q. Ask Laura what to feed the doll.
A. What should I feed the doll?

This is more difficult than Case 2 because the child must refer outside the clause to choose between two possible subjects for the verb.

A wide variety of sentences, randomly arranged, were used. Actually, two children were present: the one being questioned, and another one, who was to be *asked* or *told*.

Remember that the basic idea was to see if *ask* and *tell* were distinguished by the child. The first finding was that the children interpreted *ask* in the sense of *request* correctly, without any difficulty. The interesting developmental sequence had concerned the use of *ask* in the sense of *question*. Here C. Chomsky found five stages of development; that is, the data grouped itself naturally into five categories, and they formed an orderly sequence. The children could handle the simple cases before they could handle the more complex ones. We will look briefly at the five stages [pp. 55–59].

Stage A: Failure on all cases.

Christine M., 5;1
Q. Ask Eric his last name.
A. Handel.
Q. Ask Eric this doll's name.
A. I don't know.
Q. Ask Eric what time it is.
A. I don't know how to tell time.
Q. Tell Eric what class is in the library.
A. Kindergarten.
Q. Ask Eric who his teacher is.
A. Miss Turner.
Q. Ask Eric who this is.
A. Bozo

In every case, a *tell* interpretation is imposed on *ask*.

Stage B: Success on Case 1; failure on other cases.

Peter F., 6;9
Q. Ask Joanna the color of Micky Mouse's trousers.
A. Blue.
Q. Tell Joanna who this is.

A. Bozo.
Q. Ask Joanna who this is.
A. Who's that?
Q. Tell Joanna what color this book is.
A. Blue.

The children could distinguish *ask* and *tell* for Case 1 but not Cases 2 or 3. (There were no children who failed at Case 1 and succeeded at Cases 2 or 3.)

Stage C: Success on Cases 1 and 2; failure on Case 3

Laura S., 6;5
Q. Ask Joanne what color this book is.
A. What color's that book?
Q. Ask Joanne her last name.
A. What's your last name?
Q. Tell Joanne what color this tray is.
A. Tan.
Q. Ask Joanne what's in the box.
A. What's in the box?
Q. Ask Joanne what to feed the doll
A. The hot dog.
Q. Now I want you to *ask* Joanne something. *Ask* her what to feed the doll.
A. The piece of bread
Q. Ask Joanne what *you* should feed the doll [Case 1].
A. What should I feed the doll?

The ability to interpret *ask* in simple constructions is not enough to enable the child to succeed in the more complex Case 3. In Case 3, they interpret *ask* as *tell*.

Stage D: Success of Cases 1 and 2; partial success on Case 3.

Joanna B., 6;9
Q. Ask Peter what to feed Pluto.
A. What should you feed Pluto?

Penny O., 7;0
Q. Ask Ann what to feed the doll
A. What d'you feed the doll?
Q. Ask Ann what to put back in the box.
A. What d'ya put back?

Now the children succeed in distinguishing *ask* and *tell* in all three cases, but they get Case 3 only half right. That is, they do ask a question (not just tell, as Stage C children do), but they ask the wrong question. In particular, they assign the wrong subject.

To the instruction *Ask Lynn what to put back in the box* they answer. *What are you going to put in the box?* This is what C. Chomsky originally set out to find; a stage where *ask* and *tell* were distinguished but where the exception to the MDP had not been learned. But this occurred at a remarkably late stage. The children in this group were at an average age of about seven and one-half years. They had various ways of coping with the difficulty, and there is a wide variety of responses, but they all share the property that the correct subject is not assigned.

Stage E: Success on all Cases

Warren H., 9;7
Q. Ask Kim what to feed the doll.
A. What should I feed the doll?
Q. Ask Kim what to put back in the box.
A. What should I put back in the box?
Q. Tell Kim what color to make the circle.
A. Make the circle red.
Q. And ask Kim what color to make the square.
A. What color should I make the square?

The sequence of stages was not strongly correlated with age. One child who was 5;10 succeeded on all constructions, that is, was at Stage E. Another child, who was ten years old, was only at Stage C. There was a general tendency, of course, for the children at later stages to be older than those at earlier stages, but there was great variation. Furthermore, linguistic development in this sense did not in all cases coincide with the teacher's general assessment of the child. The one second-grade boy who was at Stage E was a child who was rated by his teacher as being below average.

Summary

Three general characteristics of child language are illustrated by the observations in this chapter. First is the autonomy of child language. In the development of questions, as elsewhere in linguistic development, children regularly produce forms they have not heard. It is doubtful that any mother would say *Why not cracker can't talk?* or *What you have in you mouth?* These questions reflect the child's stepwise construction of a grammar. The actual sentences produced by a child at any point are determined by his own grammar, not by the adult grammar he will eventually master.

A second characteristic of child language is the general superiority of comprehension over production. Although widely recognized, this disparity is difficult to understand (Maccoby & Bee, 1965, and McNeill, 1970b, discuss the problem). At the very least, it suggests that comprehension plays a more important role in language acquisition than production.

The third characteristic is the obvious preference of the child for a small number of general rules. Overgeneralizations are as common in syntax as in morphology. Just as American and Russian children overgeneralize past tense, case, and other inflections, the children in C. Chomsky's experiment overgeneralize rules relating deep and surface structure. Exceptions to rules — sentences in which the object occurs before the subject or sentences that violate the Minimal Distance Principle — are mastered only after a considerable interval.

4.1 Telegraphic Speech[*]

We adults sometimes operate under a constraint on length and the curious fact is that the English we produce in these circumstances bears a formal resemblance to the English produced by two-year-old children. When words cost money there is a premium on brevity or to put it otherwise, a constraint on length. The result is "telegraphic" English, and telegraphic English is an English of nouns, verbs, and adjectives. One does not send a cable reading: "My car has broken down and I have lost my wallet; send money to me at the American Express in Paris" but rather "Car broken down; wallet lost, send money American Express Paris." The telegram omits *my, has, and, I, have, my, to, me, at, the, in*. All of these are functors. We make the same kind of telegraphic reduction when time or fatigue constrain us to be brief, as witness any set of notes taken at a fast-moving lecture.

A telegraphic transformation of English generally communicates very well. It does so because it retains the high-information

*From Brown, R., & Bellugi, U., "Three Processes in the Child's Acquisition of Syntax," *Harvard Educational Review*, 34:2, 1964, 138–140. Copyright © 1964 by President and Fellows of Harvard College. Reprinted with permission.

words and drops the low-information words. We are here using "information" in the sense of the mathematical theory of communication. The information carried by a word is inversely related to the chances of guessing it from context. From a given string of content words, missing functors can often be guessed but the message "my has and I have my to me at the in" will not serve to get money to Paris. Perhaps children are able to make a communication analysis of adult speech and so adapt in an optimal way to their limitation of span. There is, however, another way in which the adaptive outcome might be achieved.

If you say aloud the model sentences of [Table 4-2 in this volume] you will find that you place the heavier stresses, the primary and secondary stresses in the sentences, on contentives rather than on functors. In fact the heavier stresses fall, for the most part, on the words the child retains. We first realized that this was the case when we found that in transcribing tapes, the words of the mother that we could hear most clearly were usually the words that the child reproduced. We had trouble hearing the weakly stressed functors and, of course, the child usually failed to reproduce them. Differential stress may then be the cause of the child's differential retention. The outcome is a maximally informative reduction, but the cause of this outcome need not be the making of an information analysis. The outcome may be an incidental consequence of the fact that English is a well-designed language that places its heavier stresses where they are needed, on contentives that cannot easily be guessed from context.

We are fairly sure that differential stress is one of the determinants of the child's telegraphic productions. For one thing, stress will also account for the way in which children reproduce polysyllabic words when the total is too much for them. Adam, for instance, gave us 'pression for expression and Eve gave us 'raff for giraffe; the more heavily-stressed syllables were the ones retained. In addition we have tried the effect of placing heavy stresses on functors which do not ordinarily receive such stresses. To Adam we said: "You say what I say" and then, speaking in a normal way at first: "The doggie will bite. Adam gave back: "Doggie bite." Then we stressed the auxiliary: "The doggie will bite: and, after a few trials, Adam made attempts at reproducing that auxiliary. A science fiction experiment comes to mind. If there were parents who stressed functors rather than con-tentives would they have children whose speech was a kind of "reciprocal telegraphic" made up of articles, prepositions, conjunctions, auxiliaries, and the like? Such children would be out of touch with the community as real children are not.

It may be that all the factors we have mentioned play some part in determining the child's selective imitations; the reference-making function of contentives, the fact that they are practiced as single words, the fact that they cannot be guessed from context, and the heavy stresses they receive.

SELECTED REFERENCES

Bellugi, U. The development of interrogative structures in children's speech. In K. Riegel (Ed.), *The development of language functions.* University of Michigan Language Development Program, Report No. 8, 1965. Pp. 103–138.

Bellugi, U. The acquisition of negation. Unpublished doctoral dissertation, Graduate School of Education, Harvard University, 1967.

Bloom, L. *Language development: Form and function in emerging grammars.* Cambridge, Mass.: M.I.T. Press, 1970.

Brown, R. Linguistic determinism and the part of speech. *Journal of Abnormal and Social Psychology*, 1957, **55**, 1–5.

Brown, R., & Bellugi, U. Three processes in the child's acquisition of syntax. *Harvard Educational Review*, 1964, **34**, 133–151.

Brown, R., Cazden, C., & Bellugi, U. The child's grammar from I to III. In J. P. Hill (Ed.), *Minnesota symposium on child psychology.* Vol. 2. Minneapolis: University of Minnesota Press, 1969. Pp. 28–73.

Chomsky, C. S. *The acquisition of syntax in children from 5 to 10.* Cambridge, Mass.: M.I.T. Press, 1969.

Ervin, S. Imitation and structural change in children's language. In E. H. Lenneberg (Ed.), *New directions in the study of language.* Cambridge, Mass.: M.I.T. Press, 1964.

Fraser, C., Bellugi, U., & Brown, R. Control of grammar in imitation, comprehension, and production. *Journal of Verbal Learning and Verbal Behavior*, 1963, **2**, 121–135.

Klima, E. S., & Bellugi-Klima, U. Syntactic regularities in the speech of children. In J. Lyons & R. J. Wales (Eds.), *Psycholinguistics papers.* Edinburgh: Edinburgh University Press, 1966. Pp. 183–208.

Lovell, K., & Dixon, E. M. The growth of the control of grammar in imitation, comprehension, and production. *Journal of Child Psychology and Psychiatry*, 1967, **8**, 31–39.

Maccoby, E. E., & Bee, H. L. Some speculations concerning the lag between perceiving and performing. *Child Development*, 1965, **36**, 367–377.

McNeill, D. The development of language. In P. H. Mussen (Ed.), *Carmichael's manual of child psychology*. Vol. 1. (3rd. ed.) New York: Wiley, 1970. Pp. 1061–1161. (a)

McNeill, D. *The acquisition of language: The study of developmental psycholinguistics*. New York: Harper & Row, 1970. (b)

Menyuk, P. *Sentences children use*. Cambridge, Mass.: M.I.T. Press, 1969.

Slobin, D. I., & Welsh, C. A. Elicited imitation as a research tool in developmental psycholinguistics. Unpublished paper, Department of Psychology, University of California at Berkeley, 1968.

FURTHER READING

Chomsky, C. *The acquisition of syntax in children from 5 to 10*. Cambridge, Mass.: M.I.T, 1969.

Brown, R., Cazden, C., and Bellugi, U. The child's grammar from I to III. In J. P. Hill (Ed.), *Minnesota symposium on child psychology*. Vol. 2. Minneapolis: University of Minnesota Press, 1969.

Klima, E. S., and Bellugi-Klima, U. Syntactic regularities in the speech of children. In J. Lyons and R. J. Wales (Eds.), *Psycholinguistics papers*, Edinburgh: Edinburg University Press, 1966.

Herriot, P. The comprehension of tense by young children, *Child Development*, **40** (1969), pp. 103–110.

Menyuk, P. *Sentences children use*. Cambridge, Mass.: M.I.T. Press, 1969.

5

Theories of Syntactic Development

We have been carefully avoiding a question that can no longer be avoided: How *do* children learn the syntax of their language? The previous chapters have described the course of syntactic development; they have considered the hypothesis that some aspects of language may not have to be learned in the usual sense because they are part of the child's innate capacity for language. Even if this hypothesis is correct, there is a tremendous amount that the child must learn. We do not, at the present time, have any complete theories that can be seriously considered as explanations for syntactic development in toto. Instead, we have a mixed bag of mechanisms, processes, and strategies which may play a role.

A First Attempt

A common-sense answer is that children "just imitate what they hear." This might be elaborated along the lines "parents teach them — they tell their children when they make a mistake."

The theory that the child acquires new linguistic forms from the speech of his parents through mimicking has been widely held in psychology. By repeating such forms, the child practices them, and he learns from some kind of reinforcement which situations are appropriate for the use of each form. In this account there are three processes: imitation, practice, and reinforcement. Each must be considered closely.

IMITATION

Imitation, in the broad sense of "coming to resemble a model," may play an important motivating role in language development. Children want to "be like" their parents, and speech is an obvious characteristic of adults. But motivation is not identical with the mechanism of acquisition. A young child whose older brother or sister has a bicycle wants to learn to ride the bicycle as his sibling does, but the learning does not take place by imitation. Instead, a complex kind of sensorimotor learning, relying on the child's own active efforts to ride the bicycle, usually including frequent falling, is necessary.

There is a considerable body of evidence that imitation does not play a very important role in the actual acquisition of syntax. Many of the very earliest utterances of children cannot be viewed as imitations or even reduced imitations of adult speech, such as, *Allgone sticky*. Furthermore, even when children do imitate parental speech (which is not uncommon), they reformulate the sentence using their own grammar. Children can hardly acquire new grammatical features through imitation when it is precisely these new features that are omitted in imitations.

Perhaps the most dramatic evidence against imitation is the fact that children who cannot speak at all, but who can hear normally, acquire normal linguistic competence in comprehension. Eric Lenneberg (1962) has reported the case of a boy who for unknown neuromuscular reasons was unable to articulate speech at all. Such a child could never have imitated adult speech. Indeed, he could not have been reinforced for speaking grammatically. Yet he did learn to comprehend language. Cases such as these are strong evidence against *any* theory of language acquisition that depends very strongly on the child's productions; for example, the selective reinforcement theory of the development of speech sounds from babbling. Although this case is the most striking, essentially the same phenomenon occurs for every child. The fact that comprehension is often better than production is virtually impossible to square with the view of learning through imitation.

The negative conclusion about the role of imitation in a theory of syntactic development must be qualified in several ways. Obviously, on the basis of the evidence considered so far, it can apply only to syntactic development; whether imitation is a major mechanism of articulation development and of acquisition of new vocabulary items, as is very plausible, is a separate question.

One of the most difficult problems in developmental psychology is the relation between research findings on normal children, and therapeutic methods for exceptional children. The fact that imitation may not play a role in the syntactic development of normal children does not imply that it may not be of great value for the speech therapist or other language trainer. Children are referred to the therapist precisely when the normal process of development has failed. The use of imitation must be evaluated in each appropriate context. The negative conclusion for normal children does suggest, however, that the process of imitation ought to be closely examined in the therapeutic setting. Under what conditions do children in the therapy setting successfully imitate? If the child does not match the model sentence, what changes occur? Are there regular patterns of distortion?

Finally, although new linguistic features may not enter into the child's language directly via the act of imitation, there is another route open. When the child imitates *Adam's nose is dripping* with *Nose drip*, is he aware of the difference between the two utterances? A comparison of the two would be a nearly ideal learning situation. It is paradoxical to speak of the child as understanding that his imitation does not match the model, but the finding that comprehension is superior to production renders the hypothesis more plausible. If this hypothesis is correct (and there is no evidence currently available which bears upon it), it is not imitation that explains syntactic development but, rather, the processes by which linguistic features enter the child's comprehension ability and by which adult models can be compared with his own imitations.

PRACTICE

Practice is not really an explanation of language acquisition, but presumably it is the mechanism by which features are firmly fixed in the child's language. The development of inflections in English and Russian casts doubt on the efficacy of practice. English-speaking children have the correct past tense forms of the irregular verbs and use them correctly, and Zhenya had the correct instrumental singular forms for many nouns and used them correctly; both fitting the definition of practice perfectly. But these forms are given up unhesitatingly when the regular endings are learned.

REINFORCEMENT

Parents often disapprove or approve of what their children say. But they do not really carry on an intensive teaching program of the kind necessary for second-language learning after adolescence. And in fact, such disapproval or approval does not seem to be necessary, as immigrant children pick up a second language in the streets without any reinforcement of this type.

The claim that it is direct reinforcement that leads to the predominance of grammatically correct sentences assumes that parental approval and disapproval are in fact dependent on grammaticality. Of course, even if these expressions are appropriately contingent, they may not have an effect. Brown, Cazden and Bellugi (1969) worked through several samples of data, comparing the correctness of those child utterances that were followed by a sign of approval by the parent with those child utterances that were followed by a sign of disapproval. In the majority of cases, the grounds on which an utterance was approved or disapproved were not linguistic at all but, rather, were based on the correspondence between utterance and reality, that is, the truth of the sentence. Reading 5.1 summarizes Brown's findings.

Perhaps viewing parental approval and disapproval as positive and negative reinforcers is too literal. Any parental speech to a child is a kind of attention, and children crave such attention. When the child produces his first words, he is likely to receive a great deal of attention, much of it positive. Later, the speech of the child is likely to provoke some response from the parent. However, this attention is largely independent of the form of the child's utterance; that is, attention may motivate a child to talk but necessarily not to speak grammatically.

Another possible reinforcer is satisfaction of the child's wants. This possibility is the heart of the **communication pressure hypothesis:** children learn to talk because they need to communicate their needs to others. Such an hypothesis can be correct only if satisfaction of the child's needs is more likely following a syntactically correct utterance than following a syntactically incorrect one. Although the appropriate research, analogous to Brown's evaluation of approval and disapproval, has not been performed,[1] the weight of anecdotal evidence is against the hypothesis. The child who says *mi* will receive milk; a few months later he will be saying *Want milk* or *I want milk* when *mi* would do. Mothers are highly understanding, and comunication with them is easy even with primitive linguistic systems. If acquisition of a word or linguistic feature is long overdue, a parent may actively take a hand, but what is striking is how seldom this occurs. The child produces *I want milk* before the parent might begin to disapprove more primitive forms.

Another possible reinforcer is **communication satisfaction:** it is intrinsically reinforcing for a child to understand other people talking and to make himself understood. Such a view, plausible as it is, robs reinforcement of its role as an explanatory device. The question of syntactic development is translated into a question about how children know when they have understood another person or when they have been understood.

The appeal of imitation, practice, and reinforcement in large part lies in the fact that they are easily observable and quantifiable. They reflect a passive conception of the language learner. The emphasis in the theory is on what the environment does *for* and *to* the child. An understanding of language as a creative system, with the consequence that linguistic competence must consist, in large part, of a set of rules, not a collection of elements, leads to skepticism of such explanations.

The Role of Maternal Speech

Despite any innate capacity for language, children must hear a language in order to learn to speak it. Most of what they hear is the speech of their primary caretaker, usually the mother. What kind of linguistic environment do mothers provide for their children?

Most people who have had experience speaking with children have a strong feeling that their speech to young children is quite different from their other speech. Some of the differences that have been proposed are smaller vocabulary, shorter sentences, less complex sentences, more use of intonation, and clearer articulation. In fact, we have very little information based

[1]Brown and Hanlon (1970) present some interesting data on this question.

on the only valid evidence: observations of mothers speaking to their children.

Only recently has the first controlled comparative study of speech to children and adults been performed. Phillips (1970) recorded the speech of thirty middle-class, white mothers under two conditions: first, while speaking to the experimenter; and second, while speaking to their children during a period of free play. The mothers' utterances to their children were shorter, contained fewer verbs and modifiers, and included a smaller variety of verb forms. Of the children, who were all first-born boys, ten were eight months old, ten were eighteen months old, and ten were twenty-eight months old. The speech to eight and eighteen month olds showed these differences more strongly than the speech to twenty-eight month olds.

Does simplification really help children learn language? Clearly, talking in baby talk to a child for the first four years of his life would be a hindrance; but so would speaking in the language of an encyclopedia or a diplomatic treaty. There must be an optimum level of language complexity, challenging to the child but not impossibly so. Shipley, Smith, and Gleitman (1969) studied the spontaneous responses of young children to commands that varied in structure. They found that children past the one-word stage responded appropriately more often when the command was formulated in adult form (*Throw me the ball*) than when the command was formulated in a simplified form similar to the children's own language (*Throw ball*). This finding might be interpreted as support for the hypothesis considered above, that children can distinguish between their own language and the more elaborated language of adults. More information is needed about the changes in mother's speech to young children, and on the relation between the child's speech and his mother's speech at different stages of development.

LINGUISTIC INTERCHANGE

Probably more important than the absolute quality of the mother's speech is the nature of the linguistic interchange between parent and child. Several interesting kinds of verbal interchange have been discovered by Roger Brown and his coworkers. And these may lead to the simultaneous presentation of the deep structure of a sentence and its transformed surface structure. This would provide just the appropriate information for formulating a transformation.

Prompting

One is called **prompting,** or **constituent prompting.** The parent asks a question, such as, *What do you want?* The child does not respond, and the parent tries again: *You want what?* The parent may be assuming that the second question, which is a sort of sentence-completion item, is easier to understand. If this is correct, and the child does understand the question without *wh* movement to initial position, then he has in mind something closer to the deep structure (*You want what?*) just after being presented with the surface structure (*What do you want?*). He might learn how to ask questions this way, that is, learn to formulate the transformations that invert subject and auxiliary, supply *do* if necessary, and move the *wh*-word to the initial position.

Echoing

A different exchange begins when a child utters a sentence that is in part unintelligible, such as, *I going ow nah* or *I'm gonna splay.* The mother than imitates the child insofar as she can, and replaces the unintelligible part with one of the *wh*-words of English, producing questions such as *You're going where?* and *You're gonna do what?* Such an exchange is called **echo** or **say constituent again.** The mother's question is similar to the deep structure of a well-formed *wh*-question. It does not correspond directly to the child's utterance, which was a declarative. The child's sentence is the *answer* to the question. A proper answer to *You're going where?* might be *I'm going home.* For example,

    CHILD: I going owa nah.
    MOTHER: You're going where?
    CHILD: I going . . .

The mother is asking a question to which, what the child just said, and will repeat more clearly (hopefully), are answers. As Bellugi's study of questions (Ch. 4) has shown, children cannot answer questions properly early in their development; it is something that must be learned. Notice that the answer to a *wh*-question is basically identical with the deep structure of the *wh*-question, with the *wh*-word replaced by the information desired. The question provided by the mother may help the child to learn.

In both these types of exchange, the mother is producing a form of question which Brown calls the **occasional question** because they are occasionally produced by adults in normal discourse. The children in Brown's sample whose grammatical competence advanced more rapidly had mothers who produced such occasional questions more often. Adam's mother produced them at the rate of one in fifty-seven utterances; Eve's, one in eighty; and Sarah's, only one in one-hundred forty-six. Sarah advanced more slowly than the others. However, these children differed in many other dimensions, such as socioeconomic class, so this difference is hardly proof. It should also be pointed out that the children never used the simplified forms themselves.

Expansion

The most interesting exchange between mother and child is the **expansion.** In an expansion, the mother imitates her child, but she does not reproduce the child's utterance exactly. Instead, she adds something to it. Table 5-1 illustrates some typical expansions.

TABLE 5-1. *Expansions of Child Speech Produced by Mothers*

Child	Mother
Baby highchair.	Baby is in the highchair.
Mommy eggnog.	Mommy had her eggnog.
Eve lunch.	Eve is having lunch.
Mommy sandwich.	Mommy'll have a sandwich.
Sat wall.	He sat on the wall.
Throw daddy.	Throw it to daddy.
Pick glove.	Pick the glove up.

SOURCE: Brown, R., & Bellugi, U. "Three Processes in the Child's Acquisition of Syntax," *Harvard Educational Review*, 34:2, 1964, 141. Copyright © 1964 by President and Fellows of Harvard College. Reprinted with permission.

In general, there are many possible expansions that a parent might provide. Suppose a child says *Mommy soup.* Among the possible expansions are *Mommy is having her soup, Mommy had her soup*, and *This is mommy's soup.* The decision among these cannot be made on linguistic grounds alone. Similarly, the first four child utterances in Table 5-1 are all of the same linguistic form: proper noun followed by common noun. But they are expanded quite differently. A mother selects an expansion on the basis of various extralinguistic cues; perhaps the first course is just over, in which case the expansion would probably be in the past tense, *Mommy had her soup.* If the mother read the situation correctly, then the child would have in mind a meaning, and the mother would have provided the proper surface structure.

Brown's group noticed that the middle-class parents expanded about 30 percent of the children's utterances. The parents of the working class child, Sarah, did this much less often, and Sarah advanced less rapidly. But Sarah's mother also talked less to her child in general, so expansion rate and volubility were confounded.

Dan Slobin (1968) has noticed that children's imitations of their parent's expansions of their own utterances are often grammatically more advanced than their free speech, in contrast to their other imitations, which are not more advanced grammatically. Table 5-2 illustrates such exchanges and their frequency.

TABLE 5-2. *Imitations of Expansions (percent)*

Type of imitation	Example	Relative frequency[a] Adam	Eve
a. Unexpanded	Child: Just like cowboy. Adult: Oh, just like the cowboy's. Child: Just like cowboy.	45	17
b. Reduced	Child: Play piano. Adult: Playing the piano. Child: Piano.	7	29
c. Expanded	Child: Pick'mato. Adult: Picking tomatoes up? Child: Pick 'mato up.	48	54

SOURCE: From "Imitation and Grammatical Development in Children" by Dan I. Slobin, from *Contemporary Issues in Development in Psychology* edited and with commentary by Norman S. Endler, Lawrence R. Boulter and Harry Osser. Copyright © 1968 by Holt, Rinehart and Winston, Inc. Reprinted by permission of Holt, Rinehart and Winston, Inc.

[a]These figures cover Adam from age 2;3 to 2;10 and Eve from 1;6 to 2;2.

The mismatch between the child's original utterance and the adult's expanded form may serve as a motivation for the imitation of the expansion. Like Brown's observations, these data are only circumstantial evidence for the role of expansions in the learning of syntax.

Cazden (1965) experimentally investigated the effect of this kind of experience, as distinguished from volubility. She worked with twelve Negro children aged between twenty-eight and thirty-eight months. Since they spent all day at a day care center in Boston where the child-adult ratio was 30:1, Cazden felt that it could be assumed that they were linguistically deprived. The children were grouped into four trios, with the children in each trio being approximately equal in chronological age, talkativeness, and initial level of development as judged by MLU. Within each trio, the children were randomly assigned to one of three treatment groups: (1) control, (2) expansion, and (3) what Cazden called modeling but which has since been called *expatiation*.

The expansion group received forty minutes per day of deliberate expansion. Everything the child said was expanded. The expatiation group received exposure to an equal number of wellformed sentences that were not expansions but were relevant to the child's utterances. For example, if the child said *I got apples*, the experimenter said *Do you like them?* Or if the child said *We got some more*, the experimenter said *There's a lot in here*. Children in the control group received no special treatment, but they were brought into the treatment rooms every few days so that they would remain familiar with the materials and the tutors.

Several measures of language development were obtained before and after the twelve-week experimental period, because all the children, even the controls, could be expected to advance over a twelve-week period. The measures included MLU, a copula index (use of copular *be* in sentences such as *This is red*), verb complexity, and others. For each group, an advancement score — after minus before — was computed. The expansion-receiving group had advanced somewhat more than the control group on these measures. However, the expatiation-receiving group had advanced even more. So the order of the groups was: *expatiation, expansion, control*; the difference between the first two was larger than between the second.

There are at least three explanations that can be offered for this surprising finding. In fact, the "hindsight" reasoning generated by this experiment is at least as interesting as the data from the experiment itself. The first is McNeill's suggestion (1970b) that the experimenter, just like a parent, might guess wrong and provide the wrong surface structure for an expansion. This would happen, for example, if the child had the future tense in mind, but the parent produced *This is mommy's soup* instead of *Mommy will have her soup*. This probably does not happen often in natural settings. Parents do not expand more than about 30 percent of their children's utterances; perhaps this is all that they *can* expand correctly. But in Cazden's experiment the children were given 100 percent expansions; many of these were probably based on misinterpretations of the child's utterances. Such misleading expansions may have interfered with language learning.

This process may have been aggravated by dialect differences. As we will see in Chapter 9, many black Americans speak a dialect that is somewhat different from Standard English. Because the tutors in Cazden's experiment, like most white Americans, were not familiar with the dialect, they may have been even more prone to misinterpretation. A replication of this training program with tutors from the children's own race or community might produce very different results.

A second explanation is Cazden's own proposal that richness of verbal stimulation was more important than the grammatical contingency found in expansions. The expatiations were of wide variety, since they were not connected as closely with what the child had just said. If the process of language acquisition is similar to the construction of a scientific theory, in which hypotheses are formulated and tested against the available data, then the richer the set of data, the better (but see the comments on simplification above).

A third explanation is possible. Imagine what it would be like to be with someone who expanded everything you said. After a while, it would become either boring or annoying or both. Such an artificial elevation of the expansion rate may simply have reduced the child's attention. Many studies with children have shown that stimuli of a certain degree of novelty — not too familiar and not too strange — command the greatest attention. The expatiations may have been more interesting than the expansions for the children. (This explanation is highly consistent with the Swiss psychologist Jean Piaget's view of learning.)

These processes are not mutually exclusive, and probably all of them contributed to the outcome of the experiment. But more experiments will be necessary to determine the exact contribution of each factor. An obvious experiment would be to expand those child utterances that the adult feels he can interpret confidently and expatiate on the others. The "richness" explanation predicts that such an experimental group should do no better than the expatiation-only group; while the "misinterpretation" explanation predicts even better performance.

Despite the ambiguity of the results of this experiment, it remains the only published experiment investigating the effects of a specific kind of experience on linguistic development. As we will see in Chapter 10, the lack of data of this kind is a great hindrance in the design of early education programs.

Brown, Cazden, and Bellugi (1969) have tried to assess the role of expansions, as distinguished from parental modeling of a linguistic feature, in their longitudinal data. The first five regular inflections to emerge are the plural and possessive on the noun and the present progressive, the past, and the present indicative on the verb. For each child, these inflections emerge in a specific order. (As a criterion of emergence, the child must produce the inflection in at least 90 percent of the contexts in which it is clearly required.) Does this order correlate with any aspect of the linguistic environment provided by the child's mother? Three aspects of parental speech were examined: (1) the *proportion* of times the child's omitted inflections were provided by a parental expansion, (2) the *absolute frequency* of such expansions, and (3) the *absolute frequency* with which the inflection was *used* by the parent. For each of these three aspects, an order for the five inflections was obtained for each parent.

For each child a rank-order correlation could be computed between the order of emergence of the five inflections and the order of the five inflections for each aspect of parental speech; a total of fifteen correlations in all. For all three children, the order of emergence within the child's linguistic system was more strongly related to the frequency with which the inflection was used by the parent than it was to either the absolute frequency or proportion of expansions which provided the inflection. But, with only one exception, none of the correlations were significant. The sole exception was the correlation with frequency of use by parent for Sarah. This result is at best weak support for the richness hypothesis.

In summary, at the present time there is no direct evidence that expansions as such facilitate language acquisition, but there is a small amount of evidence that providing a rich set of data does affect acquisition.

The Role of the Child

Passive models of syntactic development, such as imitation and reinforcement, appear to be inadequate. But, in addition, they seem, to almost any observer of a young child learning to talk, to miss the sense of activity, of trial and error, of continual creation, on the part of the child. Child psychology is increasingly recognizing the functioning of the child as an autonomous investigator of the world, as a "little scientist." The work of Jean Piaget has been a major factor in this trend. In a summary of Piaget's work, Ginsburg and Opper wrote:

... Piaget places major emphasis on the role of activity in intellectual development, especially in the early years of life. In Piaget's view, one of the major sources of learning, if not the most essential one, is the intrinsic activity of the child. The child must act on things to understand them. Almost from birth, he touches objects, manipulates them, turns them around, looks at them, and in these ways he develops an increasing understanding of their properties. It is through manipulation that he develops schemes relating to objects. When new objects are presented, the child may at first try to apply them to already established schemes. If not successful, he attempts, again through manipulation, to develop new schemes; that is, new ways of acting on and thereby comprehending the world [1969, p. 221].

Piaget has written, with respect to the aims of education, "the principal goal of education is to create men who are capable of doing new things, not simply of repeating what other generations have done — men who are creative, inventive, and discoverers (Piaget, 1964, p. 5)." It is difficult to imagine a more apt description of language development. In the remainder of this chapter, we will consider explanations of syntactic learning that emphasize the role of the child rather than of external reinforcers, models, expanders, and so on.

Many children go through a sort of linguistic drill before falling asleep at night; a few do the same thing upon waking up. The first systematic study of this process was undertaken by Ruth Weir and reported in her book *Language in the Crib* (1962). She recorded the presleep monologues of her son Anthony when he was about two and a half years old.

Especially fascinating are the sequences of related utterances produced by Anthony. Many of them focus on pronunciation; the child corrects his own pronunciation and drills himself on consonant clusters. Others appear to be grammatical exercises, not so different from the exercises in foreign language textbooks. The most frequent type of sequence Weir recorded is the **build up**: *Block. Yellow block. Look at the yellow block.* The **breakdown** proceeds in the opposite direction: *Another big bottle. Big bottle.* Substitutions of nouns into fixed sentence frames occur: *What color. What color blanket. What color mop. What color glass.* Practice in affirmation and negation: *Not the yellow blanket. The white. It's not black. It's yellow. Not yellow. Red.*

This example is striking because Anthony is interweaving syntactic negation — *It's yellow. Not yellow.* — with a kind of semantic negation — *Not yellow. Red.* Other sequences that occurred include tense practice, pronominal substitution, practice in formulating declaratives and questions, and others.

It is obvious from the transcripts that Anthony enjoys playing with his language. There are many examples of rhyming and alliteration. In general, the content is subordinate to the linguistic form. These presleep monologues are a kind of practice; not a passive repetition of items, but practice at actively forming new combinations. What role they play in language development is unknown.

THE CHILD AS LINGUIST

The previous chapters have contained many instances of phenomena they can best be viewed as evidence of an active, ongoing process of hypothesis testing by the child. The consistent use of overregularizations such as *comed*, early grammatical rules such as the pivot-open structure of *Allgone sticky*, systematic misinterpretation of the structure of *The doll is easy to see*, and others show that the child has for a time adopted incorrect hypotheses. But the same process must lead to the adoption of correct hypotheses as well. The Copernican model of the universe, with the planets traveling in circular orbits about the sun, was an incorrect hypothesis (the planets travel in elliptical orbits, which are quite different from circles), but it was a step in the right direction. And so is *Allgone sticky*.

How children formulate hypotheses — rules — for the language they hear remains unexplained and is likely to remain so for some time. Braine (1963) has suggested the process of "contextual generalization," mentioned in Chapter 2. By experiencing a word in a particular position in a variety of contexts, the child acquires an association between the word and the position. The word can then be used by the child in that position. The pivot words are the first result of this process. The child focusses on a position in the sentences he hears, and the words that occur in this position become pivot words. Position need not be specified with reference to the sentence as a whole. Rather, it must be specific to a phrase, which may be indicated by intonation or by characteristic morphemes such as the plural -s on a noun, which typically marks the end of a noun phrase. One criticism of this theory was discussed earlier: it appears to favor learning of word-order languages over inflected languages with freer word order. If contextual generalization can apply to an inflected language, it should first result in an early child language that is free in word order but containing appropriate inflections. However, the evidence from Russian language learning shows a strong tendency for children to produce an uninflected relatively rigid language.

A more serious criticism lies in the fact that the order of words in a sentence reflects the underlying relations among the words only indirectly. The order of words in *John is eager to please* and *John is easy to please* is the same, but the relations among the words are quite different. Conversely, in active and passive sentences the order is quite different, but the relations are identical. Braine (1965) has suggested that contextual generalization be considered only as a theory of the acquisition of simple active declarative sentences in which order is a more reliable indicator of structure. Learning of other sentence types may then be explained on the basis of a transfer of learning. Such a restriction does not solve the problem. How does the child know which sentences to learn from? He hears more than simple sentences. Brown and Hanlon (1970) analyzed mother's utterances to their children before the children began to produce anything but simple active declarative sentences. They found that less than 30 percent of the mother's speech consisted of simple active declaratives. Braine's reformulation of his theory assumes that the child can distinguish those cases in which deep and surface structure are similar in order to learn how to formulate such sentences.[2]

An alternative model of hypothesis formulation is the rationalist approach of linguists and linguistically oriented psychologists such as Chomsky and McNeill. Think of the child as a "little linguist." He is formulating hypotheses about the corpus of speech he receives. The hypotheses are confirmed if they account for the corpus already available and successfully predict future sentences; they fail otherwise. Hypotheses that are confirmed become part of the grammar of the child; the others are rejected.

Suppose that children first formulate hypotheses about the corpus in the form of phrase-structure rules. This would work for a time, but inevitably it will become very complex. Generalizations that might unify a set of linguistic facts cannot be expressed this way. Instead, the child must work with a large number of special cases. The attempt in Chapter 1 to represent the auxiliary verb system in English with phrase-structure rules

[2]An enlightening debate on the role of contextual generalization can be found in Bever, Fodor, and Weksel (1965a, 1956b) and Braine (1965).

alone resulted in eight different rules for the auxiliaries in simple declarative sentences. Additional rules would have been necessary for passives, questions, and negatives.

A linguist — at least a transformational grammarian — would resort to transformations at this point because they are inherently more powerful. One phrase-structure rule and one transformation accounted for the facts of auxiliary verbs in simple declarative sentences, and no additional rules were needed for the other sentence types (except the passive, question, and negation transformations, which were necessary for other reasons). The solution for the child is also to formulate a transformation, to distinguish between deep and surface structures.

A progression of this sort was seen in the development of questions. One of the children first had a form *d'you want* . . ., which always appeared in that form and was pronounced as a single word. This was viewed as the result of a phrase-structure rule. It does succeed in producing one type of adult question. But there are many other types of questions, and this approach would require an additional rule for every question type. Eventually the child switched to a transformation system, in which three transformations produce a wide variety of surface structures.

To claim that transformations are formulated by children because they are more powerful than phrase-structure rules leaves a great deal unexplained. For one thing, it does not explain how a child *knows* that transformations are more powerful, or even that such rules *can* be formulated. However, since all languages appear to be transformational, this much may be part of children's capacity for language. They may expect language to be transformational, but they have to learn where transformations are appropriate and what form they take. A relevant linguistic fact is that there are restrictions on the kind of operations that transformations perform. For example, no language has a transformation that permutes every pair of words in a sentence, that is, changes. *My brother plays the flute superbly* to *Brother my the plays superbly flute*. If a complex sentence is formed by conjoining two simple sentences, for example, *John came to visit* and *John stayed a month* to form *John came to visit and John stayed a month*, and if the language allows pronominalization of one of two identical noun phrases, it is always the second *John* that is changed to *he*, not the first. So we have *John came to visit and he stayed a month*, but not *He came to visit and John stayed a month*, where *he* refers to *John*. The transformations that are actually found in languages are only a small subset of those logically possible. In other words, there are formal universals in the transformational component of language, and they may be a part of children's capacity for language.

The stubborn fact of the superiority of comprehension to production haunts these and many other theories. Very little attention has been given to formulating theories that might account for this discrepancy. In Chapter 3, a proposal of McNeill (1970b) based on the use of the basic grammatical relations in comprehension was considered. Kelley (1967) has suggested an intriguing model in which syntactic development is explicitly assumed to depend on the process of comprehension. Speech production is of secondary consequence. In Kelley's model, which has been implemented in a very simple form as a computer program, the crucial feedback in hypothesis-testing does not come from external sources such as reinforcement but is internal in nature. Hypotheses are supported if they actually lead to successful understanding of the utterances encountered (see Reading 5.2). Successful understanding is taken to be the achievement of an interpretation of the sentence which is consistent with the learner's knowledge of the world. To be sure, this amounts to a translation of the question, "How do children learn to talk?" into the equally difficult questions, "How do children know when they have understood?" or "What does it mean to have a reasonable interpretation?" However, often a translation of a question is an aid to answering it.

In the early stages of language development, children produce subject-verb, verb-object, and subject-object sentences, but subject-verb-object sentences appear only later. Does the emergence of SVO sentences reflect the development of a new hypothesis, or has the three-term order been present implicitly in the shorter sentences? Bloom (1970a) has argued that the SVO order is part of the children's competence at the earlier stage, but that constraints, either linguistic or cognitive, limit the length and complexity of productions. There are many instances in which children demonstrate mastery of subparts of sentences — for example, elaborated noun phrases, negation, adverbial modifiers — in relative isolation, but much simpler forms appear when these subparts are combined. A description that is based on the most advanced language of which the child is capable will, therefore, specify sentences more complex than any the child actually produces. The constraints are gradually lifted; thus advances in productions reflect the removal of constraints rather than the acquisition of new linguistic features. The actual acquisition precedes the appearance of the feature in productions. Just what the constraints are is the puzzle. They are probably not purely cognitive, such as memory span, because the items that are deleted in combinations are not randomly selected. It is possible to specify fairly precisely which deletions will occur (see Bloom, 1970a, chap. 6 for a detailed study). There is some evidence that the linguistic features that are most likely to be retained are the latest acquisitions of the child; it is the older features that are more likely to be deleted.

Summary

The more we learn about language development, the less we understand how it is done. The child's acquisition of language is one of the major feats of his development; language acquisition is a crucial test for any theory of learning. The concepts of imitation and reinforcement, although relevant, are inadequate as explanations. The creativity of the child, and his relative independence from adult models and approval, weigh against passive mechanisms of learning. Perhaps more important is the verbal interchange between mother and child. Such exchanges may be equivalent to miniature teaching situations in which the child can learn the proper form for his intended meaning.

But most important is the role of the child himself. In some poorly understood way he formulates hypotheses about the language about him and tests them, either by formulating utterances of his own or by attempting to comprehend new utterances. The latter may be more plausible, for he can comprehend more than he can produce. Increasingly elaborated productions may reflect a loosening of constraints on a well-developed comprehension rather than a new acquisition.

Most of the processes considered in this chapter have excluded considerations of meaning; they have emphasized the formal nature of language. The child's language learning does not take place in a vacuum. The language about him, and his own speech, have meaning. How does this context help in the learning language? In the next chapter we will consider the development of meaning, and how the development of form and the development of meaning are related.

5.1 On the Role of Reinforcement in Language Acquisition*

The proposition "Syntactically correct utterances come to prevail over syntactically incorrect utterances through the selective administration of signs of approval and disapproval" is a testable one.

The proposition cannot be true for the natural case of parents and children at home unless parental approval and disapproval are in fact appropriately contingent on syntactical correctness. If the reactions are appropriately contingent, then they may or may not have the effects proposed. For this analysis . . . [The] general plan was to contrast the syntactic correctness of the population utterances followed by a sign of approval — *that's right, very good*, or just *yes* — with the population of utterances followed by a sign of disapproval — *that's wrong* or *no*. The results are simply stated: there is not a shred of evidence that approval and disapproval are contingent on syntactic correctness.

What circumstances did govern approval and disapproval directed at child utterances by parents? Gross errors of word choice were sometimes corrected, as when Eve said *What the guy idea*. Once in a while an error of pronunciation was noticed and corrected. Most commonly, however, the grounds on which an utterance was approved or disapproved . . . were not strictly linguistic at all. When Eve expressed the opinion that her mother was a girl by saying *He is a girl*, her mother answered *That's right*. The child's utterance was ungrammatical, but her mother did not respond to that fact; instead she responded to the truth of the proposition the child intended to express. In general, parents fitted propositions to the child's utterances, however incomplete or distorted the utterances, and then approved or not according to the correspondence between proposition and reality. Thus, *Her curl my hair* was approved because the mother was, in fact, curling Eve's hair. However, Sarah's grammatically impeccable *There's the animal farmhouse* was disapproved because the building was a lighthouse, and Adam's *Walt Disney comes on on Tuesday* was

*From Brown, Roger, & Courtney Cazden, & Ursula Bellugi, "The Child's Grammar from I to III," in *Minnesota Symposium on Child Psychology, Volume II*, edited by J. P. Hill, University of Minnesota Press, Minneapolis, © 1969, University of Minnesota. Pp. 70–71.

disapproved because Walt Disney came on on some other day. It seems, then, to be truth value rather than [well formed syntax] that chiefly governs explicit verbal reinforcement by parents — which renders mildly paradoxical the fact that the usual product of such a training schedule is an adult whose speech is highly grammatical but not notably truthful.

5.2 A Comprehension-Based Model of Language Acquisition*

According to [a comprehension-based] model syntactic acquisition proceeds by processing sentences, one after the other, trying to understand each in turn. To understand a sentence means to produce a correct analysis of that sentence. The component which models the process of understanding is the parsing algorithm. This component takes a sentence it has been presented with and the grammar of the model, along with any current grammatical hypotheses the model may have generated, and attempts to produce an analysis of the sentence.

To determine whether an analysis of an input sentence is correct is the function of the comparator component. This component determines whether a sentence analysis is consistent with what the child knows (on the basis of his general knowledge of the world and his particular knowledge of the situational context in which the sentence was spoken). If no analysis of a sentence is consistent in this sense with what the child knows, the sentence is simply discarded and not used at all. Only if the sentence is correctly understood is there any effect on the grammatical competence of the model.

When a sentence is correctly understood two things happen: first, all of the grammatical constructs used by the parsing algorithm to produce the correct sentence analysis are incrementally confirmed (including any grammatical hypotheses that were used); and secondly,

*From Kelley, K. L. Early syntactic acquisition. Rand Corporation Report No. P-3719, 1967. Pp. 93–95. Reprinted with permission.

the sentence itself may serve as the stimulus for the generation of some new hypotheses. After these two operations the model goes on to obtain another sentence and continue its processing.

In addition to the time scale in which sentences are presented one after the other, there is a larger developmental time scale in which the model passes through acquisition stages. [In this model there are three distinct stages.] Each stage is characterized by the generation of a different set of grammatical hypotheses about the language. During a particular stage these hypotheses are tested against the sentences the model experiences, and those hypotheses which are accurate characterizations of the language will be confirmed in the usual manner, while those which are not simply atrophy and are discarded.

The principal mechanism for acquiring a grammatical construct is for a hypothesis to be sufficiently well confirmed to become a part of the grammar.

SELECTED REFERENCES

Bever, T. G., Fodor, J. A., & Weksel, W. On the acquisition of syntax: A critique of "contextual generalization." *Psychological Review*, 1965, **72**, 467–482. (a)

Bever, T. G., Fodor, J. A., & Weksel, W. Is linguistics empirical? *Psychological Review*, 1965, **72**, 493–500. (b)

Bloom, L. *Language development: Form and function in emerging grammars.* Cambridge, Mass.: M.I.T. Press, 1970. (a)

Bloom, L. Semantic features in language acquisition. Paper presented at the Conference on Research in the Language of the Mentally Retarded, University of Kansas, February, 1970. (b)

Braine, M. D. S. The ontogeny of English phrase structure: The first phase. *Language*, 1963, **39**, 1–13.

Braine, M. D. S. On the basis of phrase structure: A reply to Bever, Fodor, and Weksel. *Psychological Review*, 1965, **72**, 483–492.

Brown, R., & Bellugi, U. Three processes in the child's acquisition of syntax. *Harvard Educational Review*, 1964, **34**, 133–151.

Brown, R., Cazden, C., & Bellugi, U. The child's grammar from I to III. In J. P. Hill (Ed.), *Minnesota symposium on child psychology.* Vol. 2. Minneapolis: University of Minnesota Press, 1969. Pp. 28–73.

Brown, R., & Hanlon, C. Derivational complexity and order of acquisition. In J. R. Hayes (Ed.), *Cognition and the development of language* New York: Wiley, 1970. Pp. 11–53.

Cazden, C. Environmental assistance to the child's acquisition of grammar. Unpublished doctoral dissertation, Graduate School of Education, Harvard University, 1965.

Ginsburg, H., & Opper, S. *Piaget's theory of intellectual development: An introduction.* Englewood Cliffs, N.J.: Prentice-Hall, 1969.
Kelley, K. L. Early syntactic acquisition. Rand Corporation Report No. P-3719, 1967.
Lenneberg, E. H. Understanding language without the ability to speak. *Journal of Abnormal and Social Psychology,* 1962, **65,** 419–425.
McNeill, D. The development of language. In P. H. Mussen (Ed.), *Carmichael's manual of child psychology.* New York: Wiley, 1970. Pp. 1061–1161. (a)
McNeill, D. *The acquisition of language: The study of developmental psycholinguistics.* New York: Harper & Row, 1970. (b)
Phillips, J. R. Formal characteristics of speech which mothers address to their young children. Unpublished doctoral dissertation, Department of Psychology, Johns Hopkins University, 1970.
Piaget, J. Development and learning. In R. E. Ripple & V. N. Hardcastle (Eds.), *Piaget rediscovered.* Ithaca, N.Y.: Cornell University Press, 1964.
Shipley, E. F., Smith, C. S., & Gleitman, L. R. A study in the acquisition of language: Free responses to commands. *Language,* 1969, **45,** 322–342.
Slobin, D. I. Imitation and grammatical development in children. In N. S. Endler, L. R. Boulter, & H. Osser (Eds.), *Contemporary issues in developmental psychology.* New York: Holt, Rinehart and Winston, 1968. Pp. 437–443.
Weir, R. *Language in the crib.* The Hague: Mouton, 1962.

FURTHER READING

Brown, R., Cazden, C., & Bellugi, U. The child's grammar from I to III. In John P. Hill (Ed.), *Minnesota symposium on child psychology.* Vol. 2. Minneapolis: University of Minnesota Press, 1969.
McNeill, D. *The acquisition of language: The study of developmental psycholinguistics.* New York: Harper & Row, 1970.
Palermo, D. S. Language acquisition. In H. W. Reese and L. P. Lipsitt (Eds.), *Experimental child psychology.* New York: Academic Press, 1970.

6

Semantic Development

A language is more than a set of rules for combining words or morphemes. Language can be used for communication, albeit imperfectly, because language has meaning: there is a connection between language and reality.

In the competition for least understood aspect of language acquisition, **semantic development** is surely the winner. This may seem surprising, for the study of vocabulary growth, one of the oldest lines of research on language development, would appear to contribute to an understanding of the growth of meaning. In recent years, interest in vocabulary growth has declined as realization has grown that such studies miss many important aspects of semantic development. First, the presence of a word in a child's vocabulary does not, by itself, tell an observer much about the meaning of that word to the child. An assumption of identity of meaning to the child and to adults is not justified in many cases. Second, vocabulary counts ignore important relationships between word meanings, relationships that make a vocabulary more than a list of words. And third, vocabulary studies do not

131

provide any information on the crucial process by which word meanings are combined into sentence meanings.

Another reason (or excuse) for the lack of understanding of semantic development is that this aspect of language is the most directly tied to the broader cognitive development of the child. The question "How do children express ideas?" cannot be neatly separated from the question "What kind of ideas do children have to express?"

Theories of Meaning

The most serious handicap in the study of semantic development, however, is the fact that we do not really understand what it is that is being developed, that is, we do not understand adult semantic competence. In the case of syntactic development, the existence of a well-articulated theory of adult competence — transformational grammar — provides a framework for the collection and analysis of data from children. Although philosophers and linguists have investigated meaning for centuries, we lack a clear understanding of the concept.

REFERENTIAL THEORY

Alston (1964) surveys some theories of meaning and the difficulties they encounter. Two theories should be mentioned briefly here because variants of them are common in the psychological literature. The first is the **referential theory.** There are many words for which, if asked the meaning, we might point to something in the world. For example, *Fido* refers to a particular dog, **red** refers to a particular class of colors, *cat* refers to a class of animals, and so on. That "something" to which a word or expression refers is its **referent.** The referential theory simply states that *the meaning of a word* is *its referent.* In other words, words are symbols that stand for something other than themselves, something in the world, namely, their referents.

This theory, and similar ones, have been popular among some psychologists because they lead to a simple explanation of how words and their meanings are learned. *Fido* is learned by hearing "Fido" spoken while seeing the particular dog; *red* is learned by hearing "red" while being shown a red object; and so on. This is entirely consistent with traditional views of learning. Nevertheless, the inadequacy of such a theory has been known for at least a century. Bertrand Russell formulated the best known example of this inadequacy. Consider the expressions "Sir Walter Scott" and the "author of *Waverley*." These two expressions have the same referents. That is, they refer to exactly the same individual, since Scott was the author of *Waverley*; but they do not have the same meanings. If they had exactly the same meaning, there could be no reason ever to say *Sir Walter Scott is the author of* Waverley, any more than to say *Sir Walter Scott is Sir Walter Scott*, which is pointless. But *Sir Walter Scott is the author of* Waverley is a reasonable sentence, it does convey information, and it does this by linking together two expressions with different meanings.

Just as two expressions can have the same referent but different meanings, the converse can occur. Consider words such as *I, you, here*, and *there*. Suppose I use the word "you" in a sentence spoken to a friend, and a few seconds later my friend uses the word "you" in a sentence to me. When I used the word "you," it referred to my friend; when he used the word "you" it referred to me. But that does not mean that the word "you" has two different meanings (one for every person spoken to in the world.) It *means* exactly the same thing, namely, "the person being spoken to." And the word "I" means "the speaker," while its referent changes constantly. Words like this have a constant meaning but many referents.

Compare the word "food" in English with its counterpart in the language of cannibals. Is the meaning of *food* different from the meaning of the cannibal term because the latter refers to human beings? Of course not; the two terms *mean* exactly the same thing — "something to eat"; here the referents are different. This example, and others like it (such as the word "beautiful," as applied to women), suggest that in many cases, specification of the referents of words is not strictly part of the language at all; it is determined by many other features of the world, including the culture of the linguistic community. In such cases, only the meanings of the words can be considered part of the language proper.

Even more damaging to the referential theory is the fact that many words either do not have a referent or it is difficult to decide what the referent is. Words and phrases such as "unicorn" and "the present king of France" are illustrations of this deficiency. Most of the "little words" of a language, such as *and, if, is*, and *but*, also fall in this category. In fact, many philosophers who have worked with the referential theory have simply denied that these "little words" have any meaning in isolation. And yet we all have feelings about these words and their meanings. For example, we can talk about the difference between *and* and *but; but* seems to mean "and, though you're not expecting this, . . ."

Of course, many words do have referents. And knowing how to use these words includes knowledge of their referents. However, Roger Brown (1958) has shown that even this simplest aspect of meaning is not so very simple. If it were the case that every object had exactly one name, and every name had exactly one referent, the situation would be quite straightforward. But neither condition is true. Almost all names actually refer to a category — the word "dog" refers to *all* four-legged animals of a certain type, the word "green" refers to *all* green objects, and so on. Conversely, every object can be named with a variety of terms. A pencil I have used can be called *a pencil, a No. 2, a writing instrument, this worn dull thing I used,* and many other terms. Some of them refer specifically to the pencil, some refer to larger categories — *a writing instrument,* for example. Brown (1958) uses the example of a dime, which can be called *dime, coin, money,* and *1952 dime,* among others. Some of the terms refer specifically to the particular dime, some to categories. And those that refer to categories may refer to larger or smaller categories — compare *dime* with *coin.* Which one of these terms should be used? In fact, the name that is most commonly used by adults to children (and in fact, by adults to adults) is the term that is most useful. *Dime* is the most useful name for this particular dime, because all dimes are equivalent for most purposes. But coins are not all equivalent for most purposes (they are equivalent for some, of course, such as making a decision by flipping). On the other hand, the fact that it is a 1952 dime is unimportant (except for coin collectors). Learning about the referents of words is really a matter of learning about how the world is organized by human beings.

As a corollary to this conclusion, Brown clarifies an old question in the study of children's thinking; namely, is children's thinking more concrete than adults' or vice versa? He argues that studies of children's vocabularies are basically irrelevant to these questions because "the sequence in which words are acquired is not determined by the cognitive preferences of children so much as by the naming practices of adults [1958, p. 20; and see Reading 6.1]."

BEHAVIORAL THEORY

Another well-known theory of meaning is the **behavioral theory.** The behavioral theory of meaning focuses on the use of language in communication. It postulates that the meaning of a word or expression is the set of responses it produces in the hearer. Often this definition is broadened to include the situation in which the word or expression is used. Leonard Bloomfield, the most famous American linguist of the first half of this century, wrote "the meaning of a linguistic term. . . [is] the situation in which the speaker utters it and the response which it calls forth in the hearer [1933, p. 139]." This theory can be a satisfactory theory of meaning only if there are features common and distinctive to all the situations in which an expression might be uttered and if there are such common distinctive features in all the responses to the expression. Consider the use of the word "pencil" in these sentences:

1. Bring me a *pencil*.
2. This *pencil* is broken.
3. I need a No. 2 *pencil*.
4. Do you have a red *pencil?*
5. *Pencils* were invented in the eighteenth century.

There is nothing common to the situations in which these sentences might be uttered. But the meaning of *pencil* seems intuitively to be the same in all these contexts.

An alternative approach is to use the behavioral theory to describe the meaning of *sentences* and not isolated words. Perhaps we could describe the specific situations in which the sentence *This pencil is broken* might be used. However, the situations in which *This pencil is broken* is uttered might also lead to the uttering of *Bring me the pencil sharpener*. We do have a choice in deciding what to say in a particular situation. To claim that there is something distinct about the situations that would lead to the uttering of these two sentences, namely, the past history and "mental state" of the speaker, is entirely ad hoc and is essentially an abandoning of the behavioral theory.

Imperative sentences appear to be the clearest example of the claim that the meaning of an utterance is the response it produces. But suppose a parent says *Come in now* to his child. Think of the range of responses possible: The child gives no response and proceeds with his activity; he refuses to reply; he says

"Why?"; he changes the subject; he runs away; he complies with request. If the last response were the most common, the life of a parent would be much easier. And so would the life of the philosopher and the linguist. But it isn't.

Some psychologists have responded to these criticisms by saying that the meaning of a word or expression is not the actual response but the disposition, or tendency to respond, it produces. Saying *Come in now* produces a tendency to come in if the hearer has an inclination to obey the speaker. But this tendency must compete with other tendencies. This modification of the theory does not escape many of the problems. Suppose you hear a historical sentence such as *Pencils were invented in the eighteenth century*. What dispositions does this produce? If you are later asked, *When was the pencil invented?* you will reply *In the eighteenth century*. But understanding this sentence includes more than this response. For example, it follows from this sentence and other knowledge (or, "one would have the disposition to say") that pencils were invented before television but after the wheel, and so on.

The behaviorial theory, like the referential theory, has been attractive because it fits in nicely with traditional psychological theories. For example, Mowrer (1954) once offered a classical conditioning explanation of the meaning of *Tom is a thief*. Because of the hearer's past experience, he had a characteristic response to the word "thief." Perhaps his disposition in the presence of a thief is to hide all his valuables, not trust the person, call the police, and so on. When he hears the sentence *Tom is a thief*, it is rather like one of Pavlov's famous experiments with dogs. You remember that Pavlov presented dogs with food, which caused them to salivate. Every time he presented food he turned on a light briefly. After a number of trials, turning on the light without presenting food produced salivation in the dogs:

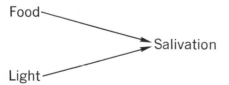

In hearing the sentence *Tom is a thief*, *thief* corresponds to *food*, which automatically produces the response, and *Tom* corresponds to the light. After hearing the sentence, the hearer will respond to *Tom* in the same way he would respond to a *thief*.

Numerous objections can be raised to such a theory of sentence meaning. Consider the sentence *Tom is not a thief*. Here *Tom* and *thief* are paired, just as in *Tom is a thief*. But the meaning is not at all the same. And what about *Tom was a thief but is honest now?* How is the hearer to respond? This theory completely ignores the structure of the sentence, that is, the way in which the words are combined, and this is a crucial element in the meaning of the sentence.

There is an even more serious confusion. Suppose you do not like thieves, are disposed to call the police, shout *Thief!*, and so forth. Now someone tells you that Tom is a thief. Do you automatically call the police? Maybe and maybe not. You may not believe the sentence. But whether or not you believe it, you understand it. Understanding — determining the meaning — must come before judgment of belief.

The referential theory and the behavioral theory do rest on valid insights about the nature of meaning, although they fail as all-encompassing definitions. Dwight Bolinger (1968) has suggested a loose but useful view of meaning as a system for segmenting reality. Word meanings serve to divide up the world. *Reality* and *world* here do not mean just the concrete world of physical objects external to the self but, rather, anything that may be talked about: dreams, pain, ideas, memories, and so on. Certainly most of what we say is not simply a running description of what is going on around us. We do not say *now I'm getting up; now I'm brushing my teeth; now I'm walking to class; now I'm getting bored*. We talk about the past — *What a dull lecture that was!* — or about the future — *If I get an A in this course I'll get into medical school* — or about wishes — *If only this were the end of the term* — or about many other situations far removed from the present one.

The way in which meanings segment reality are not given in the world; they too are arbitrary. The way in which English divides up colors into *blue* and *green* does not correspond to any natural division in physics or optics. Other languages do it differently. There are many cases where the particular distinction is not yet settled. In English we have three terms — *doctor, physician,* and *professor* — of which the last two have fairly well-defined meanings, but the first is still a matter of uncertainty and, occasionally, controversy. Often when we think about meanings, we select particularly simple cases, such as concrete nouns — *dog, sun, house,* and the like. But the majority of words divide reality in complicated and subtle ways. This is why it is extremely rare for two words to be exact synonyms. For example, we do not ordinarily say *I caught an illness* or *She caught an ailment.* Instead we say *I caught a disease. Disease* has a more concrete, separate-entity sort of meaning. *To return* and *to take back* are not perfect synonyms. *We took Junior back to the zoo* might refer to a second trip to the zoo for an afternoon or it might refer to an inmate; while *We returned Junior to the zoo* indicates that the zoo is indeed Junior's home. This is the reason that dictionaries are always very long and always inadequate, as anyone who has tried to learn a second language using a dictionary has discovered.

If word meanings are viewed as subtle divisions of reality, determination of the meaning of a word for a particular speaker, such as a child, will require extended and careful observation of the speaker's use and comprehension of the word, in linguistic and nonlinguistic contexts.

Vocabulary Growth

Many studies of vocabulary growth are reviewed in McCarthy (1954). The most comprehensive investigation is that of Smith (1926); the results of her study are shown in Table 6-1. The data on which this table is based were collected approximately forty-five years ago, however, and some caution is appropriate in generalizing the findings. The study of child development is continually changing; not only because of improvements in methodology and refinements in theory, but because of changes in the subject matter itself, namely, children. Many aspects of development have increased in rate during the past half century, ranging from the physiological, such as the onset of puberty, to the intellectual, such as performance on the Stanford-Binet Intelligence Scale. It is likely that the rapid rate of vocabulary development in the table is an underestimate of the growth of vocabulary today.

Word Meanings for Children

Determination of the meaning of a word for a child is exceptionally difficult, and it is not surprising that most of the information available comes from careful observation by linguists and psychologists of their own children, rather than from carefully controlled experimental studies. This tradition of diary

TABLE 6-1   *Vocabulary Growth as a Function of Age*

Age (years, months)	Number of words	Increment
0; 8	0	
0; 10	1	1
1; 0	3	2
1; 3	19	16
1; 6	22	3
1; 9	118	96
2; 0	272	154
2; 6	446	174
3; 0	896	450
3; 6	1222	326
4; 0	1540	318
4; 6	1870	330
5; 0	2072	202
5; 6	2289	217
6; 0	2562	273

SOURCE: Adapted from Smith, M. E. An investigation of the development of the sentence and the extent of vocabulary in young children. *University of Iowa Studies in Child Welfare*, 1926, **3**, No. 5.

studies begins with the investigations of Darwin, Taine, and others in the middle of the nineteenth century. Many interesting excerpts are collected in Bar-Adon and Leopold (1971).

The words "mama" and "papa" (or "dada") are often the first words to be acquired. At this first stage, it is evident that words can have different meanings for children from those of adults. How many parents have been chagrined when their year-old child cheerfully called every adult male *daddy*. Although *mama* is often the first word, it is not unusual for it to follow *papa* as the first truly linguistic expression. Jakobson (1962, reprinted in Bar-Adon & Leopold, 1971) has identified a common transitional system, in which *papa* refers to a parent who is present, while *mama* is used to request fulfillment of a need or to request the presence of a parent who can fulfill the needs. Jakobson quotes Gregoire's observation: "Edm. appeared to call back his mother, absent for the day, by saying 'mam-am-am'; but it is 'papa' which he declared when he saw her return . . . Edm. saw me prepare a slice of bread for him; he said 'mama,' and not 'papa.'"[1] A frequent speculation, difficult to test, is that the first word for 'moth-

[1]Translation from the French by the author.

er,' which in the majority of languages tabulated by Murdock (1959) begins with a nasal consonant, is based on the nasal murmur which often accompanies the sucking of infants.

However, even after the stage of the first words has passed, there may be major differences in meaning. Chukovsky's observation, reported in Chapter 2, of a child who said "Can't you see? I'm barefoot all over!" is a good illustration. The meaning of *barefoot* is extended from bare feet to apply to a "bare body." In another observation, a child comments that a mint candy made "a draft in the mouth." For this child, the word *draft* primarily refers to a sense of coolness and not to the breeze that normally produces the coolness.

Still later in development, many interesting aspects of cognitive development can be interpreted as differences in word meaning. For example, Piaget has observed that a child below the age of five or so can correctly identify his left and right hands, but when asked to identify the left and right hands of a person who is facing him, he will produce precisely the opposite of the correct response. Examples such as this one are illustrative of the important role of cognitive maturity in the development of word meaning; the inability to master the relational meaning of left and right is just one instance of the child's egocentrism, his inability to take another perspective in a wide variety of situations, linguistic and otherwise.

It is not difficult to produce many examples of idiosyncratic word meanings. However, there is little understanding of the general patterns of meaning and its development. A dimension that is often considered is from generalized to differentiated meaning. Children's word meanings are often wider than those of adults. But this overgeneralization is not universal. Leopold called a page in a book his daughter was examining, *weiss* ("white"). Hildegard's reaction was *schnee? no!* ("snow? no!"). For her the word "white" was associated with snow; applying it to a different substance was puzzling (Leopold, 1948). Learning word meaning is basically a problem of concept formation. The child hears a word in a wide variety of situations which are seldom if ever identical. He must extract the common characteristics, the "critical attributes." In fact, there may be no hard-and-fast common characteristic. What do all games have in common? There is a core of characteristics, some of which are found in every game, including competition, withdrawal from "reality," explicit rules, pleasure, and more. But none of these is found in every game.

If learning a word meaning is formation of a concept, errors of two kinds can be expected: overextension of the word to inappropriate cases and failure to apply the word in appropriate cases. Both widening and narrowing undoubtedly occur. Just how subtle the learning must be can be seen by comparing the words provided by different languages for the same domains (Leopold, 1948). The word "brush" in English includes not only hairbrushes, but shoebrushes, clothes brushes, and toothbrushes ("brush your teeth"). If a child who has learned this word extends it to a painter's brush, calling it *brush*, he is correct, and the phenomenon will be unremarkable to an English-speaking adult. If a German-speaking child performs the same generalization, it will immediately be noticed, perhaps as an amusing incident, because in German the word for a painter's brush (*pinsel*) is not the same as for a hairbrush (*burste*). Conversely, a German-speaking child can extend the range of application of *tuch* ("cloth") from handkerchiefs to towels and napkins, although an English-speaking child who does the same thing with one of his words is inappropriately grouping the objects together.

Another dimension of semantic development is from predominantly emotional and volitional meaning to more objective usage. The young child uses *more* not as an indication of quantity but as an expression of "I want more." *Ball* is likely to mean, "I want the ball." With further development, linguistic and cognitive, the emotional and objective functions are distinguished. Eventually they are expressed by different elements of the sentence, as in *I want more*, and *Give me the ball*.

Piaget suggested another dimension along which word meaning may be considered to develop. He has studied the development of the symbolic function, that is, the use of one action or object, either concrete or mental, to stand for another. On the basis of his investigations of adaptive behavior, play, and imitation, he has distinguished three stages (Ginsburg and Opper, 1969). A summary of these stages follows.

1. A presymbolic stage, in which substitution does not occur.
2. A symbolic stage, in which symbols do occur, but they are essentially personal, not shared; furthermore, they must have some resemblance or connection with the object or event being symbolized. For example, (at fifteen months Jacqueline) ". . . saw a cloth whose fringed edges vaguely recalled those of her pillow; she seized it, held a fold of it in her right hand, sucked the thumb of the same hand and lay down on her side, laughing hard. She kept her eyes open, but blinked from time to time as if she were alluding to closed eyes [Piaget, 1951, p. 218]."

That is an example of symbolic behavior, the cloth symbolizing the pillow, and not a simple confusion of the cloth and pillow, as the child's playfulness demonstrates. It is an instance of a concrete symbol; Piaget's studies have shown that mental symbols also begin to emerge at this stage.

> 3. Finally, a stage in which signs are used; that is, symbols which are shared and arbitrary. There need not be a connection or resemblence between the sign and what it signifies.

These stages appear to be good descriptions of the early stages of semantic development. At first, words are not truly symbolic. The child who says *No* to his mother who is trying to put him to bed, or says *Milk* when he wants milk, is not making a symbolic reference to something else. He is simply vocalizing his own feelings. Next, words begin to be used in a symbolic way. At twenty-one months, after returning from a trip Jacqueline told her father, "Robert cry, duck swim in lake, gone away [Piaget, 1951, p. 222]." Here the words refer to events that occurred in the past. However, the words are still somewhat personal in their meaning. We have already seen several examples of this, but here is another from Jacqueline (at thirty-one months):

> . . . seeing Lucienne in a new bathing suit, with a cap, Jacqueline asked: "What's the baby's name?" Her mother explained that it was a bathing costume, but Jacqueline pointed to Lucienne herself and said: "but what's the name of that?" (indicating Lucienne's face) and repeated the question several times. But as soon as Lucienne had her dress on again, Jacqueline exclaimed very seriously: "It's Lucienne again," as if her sister had changed her identity in changing her clothes [Piaget, 1951, p. 224].

Here *Lucienne* does not refer to a single person who retains identity despite clothing changes; instead, the word is tied to a particular combination of child and costume. Only later do words attain the status of signs: sequences of sounds which are arbitrarily connected with reality, but in a shared fashion.

Many examples of child word meanings are difficult to place into any of these dimensions. One of the most interesting is the development of the meaning of terms for negation. Both McNeill (1970b) and Bloom (1970a) have observed a three-stage progression in the meanings of negative expressions. McNeill, studying the development of negation by two Japanese children, observed first negations that were denials of the truth of other statements (*That's not a pear* in response to someone saying that it was a pear) or denials of the existence of objects (*There's no pear here*). Later, negations based on internal grounds, for example, *I don't want it*, appear. And still later, negations that serve to "entail" or imply the truth of another statement, for example, *That's not an apple, that's a pear*, in which the intention is to establish the truth of *That's a pear*, emerge. In Bloom's (1970a) study of the acquisition of English, she found a similar, although not identical, division of meaning into three categories: denials, *No girl*, denying a previous statement that a boy was a girl; rejections, *No wash*, meaning "don't wash me"; and nonexistence, *No wet*, meaning "dry." The order of emergence is not identical in the two studies, however. Bloom observed first nonexistence negations, then rejections, and finally denials.

Relationships among Word Meanings

The vocabulary of a language is more than a list of words and their meanings. There are important relationships among word meanings, some of which have been studied in detail by linguists, although they have largely been ignored by psychologists.

The most obvious such relationship is **synonymy** — having similar meanings. The two sentences *I saw an eye-doctor yesterday* and *I saw an oculist yesterday* have the same meaning because they are identical except for "eye-doctor" and "oculist," and these two words have the same meaning. Synonyms as good as these are very rare (and are almost always technical terms). In virtually every case two synonyms will differ in their meaning in some way. Consider the synonyms *hitch* and *tether;* they both mean "to make fast." In some cases, either may be used correctly. But if the important aspect of the situation was making something fast to a vehicle in order to move it, we would use *hitch*, whereas if the important aspect of the situation was connecting a vehicle to a post or other object in order to prevent its motion we would use *tether*. And if we think about it, this lack of perfect synonymy is not surprising. Why bother to have two words with exactly the same meaning? After all, the great merit of having so many words and so many syntactic processes is that we can express a tremendous variety of messages. Perfect synonyms are of little use in this respect.

The opposite of synonymy is **antonymy** — having opposite meanings. But the relation between synonymy and antonymy is really not this simple. In fact, antonyms have similar meaning. *Hot* and *cold* both refer to extremes of temperature, *always* and *never* refer to extremes of frequency of occurrence, *full* and *empty* refer to degree of fullness, and so on. In each case, the two antonyms share a considerable degree of meaning, just as synonyms do. It is hard to be precise about what it is that makes us feel that some related words are synonyms and some are antonyms, but we all can tell which is which. One difference is that antonyms will never be substituted for each other as synonyms can be. An object that can be described as hot might also be described as warm, although *hot* and *warm* are not very good synonyms; but that object would never be described as cold. *Hot* and *cold* are antonyms. Some words have two antonyms, for example, "noise" and "silence" and "noise" and "music." The two antonyms share different parts of the meaning of noise.

Another relationship between meanings is **reciprocity.** *Buy* and *sell* are reciprocals, as are *give* and *receive*. What distinguishes these from antonyms (which they are, in a sense) is that whenever a sentence using one of them is appropriate, there is another appropriate sentence using the other member of the pair. For example, *John buys books from Bill* has the same meaning as *Bill sells books to John*. *He gave flowers to her* has the same meaning as *She received flowers from him*. This is a sort of "semantic passive" — like the passive transformation in syntax, it presents the same meaning from a different point of view.

One of the most important relationships between meaning is **inclusion** — the meanings of *heart, stomach,* and *liver,* include that of *organ;* the meanings of *piano, trumpet, violin* include that of *instrument;* the meanings of *red, green, blue* include that of *color,* and so on. It is this kind of relationship that allows us to go beyond the actual words in a sentence. For example, *Colorless green ideas sleep furiously* is bizarre, and one reason for this is the phrase "colorless green." Actually, these two words do not directly contradict each other in the way that "ungreen green" does. But *green* and *color* are in an inclusion relationship, and *color* and *colorless* do contradict each other. The sentence *The bachelor saw herself in the mirror* is bizarre because *bachelor* and *male* are in an inclusion relationship, and *male* is contradicted by *herself*.

Essentially nothing is known about the development of the network of relationships among word meanings. There is no evidence that related words enter a child's vocabulary simultaneously. *Hot* is usually acquired before *warm*, *up* before *down*, and *give* before *receive*. If the acquisition of vocabulary items is largely a function of adult usage of words, this is not surprising. But in some sense, the full meaning of words such as *hot, up,* and *give* is not mastered until the related words are added. It is difficult to conceive of tests that might measure knowledge of the relationships between such pairs.

A quite different relationship between word meanings is tapped by the **semantic differential technique** developed by Osgood and his colleagues (Osgood, Suci, & Tannebaum, 1957). The semantic differential is often viewed as a measure of connotative meaning. When adults are asked to rate concepts, objects, or individuals on a variety of bipolar scales, such as *heavy-light, clean-dirty,* and *fast-slow,* **factor-analytic** studies reveal an underlying system of three independent dimensions of connotative judgment: evaluative (*good-bad, clean-dirty, happy-sad*); potency (*heavy-light, strong-weak,* and *large-small,*); and activity (*fast-slow* and *active-passive*). The bipolar scales correlated with each dimension share a part of their connotative meaning. Di Vesta (1966) has investigated the development of connotative meaning using the semantic differential scales. The three dimensions of the child's "semantic space" appear to be stable by age eight. It is difficult to utilize this technique with younger children, and therefore the course of development is not known. Di Vesta's results do suggest that the system may begin with a primarily evaluative dimension that differentiates into an evaluative and a dynamic dimension, the latter eventually differentiating into the potency and activity dimensions of adulthood. Ervin and Foster (1960) have demonstrated a confusion among meanings of terms that lie along the same dimension. They studied the potency factor by asking first- and sixth-grade children to make judgments of weight, strength, and size with respect to two objects (two balls, two wires, two shakers, and so on) that differed in only one of these dimensions. For example, a child was given two jars identical except for weight. The child was asked, "Is one of these heavier and one lighter, or are they both the same?" Then similar questions were asked for size and strength. Surprising proportions of the first-grade children indicated that if an object was heavy, it was also strong (66 percent) and big (39 percent); if an object was strong, it was also big (40 percent) and heavy (41 percent); and that if an object was big, it was also strong (52 percent). The sixth graders more accurately differentiated the terms, but there remained a substantial tendency to confuse them (proportions in the range of 21–44 percent). A similar study of the evaluative factor using drawings of faces, found that the terms *happy,* *good*, and *pretty* were confused in over 61 percent of the responses of the first graders, and a smaller but significant proportion of the sixth graders. Ervin and Foster conclude that for adults, these words have specific denotative meanings but shared connotative meanings, whereas young children do not yet have specific denotative meanings. The first set of results are probably due to the fact that the physical dimensions of size, weight, and strength are empirically correlated; large objects are heavy, and so on. This correlation may delay discrimination of the attributes. It is less plausible to assume that happiness, goodness, and beauty are empirically correlated.

Sentences and Word Meanings

Although the previous discussion has focussed on the meaning of individual words, a crucial question for the understanding of semantics in language is the process by which the meanings of the individual words are combined into the meaning of the sentence. Most words have more than one meaning. This fact raises the possibility that every sentence might be ambiguous in many ways. If there are four words in a sentence with two meanings each, the sentence should have $2 \times 2 \times 2 \times 2 = 16$ meanings. But such a high degree of ambiguity is rare. Only certain combinations of meanings are compatible. For example, the word *bat* is ambiguous; it may mean a kind of flying mammal or it may mean an implement used in baseball. But the phrase *baseball bat* has no ambiguity at all; the use of *baseball* rules out one meaning of *bat*. Similarly, *The bat bit the girl* is unambiguous; the predicate *bit the girl* rules out one meaning of *bat*. In the sentence *The baseball bat bit the girl*, baseball eliminates one meaning of *bat*, and *bit the girl* eliminates the other. As a result, it is **anomalous.**

This kind of reasoning led Katz and Fodor (1963) to formulate their linguistic theory of meaning, which is the best known and most ambitious attempt to handle meaning in linguistics. Their theory is unsatisfactory in a number of respects (see Bolinger, 1965), but one of its more positive aspects is the attempt to be explicit about what a theory of semantic competence should do. The goals of their theory are very similar to the goals of syntactic theory. Just as the syntactic theory of a language, a grammar, attempts to account for the knowledge which a native speaker has that permits him to recognize some strings as grammatically well-formed, some as ungrammatical, some as ambiguous, and so on, the goal of a semantic theory is to account for the knowledge native speakers have that they can use to judge some sentences as meaningful, some as ambiguous, and some as anomalous, that is, semantically ill-formed.

To this, Katz and Fodor postulate two parts to the meaning of a word. The first is a set of **semantic features,** or markers, each of which expresses a part of the meaning of the word. For example, *bachelor* has, among other semantic features, the set (human) (male) (unmarried). *Wife* has, among other semantic features, the set (human) (female) (married).

In addition to these semantic features, there are **selection restrictions** for every word. These are restrictions on possible combinations of words. *Bachelor's wife* obviously violates these restrictions, because *bachelor* includes the feature (unmarried) while *wife* includes the feature (married). One semantic feature for one of the senses of *bat* matches the selection restrictions of *baseball*, used as a modifier, so the phrase *baseball bat* is not only meaningful but unambiguous, because the other meaning of *bat* does not match the selection restrictions.

Thus, the dictionary entries for word meanings, according to this theory, consists of two parts: (1) the semantic features of the individual words and (2) the selection restrictions that govern how word meanings are combined to form the meaning of the sentence.

Semantic features appear in more than one dictionary entry. In many cases a feature may occur in a great many dictionary entries. The feature (living) occurs in the meaning of *dog*, *rose*, *plant*, and *man*, as well as in many other words. The appearance of a given feature in a set of words indicates that their meanings have something in common. We can only guess at how such a word dictionary might be constructed by the child. The simplest hypothesis is that semantic features are added, one at a time, to dictionary entries. This is undoubtedly too simple because features are often related to other features and may enter a dictionary together. But it is a reasonable initial hypothesis.

If the development of word meaning is a gradual response, which is only initiated by the acquisition of the word into vocabulary, it can be predicted that sentences which adults would consider anomalous, that is, not semantically well-formed, will be regarded as acceptable by young children. Remember that one function of the selection restrictions is to rule out certain sentences as being anomalous, such as *The baseball bat bit the girl*.

But if the child lacks knowledge of certain semantic features, he will also be lacking the selection restrictions that are based on them. Therefore he will accept grammatical combinations of words that an adult, with a complete semantic dictionary, would mark as anomalous.

Miller and Isard (1963) asked adult subjects to listen to three different kinds of verbal strings through a masking noise. Their task was to shadow the strings, that is, to repeat what they heard as closely as possible. The strings were of three types:

Fully grammatical: The academic lecture attracted a limited
audience.
Anomalous: The academic liquid became an odorless
audience.
Scrambled: Liquid the an became audience odorless
academic.

The anomalous strings were produced by selecting one word from a number of fully grammatical sentences; and the scrambled sentences were produced in the same way, but then the words were scrambled. In this way, the same words were used in all three kinds of strings. Since the noise obliterated part of the signal, performance depended on the subjects' ability to fill in the obliterated parts on the basis of what was heard.

At several noise levels, Miller and Isard's subjects did best on the fully grammatical strings, next best on the anomalous strings, and least well on the scrambled strings: *fully grammatical, anomalous, scrambled.*

The difference in performance between the scrambled strings and the anomalous strings reflects the subjects' ability to use syntactic information. If a subject heard *The academic _____ became an odorless audience,* he could at least infer that the unknown word was a noun. The difference in performance between the anomalous strings and the fully grammatical strings reflects the ability to use semantic information, namely, selection restrictions. If a subject heard *The academic _____ attracted a limited audience,* he could infer not only that the missing word was a noun, but that it was of a fairly limited type.

McNeill (1970a) repeated the Miller and Isard experiment with children aged five, six, seven, and eight. He used more familiar words, and the task was immediate recall rather than shadowing. If a child lacks some semantic features and selection restrictions, he should be less able than an adult to guess the words of a fully grammatical sentence obliterated by noise. But for the anomalous sentences, McNeill predicted that adults and children should do about equally well, as the semantic features and selection restrictions are of no use. In other words, to the extent that the child lacks full knowledge of semantic features, his performance on fully grammatical and anomalous sentences should be the same. Figure 6-1 illustrates the results of this experiment. The five year olds are clearly less able than the eight year olds to take advantage of semantic consistency in sentences. But performance on anomalous sentences changes very little between ages five and eight, as predicted on the grounds that lack of semantic markers does not affect accuracy of guessing on such sentences. The third curve summarizes the performance on scrambled sentences. The difference between the curves for scrambled and anomalous strings is a measure of the ability to use syntactic information, and it is constant between five and eight. The syntax relevant to this experiment is mastered

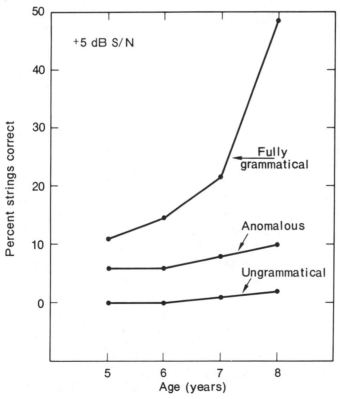

FIGURE 6.1   Percentage of strings correctly recalled by children 5, 6, 7, and 8 years old.

SOURCE: McNeill, D. The development of language. In P. H. Mussen (Ed.), *Carmichael's manual of psychology.* Vol. 1 (3rd ed.) New York: Wiley, 1970. P. 1122, fig. 8. Reprinted with permission.

before the age of five, while the semantic development lags behind.

Anomalous sentences similar to these have been observed in the linguistic productions of children by Turner (1966). She asked children to describe pictures, such as a farmer driving a tractor or a girl riding a pony. The children sometimes produced sentences such as *The tractor drives the farmer* and *The pony rides the girl.* What is interesting about these is not that they are incorrect, but that they are anomalous, that they could not possibly be a correct description of a picture.

Syntax and Semantics

In most kinds of linguistic performance, the meaning of a sentence interacts with its syntactic form. Dan Slobin (1966b) asked kindergarten, second-, fourth-, and sixth-grade children, and adults to judge the truth of a sentence with respect to a picture scene. (Sentence verification has become a popular experimental technique in psycholinguistics in recent years.) A typical picture showed a dog in pursuit of a cat. A true sentence for this picture is *The dog chases the cat;* and a false one, *The cat chases the dog.* Slobin presented sentences of different syntactic forms, using the negation and passive transformations, separately and in combination. For example, *The dog is not chasing the cat* is a false negative active sentence; while *The dog is not being chased by the cat* is a true negative passive sentence. Two measures of difficulty were used: number of errors and length of reaction. In fact, the two measures gave virtually identical results. In particular, erroneous responses took longer than correct ones.

There are two kinds of "negation" involved here. The first is syntactic: the sentence could be the result of the application of the negation transformation. The second, the sentence could be either true or false. This is a kind of semantic negation. Slobin found that negative sentences (in the syntactic sense) were more difficult to verify than affirmative ones; this is a result we would expect merely on the ground of increased syntactic complexity. The mean (average) reaction time for affirmative sentences (both active and passive) was 1.62 seconds; for negative sentences (both active and passive) was 2.03 seconds.

The breakdown into true and false was more interesting. Judgments of false were more difficult than judgments of true when the sentences were affirmative; mean response times of 1.68 and 1.55 seconds, respectively. But the reverse held for negative sentences. That is, true judgments were more difficult than false judgments when the sentences were negative; mean response times of 2.14 and 1.41 seconds, respectively. The two kinds of negation — syntactic and semantic — interact. The difficult cases are the ones in which the two forms conflict.

It may be useful to view this result as an indication of the entanglement of the denial and nonexistence functions of negation, following Bloom's analysis (see page 143). Syntactic negation is essentially one of nonexistence: *The dog is not chasing the cat* is equivalent to *There is not a dog chasing a cat here.* Semantic negation — truth or falsity — is an instance of denial negation: *It* (is) (is not) *true that the dog is chasing the cat.* When one type of negation is operative, there is a strong tendency for the other to be activated; hence the errors and longer decision times for the mixed instances, false-affirmative and true-negative.

The second major semantic consideration in this study (along with negation) is **reversibility,** a variable that has received much attention since Slobin (1966b) pointed to its importance. A picture of a dog chasing a cat is reversible. Cats can chase dogs as well as conversely. To decide if a given sentence is true, it is necessary to decide which of the two words "cat" and "dog" is the subject (in the deep structure sense) of the sentence and which is the object, and then compare this decoding of the sentence with a picture. It is, as would be expected, more difficult to do this for passive sentences; the deep structure subject is not the same as the surface structure subject. The problem of verification is simplified for *nonreversible* pictures, such as a girl riding a pony. If a child understands the sentence *The girl is being ridden by the pony;* that is, if he understands that *the girl* is the object of the verb, and *the pony* is the subject of the sentence, he can make a correct judgment immediately, without comparing the sentence with the picture. The sentence is anomalous; it could not be a description of a picture. Conversely, if the sentence is not anomalous; for example, *The girl is riding the pony*, as soon as this fact is realized, a judgment of true can be made. Because the situation is nonreversible, it could not be the other way around. Here a semantic factor simplifies verification by making possible a judgment on internal grounds alone.

Slobin's subjects found nonreversible verification easier than reversible ones. More striking is the fact that passive nonreversible sentences were as easily verified as active nonreversible sentences (average reaction times: passive nonreversible, 1.60 seconds; active nonreversible, 1.64 seconds). In other words, although passivization usually increases difficulty of verification, it does not do so for nonreversible situations.

Recently this experiment has been repeated with younger children by Bever, Mehler, and Valian (reported in Bever, 1970). Their task was slightly different from that used by Slobin: acting out sentences with toys. Slobin had found improvement in performance on nonreversible pictures. Bever's group found with their subjects that there was no difference at all between the reversible and nonreversible situations for the active sentences. The ability to exploit nonreversibility depends on the development of semantics and knowledge of the world; these lag behind the development of syntax.

The findings for the passive sentences were even more interesting. The youngest children, who were two years old, performed at about chance level on passive sentences. Children somewhat older performed better on almost all sentence types, with two exceptions: the first, the "reversed nonreversible" sentence, such as *The candy eats the policeman.* An impossible reversed sentence is constructed for a nonreversible situation. The other exception is similar, but not quite so clearly bizarre, such as *The cup holds the girl* or *The dog pats the mother.* These sentences are not impossible, but they are highly improbable. Performance on these two types of sentences actually deteriorates from age 3;0 to 4;0: from 30 percent and 49 percent for impossible and improbable sentences, respectively, to 17 percent and 38 percent. This change indicates an increasing role for semantic constraints in sentence interpretation. It is almost as if the children now ignore syntactic information; they simply identify the elements of the sentence and combine them in the most semantically plausible fashion.

This stage is followed by a brief but remarkable period in which performance on regular reversible passives, such as *The truck is pushed by the car,* deteriorates. In the data from Bever's group, the drop occurred from 3;8 to 4;0 for girls (from 55 percent in the preceding four month interval to 30 percent) and from 4;0 to 4;4 for boys (from 82 percent in the preceding four month interval to 43 percent). They argue that at this stage the children adopt a new strategy: interpret any noun-verb-noun sentence as actor-action-object acted upon. If it is the case that most sentences that children hear are active (which seems plausible, although there is little data), this is a reasonable strategy for them to adopt. Unfortunately, such a strategy will be misleading for reversible passive sentences such as *The cat is being chased by the dog.* This sentence will be interpreted as actor (cat)-action (chase)-object (dog). Such an interpretation will be coherent, since cats do chase dogs on occasion. Because the interpretation is coherent, the full syntactic analysis is skipped (although it is available when needed, that is, when the strategy produces an incoherent interpretation). This kind of error will not be made for nonreversible situations because they lead to incoherent interpretations. *The pony is being ridden by the girl* is interpreted as actor (pony)-action (ride)-object (girl). This interpretation is rejected, and the full syntactic analysis is applied. The performance during the previous stage shows that the child is aware of semantic constraints. The adoption of a noun-verb-noun strategy thus explains why comprehension of nonreversible passives improves during this stage while comprehension of reversible passives deteriorates.

The Rate of Semantic Development

The small body of evidence available on semantic development — Ervin and Foster's study of evaluative and potency terms, McNeill's experiment with fully grammatical, anomalous, and scrambled strings, and the Slobin and Bever verification studies — indicates that this development continues at least as late as age eight. Additional evidence for this conclusion comes from research on word associations. Associations are often classified into two categories. If the response is in the same grammatical class as the stimulus, for example, *hot-cold*, it is called **paradigmatic;** if it is in a different grammatical class from that of the stimulus, for example, *hot-bath*, it is called **syntagmatic.** Young children respond mostly with syntagmatic responses, while older children respond mostly with paradigmatic responses (Brown & Berko, 1960; Ervin, 1961). The shift occurs roughly in the six to eight year old period.

Until recently, this slow rate of development appeared to be in striking contrast to syntactic development, which was taken to be complete by age four or five. The work of Carol Chomsky (1969) discussed in Chapter 4 has shown that syntactic development is by no means complete, so the contrast between syntactic and semantic development is not as striking as at first appeared. It is difficult, if not impossible, to compare the rates of the two processes of development; but it is hard to resist the conclusion that semantic development proceeds at a much slower pace than syntactic development.

Until we have a better understanding of semantic development, we cannot offer explanations of this lag with any confidence. In Reading 6.2, McNeill considers several factors that may be relevant, including complexity, abstractness, dependence on cognitive maturity, and the uselessness of explicit definitions.

Summary

Mastery of the semantic system of a language includes a wide variety of achievements: addition of words to the vocabulary, development of the meaning of each word (which is basically a problem in concept formation), establishment of the network of relationships among word meanings, and mastery of the complex and poorly understood process by which word meanings are combined to form sentence meanings. The small amount of evidence currently available indicates that each of these achievements requires a considerable period for development. Young children's vocabularies are small (although larger than was once suspected), their meanings for words are not identical with those of adults, there is little evidence for the existence of relationships among word meanings, and combinations which would be rejected as anomalous by adults appear to be accepted. In addition, mastery of the meaning of many words, such as "left" and "right," requires an advanced level of cognitive maturity.

Although an exact comparison is impossible, it is difficult to resist the conclusion that semantic development is in many cases slower than syntactic development. Why this is the case is a mystery and will probably remain so until better methods are developed for assessing semantic development.

6.1 Is the Child's Thinking Concrete or Abstract?*

It is a commonplace saying that the mind of a child is relatively "concrete" and the mind of an adult "abstract." The words "concrete" and "abstract" are sometimes used in the sense of subordinate

*Reprinted from *Psychological Review*, 1958, **65**, 18–21, How shall a thing be called? R. Brown, by permission of the American Psychological Association.

and superordinate. In this sense a relatively concrete mind would operate with subordinate categories and an abstract mind with superordinate categories. It is recorded in many studies of vocabulary acquisition that children ordinarily use the words milk and water before the word liquid; the words apple and orange before fruit; table and chair before furniture; mamma and daddy before parent or person, and so on. Very high-level superordinate terms like article, action, quality, and relation, though they are common in adult speech, are very seldom heard from preschool children . . .

There are two extreme opinions about the direction of cognitive development. There are those who suppose that we begin by discriminating to the limits of our sensory acuity, seizing each thing in its uniqueness, noting every hair and flea of the particular dog. Cognitive development involves neglect of detail, abstracting from particulars so as to group similars into categories. By this view abstraction is a mature rather than a primitive process. The contrary opinion is that the primitive stage in cognition is one of a comparative lack of differentiation. Probably certain distinctions are inescapable; the difference between a loud noise and near silence, between a bright contour and a dark ground, and so on. These inevitable discriminations divide the perceived world into a small number of very large (abstract) categories. Cognitive development is increasing differentiation. The more distinctions we make, the more categories we have and the smaller (more concrete) these are. I think the latter view is favored in psychology today. While there is good empirical and theoretical support for the view that development is differentiation, there is enbarrassment for it in the fact that much vocabulary growth is from the concrete to the abstract. This embarrassment can be eliminated . . .

It seems likely that things are first named so as to categorize them in a maximally useful way. For most purposes Referent A is a spoon rather than a piece of silverware, and Referent B is a dime rather than a metal object. The same referent may have its most useful categorization on one level (Prince) for one group (the family) and on another level (dog) for another group (strangers). The categorization that is most useful for very young children (money) may change as they grow older (dime and nickel).

With some hierarchies of vocabulary the more concrete terms are learned before the abstract; probably the most abstract terms are never learned first, but it often happens that a hierarchy develops in both directions from a middle level of abstraction. Psychologists who believe that mental development is from the abstract to the concrete, from a lack of differentiation to increased differentiation, have been embarrased by the fact that vocabulary often builds in the opposite direction. This fact need not trouble them, since the sequence in which words are acquired is not determined by the cognitive preferences of children so much as by the naming practices of adults . . .

6.2 Why is Semantic Development So Slow?*

There must be numerous reasons [why semantic development is slow], and we can barely guess at them. Nevertheless, a few possibilities come to mind. One certainly is the complexity of the information that is encoded in a dictionary. Another is that developments in a child's lexicon, far more than developments in syntax, depend on achieving a certain level of intellectual maturity. A child capable of saying of 20 wooden beads, 15 white and 5 green, that white beads outnumber wooden beads is also likely to say Lassie's not an animal, she's a dog. Presumably it is with reference to semantic development that Piaget comments, ". . . (intellectual) operations direct language acquisitions rather than vice versa."

A third reason for the slow course of semantic development must have to do with the abstractness of semantic features. There is *nothing* in the superficial form of sentences capable even of hinting at underlying semantic regularities. Unlike syntactic abstractions, which are systematically related to surface structure by means of transformations, the semantic relations between surface and deep structure are unsystematic. No general relation holds between the phonemic form of *school* or *uncle* or *space ship* and the meaning of these words. It is one measure, perhaps, of how little insight we have into the acquisition of word meaning that it should thus seem impossible.

*From McNeill, D. The development of language. In P. H. Mussen (Ed.), *Carmichael's manual of child psychology*. Vol. 1. (3rd. ed.) New York: Wiley, 1970. Pp. 1123–1124. Reprinted with permission.

Occasionally, one hears the hypothesis that children acquire semantic knowledge from explicit definition. A parent may say *the zebra is an animal,* from which a child may acquire the semantic feature (animal). Perhaps the slow advance of semantic development is a result of a dependence on definitions; unlike syntax, adults may have to provide explicit instruction in semantics.

This argument is fallacious and is so for a simple reason. The sentence *the zebra is an animal* may indeed serve to introduce the marker (animal) into a new point in a child's dictionary, but it cannot affect his basic semantic competence. Explicit definitions may work to expand vocabulary, but they are irrelevant to the problem . . . [which is] the addition of semantic features to a dictionary. In order for the sentence *the zebra is an animal* to influence the dictionary entry for *zebra,* the feature (animal) must already be in the dictionary entry for the word *animal.* If it were not, the sentence *the zebra is an animal* would be without effect on a child's dictionary. But if *animal* contains the feature (animal), then obviously (animal) is already acquired, and the defining sentence merely locates it in a new entry. Explicit definitions are not the vehicle for enlargement of a child's stock of semantic features.

Not all semantic development is slow. The emergence of various semantic distinctions in negation [for example] . . . They apparently are fully developed by children of two and a half years. Greenfield has made a similar analysis of the infant term *dada,* tracing the development of its meaning in the speech of her eleven-month-old daughter. The relevant semantic distinctions (for example, male versus female; caretaker versus noncaretaker) had all appeared by the first birthday!

It is clear that only some aspects of semantic organization develop slowly. Negation and the idea of a parent emerge very early. So must many other semantic distinctions. Yet five year olds fail to distinguish anomalous from fully grammatical sentences in McNeill's experiment [1970a] and they describe a picture of a girl on a pony as *the poney rides the girl* in Turner and Rommetveit's experiment [1967]. It is a fair measure of our understanding of semantics that we cannot say how the last two examples differ from the first two . . .

SELECTED REFERENCES

Alston, W. P. *Philosophy of language.* Englewood Cliffs, N.J.: Prentice-Hall, 1964.

Bar-Adon, A., & Leopold, W. F. (Eds.) *Child language: A book of readings.* Englewood Cliffs, N.J.: Prentice-Hall, 1971.

Bever, T. G. The cognitive basis for linguistic structures. In J. R. Hayes (Ed.), *Cognition and the development of language.* New York: Wiley, 1970. Pp. 279–362.

Bloom, L. *Language development: Form and function in emerging grammars.* Cambridge, Mass.: M.I.T. Press, 1970. (a)

Bloom, L. Semantic features in language acquisition. Paper presented at the Conference on Research in the Language of the Mentally Retarded, University of Kansas, February, 1970. (b)

Bloomfield, L. *Language.* New York: Holt, Rinehart and Winston, 1933.

Bolinger, D. The atomization of meaning. *Language*, 1965, **41**, 555–573.

Bolinger, D. *Aspects of language.* New York: Harcourt Brace Jovanovich, 1968.

Brown, R. How shall a thing be called? *Psychological Review*, 1958, **65**, 14–21.

Brown, R., & Berko, J. Word association and the acquisition of syntax. *Child Development*, 1960, **31**, 1–14.

Chomsky, C. S. *The acquisition of syntax in children from 5 to 10.* Cambridge, Mass.: M.I.T. Press, 1969.

Ervin, S. Changes with age in the verbal determinants of word association. *American Journal of Psychology*, 1961, **74**, 361–372.

Ervin, S. M., & Foster, G. The development of meaning in children's descriptive terms. *Journal of Abnormal and Social Psychology*, 1960, **61**, 271–275.

Ginsburg, H., & Opper, S. *Piaget's theory of intellectual development: An introduction.* Englewood Cliffs, N.J.: Prentice-Hall, 1969.

Jakobson, R. Why "mama" and "papa"? In *Selected Writings of Roman Jakobson.* The Hague: Mouton, 1962. Pp. 538–545.

Katz, J. J., & Fodor, J. A. The structure of a semantic theory. *Language*, 1963, **39**, 170–210.

Leopold, W. F. Semantic learning in infant language. *Word*, 1948, **4**, 173–180.

McCarthy, D. Language development in children. In L. Carmichael (Ed.), *Manual of child psychology.* New York: Wiley, 1954. Pp. 452–630.

McNeill, D. The development of language. In P. H. Mussen (Ed.), *Carmichael's manual of child psychology.* Vol. 1. (3rd. ed.) New York: Wiley, 1970. Pp. 1061–1161. (a)

McNeill, D. *The acquisition of language: The study of developmental psycholinguistics.* New York: Harper & Row, 1970. (b)

Miller, G. A., & Isard, S. Some perceptual consequences of linguistic rules. *Journal of Verbal Learning and Verbal Behavior*, 1963, **2**, 227–228.

Mowrer, O. H. The psychologist looks at language. *American Journal of Psychology*, 1954, **9**, 660–694.

Murdock, G. P. Cross-language parallels in parental kin terms. *Anthropological Linguistics*, 1959, **1**, 1–5.

Osgood, C. E., Suci, G. J., & Tannenbaum, P. H. *The measurement of meaning.* Urbana: University of Illinois Press, 1957.

Piaget, J. *Play, dreams, and imitation in childhood.* Translated by C. Gattegno & F. M. Hodgson. New York: Norton, 1951.

Slobin, D. I. The acquisition of Russian as a native language. In F. Smith & G. A. Miller (Eds.), *The genesis of language*. Cambridge, Mass.: M.I.T. Press, 1966. Pp. 129–148. (a)

Slobin, D. I. Grammatical transformations and sentence comprehension in childhood and adulthood. *Journal of Verbal Learning and Verbal Behavior*, 1966, **5,** 219–277. (b)

Slobin, D. I. Soviet psycholinguistics. In N. O'Connor (Ed.), *Present-day Soviet psychology*. Oxford: Pergamon Press, 1966. (c)

Smith, M. E. An investigation of the development of the sentence and the extent of vocabulary in young children. *University of Iowa Studies in Child Welfare*, 1926, **3,** No. 5.

Turner, E. A. Developmental studies of sentence voice and reversibility. Unpublished doctoral dissertation, Cornell University, 1966.

Turner, E. A., & Rommetveit, R. The acquisition of sentence voice and reversibility. *Child Development*, 1967, **38,** 649–660.

di Vesta, F. J. A developmental study of the semantic structure of children. *Journal of Verbal Learning and Verbal Behavior*, 1966, **5,** 249-259.

FURTHER READING

Bever, T. G. The cognitive basis for linguistic structures. In J. R. Hayes (Ed.), *Cognition and the development of language*. New York: Wiley, 1970. Pp. 279–372.

Bolinger, D. *Aspects of language*. New York: Harcourt Brace Jovanovich, 1968. Ch 12.

Huttenlocher, J., & Strauss, S. Comprehension and a statement's relation to the situation it describes. *Journal of Verbal Learning and Verbal Behavior*, 1968, **7,** 300–304.

Luria, A. R. The directive function of speech in development and dissolution. *Word*, 1959, **15,** 341–352.

McNeill, D. *The acquisition of language: The study of developmental psycholinguistics*. New York: Harper & Row, 1970.

7

Phonology and Reading

Although **phonology** is in many ways the most concrete aspect of language, its development is poorly understood. Linguists have developed a very comprehensive theory of adult phonology and one very sweeping theory of phonological development as well. But the data needed to test such theories is not available. This chapter, therefore, is concerned more with phonological theory than with data from children.

All the organs that are used in speech have other functions: the lips and tongue are used in eating and swallowing, the windpipe (or trachea) is the major pathway for air from the mouth and nose to the lungs, and so on. Because of this, and because these organs are possessed by other animals, especially higher primates such as the orangutang and chimpanzee, it is often said that speech is simply an **overlaid** function, that is, a new use for an old structure. However, there are small but important differences in the structure and function of these organs in man (Lenneberg, 1967). For example, the muscles in the lips and tongue of human beings are more highly developed and more agile than the corresponding muscles in other animals. This added flexibility is of no use whatever in eating and swallowing but is extremely useful in producing rapid, articulate speech. The respiratory cycle is quite different during speech than during normal breathing. The air intake is much larger, but much more rapid, while the outflow (which is primarily through the mouth, rather than through the nose), is controlled by a different interplay of muscles.

In normal breathing, air flows through the windpipe, mouth, and nose in an unrestricted manner. Speech is produced by placing some kind of restriction in the way. All languages have two major types of sounds. In the first type, the air flows freely through the mouth cavity once it passes over the vocal cords (see Figure 7-1). These sounds are called **vowels.** In the second

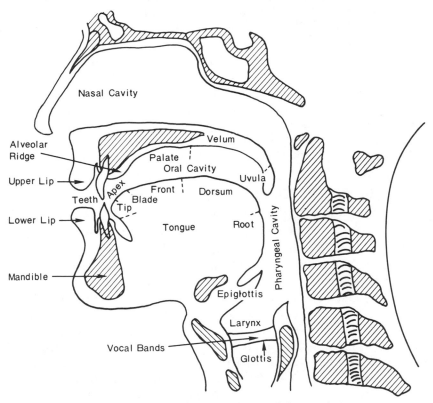

FIGURE 7.1 Cross-section of head showing principle speech organs.

SOURCE: *The Structure of American English*, W. Nelson Francis, Copyright (©) 1958, The Ronald Press Company, New York.

type of sounds, there is further obstruction in the way of the flow of air. These sounds are called **consonants.**

Vowels

In the case of the *vowels*, the basic sound is produced by vocal cords. These are two elastic membranes near the top of the windpipe. They function somewhat like the double reed of the oboe or the lips in playing the trumpet. When they are held at just the right tension, not too loose and not too taut, air passing through them will set up a regular vibration, called **voicing.** This voicing is actually made up of many different sounds, each having a distinct frequency. The lowest of these is called the **fundamental frequency.** Despite the fact that the air then passes unimpeded through the mouth, the sound may be modified greatly. This is similar to playing the various brass instruments — the lips are producing basically the same sound at the mouthpiece of the trumpet, French horn, or trombone, but the shape of the instrument determines the nature of the final note. Each particular way we can form our mouth cavity, which depends primarily on the position of the tongue and lips, will emphasize some of the sounds emerging from the vocal cords. So by moving the tongue and lips we can vary the frequencies which are emphasized, and, thus, the quality of the produced vowel.

ENGLISH VOWELS

For English vowels, it is the position of the tongue that is most important. The tongue is extremely flexible, and it may be moved in an up-and-down direction and also in a front-to-back direction. The difference between the sounds [i] and [u], as in *beat* and *cooed*, is that in [i] the tongue is raised to a position near the ridge just behind the upper teeth, that is, the **alveolar** ridge. This is quite far forward for a vowel. For [u] the back of the tongue is raised to a position near the rear of the roof of the mouth, the **palate.** This is quite far back. The [i] sound is said to be a **front vowel;** [u], a **back vowel.** To produce [a], as in *cod*, the tongue is almost as far back as it is to produce [u], so [a] is also a back vowel.

These three vowels are the extremes of the English vowels; all the other vowels fall in between them along the front-back and low-high dimensions. There are twelve major vowels in English (see Table 7-1).

TABLE 7-1   *The Vowels of English*[a]

	Front		Back
high	[i] beat		[u] cooed
	[I] bit		[U] could
	[e] bait	[ə] roses	[o] code
	[ɛ] bet		[ɔ] cawed
low	[æ] bat	[ʌ] but	[a] cod

[a]Regional differences in American English are most commonly differences in vowel pronunciation. In some areas, for example, *cot* and *caught* are pronounced alike, combining the vowels symbolized by [a] and [ɔ] into a single sound type.

The position of the tongue determines the basic quality of a vowel. Four techniques are available for modification of the basic quality: **nasalization, length, tone,** and **rounding;** but only one plays a significant role in English. If you pronounce [i] and then [u], you will notice that for [i] the corners of the mouth are drawn back, while in [u] the lips are rounded and slightly protruded. The [u] sound is a **rounded** vowel, while [i] is an **unrounded.** Four of the English vowels are rounded: [u], [U], [o], and [ɔ]. Those are all of the back vowels, with the exception of [a]. It is neither logically nor physically necessary for just the back, but not the front, vowels to be rounded, although this is the case in English. For example, it is easy to produce a sound which is like [i] but rounded (try it); in fact this is a sound used in French. French has a series of rounded front vowels as well as a series of unrounded ones, and this difference is enough to change meanings of words. *Fee,* "fairy," and *feu,* "fire" differ only in that the second is pronounced with lips rounded.

Consonants

The second major type of sound is the *consonant.* The chief characteristic distinguishing consonants from vowels is that the flow of air is either closed off completely or almost completely. When the flow is closed off, as in [t], it is called a **stop.** When the flow is partially blocked, it becomes very turbulent and produces a hissing sound, as in [s], which is called a **fricative.** The stops are produced by blocking the flow of air and letting pressure build up, then releasing it in a sudden burst. The fricatives are produced by moving the tongue or lips to a position very close to that of a stop, but not quite. Notice that [t] and [s] are produced with the tongue in very similar positions.

ENGLISH CONSONANTS

The closure, whether it is complete or partial, may occur at any position in the mouth. There are five important positions for English stops and fricatives.

1. *With the lips.* The [p] and [b] in *paste* and *baste* are stops produced with the two lips. They are called **bilabial stops.** English does not have any *bilabial fricatives.* It does, however, have fricatives produced with the lower lip against the upper teeth; the [f] and [v] in *file* and *vile.* Because they are produced with the lips and the teeth, they are called **labiodentals.**

2. *With the tip of the tongue on the upper teeth.* English does not have any stops in this position, but it has two fricatives, the initial sounds in *thin* and *that.* These are quite distinct sounds, even though they are spelled in the same way. To distinguish them, the symbols [θ] (as in *thin*) and [ð] (as in *that*) are used. These sounds are called **linguadentals.**

3. *With the tip of the tongue on the ridge just behind the upper front teeth.* Because this ridge is known as the alveolar ridge, sounds produced in this way are called **alveolars.** The [t] and [d] of *tear* and *dare* are **alveolar stops;** while the [s] and [z] of *seal* and *zeal* are **alveolar fricatives.**

4. *With the entire front of the tongue on the palate.* English does not have any stops of this type, but there are two fricatives, the final sounds of *hash* and *rouge.* These are written phonetically as [š] and [ž]. They are called **palatal** fricatives.

5. *With the back of the tongue against the velum,* that is, the back of the palate. English has two such **velar stops,** the [k] and [g] of *came* and *game.* Although English does not have any **velar fricatives,** many languages do, such as German, in *Bach.*

In addition to the stops and fricatives, there is a third, "combination" type consonant. The first sounds of [ch]eap and [j]eep are examples of these sounds. They are produced by first blocking the airflow as for a stop and then releasing it; not quickly as for *stop,* but slowly, so that the tongue is briefly in a position for a fricative. The initial sound of *cheap,* for example, is produced by starting with a [t] and then releasing it slowly so that an [š] is pronounced. These sounds are called **affricates,** and are written [č] and [ǰ], respectively.

When some of the consonants we have discussed are voiced, the vocal cords are vibrating. This can be detected by holding a finger on the Adam's apple. Those consonants that are pronounced with vocal cord vibration are called **voiced consonants;** those which are not, **voiceless consonants.** In general, voiceless and voiced consonants occur in pairs, identical save that one is voiceless, one voiced: [p] and [b], [s] and [z], [č] and [ǰ], [θ] and [ð], and so on. Vowels are almost always voiced. The only exception is the initial sound of [h]eat. This sound is produced by starting the vowel without voicing, and then adding the voicing. Sometimes this is called a **voiceless vowel,** sometimes a **glottal** (meaning vocal cords) **fricative.** We will call it a glottal fricative because there is some friction heard before the vowel starts.

There are three **nasalized consonants** in English: the [m] in *me*, the [n] in *no*, and the final sound of walking, [ŋ], which is a single consonant despite the fact that it is conventionally written as two. Nasalized consonants are produced by letting air through the nasal cavity when pronouncing the sound.

Table 7-2 summarizes the consonants on the basis of where the constriction is produced, whether it is complete or partial, whether the sound is voiced or voiceless, whether it is a nasal.

TABLE 7-2 *Some Consonants of English*

	Bilabial	Labiodental	Dental	Alveolar	Palatal	Velar	Glottal
Stops							
Voiceless	p			t		k	
Voiced	b			d		g	
Fricatives							
Voiceless		f	θ	s	š		h
Voiced		v	ð	z	č		
Affricates							
Voiceless				č			
Voiced				ǰ			
Nasal							
(All voiced)	m			n		ŋ	

Liquids and Glides

Two additional groups of sounds fall in between vowels and consonants. Sometimes they are classified with vowels, sometimes with consonants. They are the **liquids** and the **glides.**

English has two liquids, r and l. These are very common in the languages of the world, but their pronunciation varies greatly from language to language. The English [l], as in *lazy*, is pronounced with the tip of the tongue on the alveolar ridge, but with air passing over the sides of the tongue. Since there is neither complete closure nor any turbulence, [l] resembles a vowel. In [r] as in [l], it is the special shape of the tongue that gives them their character. The tongue is raised toward the roof of the mouth, forming something like a cup shape. A related kind of [r] is heard in very rapid pronunciations of [t] and [d] in *butter* and *ladder*. Here the tongue flaps against the alveolar ridge. Some languages have trilled r's, where the tongue flaps repeatedly against the roof of the mouth. The Spanish word *pero*, "but", has a single flap, while *perro*, "dog" has a trilled r. Some languages form a trill, not with the tongue, but with the *uvula*, which is the very back part of the velum.

The glides in English, [w] and [y], are characterized by movement of the articulatory organs. The glide [w], as in *wow*, is pronounced by starting in the position for [u], with the lips rounded and the tongue high and back. But instead of producing [u], the vocal organs glide into the next sound of the word, here the vowel [a]. After the [a] has been produced, the vocal organs glide back toward the position for [u]. The production of [y] is very similar, but it is the position for [i] from which, or to which, the vocal organs glide.

The Phoneme

We have just seen that there are twenty consonants, two liquids, two glides, and twelve vowels in English, for a total of thirty-six. Lets look at one of them closely, say, [k]. This consonant occurs in the English words *key*, *ski* and *caw*. How do we decide that [k] is a consonant of English? There are really two steps. First, we see that there are instances where the presence of a [k], and not some other consonant, changes the meaning of a word (or more accurately, morpheme). The pair of words *key* and *tea* differ in just this way, and they demonstrate that [k] and [t] are different sounds. When we can find pairs of words that *differ in just one sound* and also *differ in meaning*, we can conclude that the two sounds differ significantly. Such pairs of words are called **minimal pairs.** But there is another step necessary to identify the sounds of a language. The consonant [k] occurs in *ski* and *caw*, as well as in *key*; how do we know that these three *k*'s are the same sound? The first answer that comes to mind is simply that they "sound alike." But this is not quite right; the different *k*'s *are* different. A speaker of Arabic might object that the sounds in *key* and *caw* are quite distinct. In fact, [k] in *key* is pronounced with the tongue considerably further forward than it is in the pronunciation of the [k] in *caw*. In Arabic, there are minimal pairs that differ only in that one has the [k] of *key* and the other had the [k] of *caw*. Similarly, a speaker of Hindi might protest that *key* contains a different sound than *ski*, and there is an important difference. If you hold your hand in front of your mouth when you pronounce the two words, you will feel a puff of air when you release the [k] of *key*, but either no puff or a much weaker one when you pronounce the [k] of *ski*. This puff of air, when a stop is released, is called **aspiration.** This is often symbolized by a small raised *h*, as in [k^h]. In Hindi, there are minimal pairs in which the only difference is aspiration.

"That's all very well," you might answer, "but Arabic and Hindi are not English. And in English, the [k]'s in *key*, *ski*, and *caw* are the same." And that's really the right answer. Each language has its own way of deciding which sounds are the same and which are different. A class of sounds that are considered equivalent by a language is called a **phoneme** of that language. We have just seen that the three different sounds in *key*, *ski*, and *caw* are each instances of the same phoneme of English. There are no pairs of words with different meanings that differ only in that one has the [k] of *key*, and one has the [k] of *ski*.

There are an unlimited number of possible speech sounds. For example, there are an unlimited number of positions for the tongue along the roof of the mouth in producing the stops. But there are only two possible stops in English — [t] and [k] (or their voiced counterparts [d] and [g]). What we do is ignore small variations in position and only notice if the tongue is basically near the alveolar ridge or further back. In the production of vowels, there are an infinite number of positions for the tongue, both along the high-low dimension and along the front-back dimension. English distinguishes five levels along the low-high dimension, and three levels along the front-back dimension. But this is neither logically nor physiologically necessary; it is just the way English does it.

PRONUNCIATION AND MEANING

What is the function of pronunciation? As we have seen, language is basically arbitrary. There is no logical connection between the pronunciation of a word and its meaning. It doesn't really matter what the word that means "a small device for opening locks" *sounds like*. But it *does* matter that the *pronunciation* of this word *not* be the same as the pronunciation of the word that means "a beverage made from the leaves of a white-flowered plant grown in the Far East." That is, *key* is different from *tea* and that is all that matters. If the function of the sounds of a language is to distinguish different morphemes, the language only needs a small number of different sounds, a small number of phonemes. Out of the unlimited number of possible sounds a human being can make, English distinguishes only thirty-six different classes, or phonemes. Some other languages have more, some have less. And they make their distinctions in different ways. For example, in English we pay attention to whether or not a stop is voiced. We distinguish *baste* from *paste* on the basis of whether or not the first consonant, which is a bilabial stop, is voiced or not. The same distinction is shown in *tear* and *dare*, and in *came* and *game*. On the other hand, we ignore aspiration. There are no minimal pairs in English of words which differ only in aspiration: *cʰake* and *cake* have the same meaning. There are languages which do not exploit the voiced-voiceless distinction. These languages do not have any minimal pairs similar to *paste-baste*. Either all the stops are voiceless, or the voiced and voiceless versions are used interchangably (this amounts to *paste* and *baste* meaning the same thing). But some of these languages distinguish sounds on the basis of aspiration.

To summarize, *a phoneme is a class of sounds treated as equivalent by a language.* Two sounds fall in different phonemes if there exists a minimal pair of morphemes which differ only in having the two sounds. They fall in the same phoneme if they do not contrast in this way. There are two basic ways in which sounds are combined into a phoneme. In the first, there are several sounds, but each is used in a specific context. We have seen that there are at least three [k]'s: the unaspirated [k] in *ski*, the front aspirated [k] in *key*, and the back aspirated [k] in *caw*. These distinct "versions" of [k] are the **allophones** of [k]. The first is always used after [s], the second before front vowels, and the third before back vowels. Because each allophone has its specific contexts, there can be no minimal pairs of words which differ only in having different versions of [k]. This type of combination of sounds into phonemes is called **complementary distribution.** Another example is the pronunciation of [n]. In most cases it is pronounced with the tongue on the alveolar ridge, but when it occurs before a [θ], as in *tenth*, the tongue moves forward to a position touching, or nearly touching, the front teeth.

The other process of combination is **free variation.** As the term indicates, any of several possible versions of the phoneme can occur, with no change in meaning. This is actually just another way of saying that no two sounds are ever exactly identical. If you pronounce the word *key* ten times, there will be ten different positions of the tongue on the palate in pronouncing the [k] and ten different tongue positions for the vowel. These variations are simply ignored; the ten versions are in free variation. Both processes of combination can, and usually do, occur for a single phoneme.

Learning a language consists in part of having your perception of speech sounds changed. Speakers of English can hear many very subtle differences between sounds — those that correspond to distinctions between phonemes — and at the same time cannot hear many other distinctions of the same physical magnitude — the distinctions between sounds within a single phonemic category. It is not clear yet whether this is due to sharpened perceptual ability at the boundaries of phonemes or diminished ability within categories, or some combination of the two.

PHONETIC AND PHONEMIC TRANSCRIPTION

It is important to distinguish between a **phonetic transcription** and a **phonemic transcription.** A *phonetic* transcription is simply as accurate a recording as possible of the exact pronunciation of an utterance. It is written with square brackets. For example, a phonetic transcription of *coat* might be [kʰoʷt] and a phonetic transcription of *skit* would be [skɪtʰ]. The aspiration of [k] is indicated by the raised ʰ, and the rounding of [o] in *coat* is indicated by the raised ʷ. A *phonemic* transcription merely indicates the phoneme to which each sound belongs, and is written with diagonal slashes. Phonemic transcriptions for *coat* and *skit* are /kot/ and [skɪt/. These phonemic transcriptions also indicate how the words are to be pronounced, *if the general rules of English* *are known:* all initial voiceless stops are aspirated, and all back vowels except /a/ are rounded.

Phonetic and phonemic transcriptions serve very different purposes. A phonetic transcription can be read by a person totally ignorant of the language, assuming he knows the principles of the transcription. Even if he does not know English, he will pronounce [tʰɛd] with approximately the same pronunciation with which a native speaker would pronounce *Ted.* The phonemic transcription /tɛd/ however, can only be read by someone familiar with the phonology of the language transcribed. Information about the pronunciation that follows general rules, such as the fact that initial stops are aspirated, is removed from a phonemic transcription. Only one symbol is needed for each phoneme. This distinction is important for the question of alphabets for reading, which will be considered later in this chapter.

Producing, Perceiving, and Acoustics

The sounds of English have been described and classified in terms of their manner of production. A hearer does not have any information about how the speaker produces, or **articulates,** sounds. He receives only an **acoustic signal** through the air. The relation between the articulation of sounds and the acoustic signal, and the relation between the acoustic signal and the sound perceived by the hearer, are complex and not well understood. They comprise the subjects of the sciences of acoustic phonetics and speech perception, respectively.

The acoustic signal is a continuous stream; it is not divided into distinct segments corresponding to phonemes or into words, even though we think we hear a sentence as a string of words. Listening to a speaker of a foreign language is often unsettling, just because it appears to be a rapid, continuous stream. In fact, segmentation into phonemes is, in principle, impossible; within a syllable, the acoustic signal is at every moment a function of all the phonemes of the syllable. These and other complexities of the phoneme-acoustic signal relationship have lead many psychologists to consider the hypothesis of *analysis by synthesis:* speech is analyzed by generating (synthesizing) internally a signal which matches the incoming signal (Neisser, 1967; Liberman, 1970).

Prelinguistic Development

Sound types, or **phones,** such as the initial sound of *key*, [k], and phonemes, such as the English /k/ phoneme, are very different kinds of entities. The study of the development of sound types is a very old tradition in research on child language. But it is the second, the development of the phonemic system, which is important for the understanding of language development. An explicit theory of phonemic development has existed for thirty years; but the data for evaluating it are not available. The difficulty is similar to that which afflicted studies of syntactic development until recently: investigators simply collected and counted sounds, categorizing them in terms of the sounds of the adult language, rather than determining how they were used by the child. It is even possible to find claims that, for example, a nine-month-old infant has developed eight phonemes. This is logically impossible, for an infant who does not yet produce meaningful speech simply cannot have phonemes, which are defined in terms of contrasts between meaningful items, as between *tea* and *key*.

BABBLING

Much attention has been given to the prelinguistic verbal behavior of the child. Infants during the second half of the first year produce a wide variety of speechlike sounds. This is usually called the **babbling stage.** Among the sounds babbled are many that are not present in the language of adults around them. Children learning English, and who hear only English, may produce sounds resembling German umlaut sounds, French uvular *r*'s, clicks similar to those found in certain African languages, and sounds that are not utilized in any known human language. When the child has successfully mastered his language, he no longer makes these sounds. This observation is the basis of the selective reinforcement theory of development. When the infant produces a sound that does occur in the language he is learning, he is reinforced (either by an external agent or by secondary reinforcement due to similarity to sounds the infant has heard); when he produces a sound that does not occur in the language, he is not reinforced. Eventually the latter category simply disappears.

In the 1940's O. C. Irwin conducted several large-scale studies of the development of speech during the first few years of life (Irwin, 1947a, 1947b, 1947c, 1948; Irwin & Chen, 1946). These were of the first type discussed above, that is, collections of sounds. Some of Irwin's results cast doubt on the selective reinforcement explanation. During the first year of life the direction of development for consonant-type sounds is from the back of the mouth to the front. Young infants vocalize sounds similar to [k], [g], and [x] (the velar fricative in *Bach*). Sounds such as [t] and [p], which are articulated farther forward, appear later in the first year. For vowel-type sounds, the direction of development is the reverse. First to appear are front sounds similar to [i] and [e]; [o] and [a] appear later.[1]

During the second year, the direction of development is exactly the opposite. When children begin to produce meaningful words, they usually consist of a front consonant, such as /p/ or /m/, and a back vowel, usually /a/. There is much anecdotal and other evidence that this is the case in a wide variety of languages. The linguistic system begins with a very small number of phonemes; many of the sounds which were babbled will not be added to the language for many months. The back consonants and front vowels, which were among the first to be babbled, are among the last to be added to the system. Indirect evidence for the generality of this development comes from studies of baby talk. Charles Ferguson (1964) surveyed baby talk in six languages, and he found a widespread tendency for back consonants to be replaced by more forward ones, especially for velar consonants, such as [k], to be replaced by dental ones, such as [t]. An example of this in English would be the use of *tate* for *cake*. This is common in the speech of adults addressed to children in Syrian, Malathi, Comanche, Spanish, and English. Presumably the conventions for baby talk are similar in these languages because the child languages in each case are similar. The two exceptions to this trend were languages in which velar consonants are very important — Gilyak and Arabic.

These opposite trends in development in the babbling and speech periods suggest that the fact that a sound is babbled is not very relevant for language. Additional evidence for this claim is the fact that sounds which later present serious articulatory difficulties to children may have been babbled frequently (Berry, 1969). There appears to be a true discontinuity in development at the transition from babbling to speech. In fact, in some cases, the two may be separated by a brief period of silence — a remarkable phenomenon for a child.

[1]Other investigators have not always found the same pattern of development; see Muria, 1960.

The difference is probably one of voluntary, controlled action versus random, unintentional action. Or as Jesperson put it, the distinction between *plan* and *play:*

> It is strange that among an infant's sounds one can often detect sounds — for instance k, g, h, and uvular r — which the child will find difficulty in producing afterwards when they occur in real words . . . The explanation lies probably in the difference between doing a thing in play or without a plan — when it is immaterial which movement (sound) is made — and doing the same thing in fixed intention when this sound, and this sound only, is required . . . [1925, p. 106].

INTONATION

One aspect of language does appear in the prelinguistic period in essentially the adult form. This is the **intonation contour.** Philip Lieberman (1967) has argued convincingly that speech is organized in units corresponding to the expiratory airflow from the lung. The muscles of the larynx, chest, and abdomen are carefully coordinated to produce a unified pattern of expiration. The most common pattern has a fall in the **fundamental frequency** — the basic frequency of the vocal cords — at the end of a sentence. This is true of virtually all languages. The exceptions are certain predictable constructions, such as questions, in which the sentence ends with a rise in fundamental frequency. Lieberman has hypothesized that the purpose of the breath group — this basic intonation contour — is to segment the continuous flow of speech into sentences (and sometimes into clauses).

Although languages differ in the exact shape of the contour, the general pattern appears to be the same. The fundamental frequency of very young infant vocalization is of this form also. There is much anecdotal evidence about the presence of normal adult intonation contours (the normal contour and the question contour) during babbling. This is probably the reason one often has the feeling that a babbling infant is actually speaking fluently, but in a foreign language.

Although the productions of infants during this stage may have little relevance for later language development, there can be little question that much important listening is occurring. Wolff (1966) has found that infants can distinguish between the human voice and other sounds from the end of the first month. The voice is much more effective in stopping crying. Even more striking is the apparent ability of one-month-old infants to make at least some phonemic discriminations. Eimas, Siquiland, Jusczyk, and Vigorito (1971) allowed infants to suck on a pacifier connected to an electronic monitoring device that controlled a continuous recording of either /pa/ or /ba/. As long as the infant sucked, the volume was kept up. Eventually, the baby tired, and the sucking began to diminish. At this point, the other syllable (/ba/ or /pa/, respectively) was turned on. Very quickly the infants began to suck more strongly again to keep the new syllable audible. The syllables were electronically synthesized so as to be identical except for an extremely short 20 millisecond period in which the two sounds have different characteristics. It is difficult to say which is more remarkable: the infants' ability to discriminate the two syllables, or their interest in repeated listening to each new syllable as it appeared.

Other investigators have found an especial sensitivity of infants to intonation patterns (see Kaplan & Kaplan, 1971, for a comprehensive review of prelinguistic development). This is true both of intonation patterns of individual syllables (/ba/ pronounced with a rising versus falling intonation) and of sentences (*See the cat?* versus *See the cat*). Young children often appear to respond appropriately to the speech of others before producing any true language themselves, and this undoubtedly is largely based on intonation. Simply saying *No!* to an infant, and observing him cease his activity, is not proof of comprehension of the word itself; more likely it is a response to the intonation (and intensity) of the utterance.

Children quickly learn to mimic intonation and other pitch information in the speech they hear. Lieberman recorded the babbling and the crying of a ten-month-old boy and a thirteen-month-old girl when each was alone, when each was with the mother, and then with the father. Normally the fundamental frequency of adult women is higher than that of adult men, and the fundamental frequency of children is higher than that of adult women, for reasons of size. The fundamental frequency of the boy's babbling when alone averaged 430 Hz (cycles per second), but this lowered to 390 Hz when he was with his mother and 340 Hz when he was with his father. The girl was not recorded alone, but the fundamental frequency of her babbling was 390 Hz when she was with her mother and 290 Hz when she was with her father. The fundamental frequency of the children's crying did not vary with the situation.

Phonemic Development

The problems of studying the development of phonemes are at least as great as those of studying the development of syntax. Ordinarily, the phonemes of a language are determined by establishing minimal pairs — pairs of words which differ in just one sound. For example, *pin* and *bin* differ only in their initial consonant. This allows us to distinguish at least two consonants in English. *Din* establishes a third. And so on. This is all but impossible with children. Imagine asking an eighteen month old, "Are these the same, pin, and bin?" Instead, we can only record whatever the child says and try to guess which utterances have distinct meaning. The problems are multiplied by the fact that children are probably less consistent in the pronunciation and, in general, less precise than adults. Because it is necessary to catch the sounds "on the fly" and identify them, most of the relatively few studies of phonemic development which have been done have been studies by linguists of their own children (Burling, 1959, Leopold, 1953; Moskowitz, 1970; Velten, 1943). Typically, such studies result in a large number of interesting, but unique facts about the child. The problem is one of finding a general pattern. An additional source of information which is often used is the nature of the children's **substitutions:** those cases in which he uses one sound in place of the proper one for the particular word being produced. The production of [ta] for *car*, in which [t] is substituted for [k], is an example of this. If the observer has correctly guessed the intended word (which is not always easy), he can use this substitution as evidence that the two sounds, [k] and [t], are equivalent for the child; that is, they belong to the same phoneme.

The very first question about the development of phonemes must be: Is the sound system of a child's speech during development actually a structured, phonemic system? This is analogous to the question, Is the child's speech grammatically structured? If this question can be answered affirmatively (as the latter was, in Chapters 2 and 4), then we can consider how the systems develop.

The question can be answered affirmatively, with some caution given to the difficulties of studying phonemic development. Velten's daughter Joan, for example, near her second birthday had the following phonemes: /p/, /t/, /w/, /f/, /s/, /a/, /m/, /n/, and /u/ (1943). This does *not* mean that these were the only sounds Joan produced. She produced [b] as well as [p], for example. In fact, [b] occurred at the beginning and in the middle of words while [p] occurred in the final position. And [p] and [b] never contrasted, so they belonged to a single phoneme. Whether to call the phoneme /p/ or /b/ is arbitrary. And there was variation within the other phonemic categories as well. But these were the only contrasts. Words such as *black, pat, spot, block, bite,* and *pocket* were pronounced /pat/ (with an initial *b* phonetically). There was also a great deal of free variation in the /a/ phoneme, so these words might sound like [bæt/, [bayt], and [bat]. *New, knee, nail, no,* and *near* were all pronounced [nu].

Although a child's sound system can, as a whole, usually be described as a phonemic system, there are often exceptions. Although Joan eventually developed a /u/ phoneme, for a long period (seven months) she had only the /a/ vowel phoneme. During this period, the [u] sound did occur in a very few words, but almost as a rare, "foreign" sound. There was no consistent contrast between /a/ and /u/. Only after this extended period was a new phoneme established, which was used for the adult English phonemes /u/, /U/, /o/, /i/, and others.

This is not very different from a common kind of historical change in language. The voiced fricatives /v/ and /z/ worked their way into English from French in just this way. English has voiceless fricative phonemes such as /f/ and /s/, and in some contexts they were pronounced [v] and [z], respectively, but there were no consistent contrasts. After the Norman invasion, there was a massive infusion of French words into English, and these included many that contain voiceless fricatives, including the words *very, veal, zeal,* and *zest.* For a brief period these existed as "foreign words," with no effect on the fricatives of English words. Eventually the situation was resolved by the establishment of two new phonemes: /v/ and /z/. And now we have minimal pairs illustrating the contrasts: *file-vile,* and *seal-zeal.*

If a child can be considered to have a phonemic system at each point in development (albeit with qualifications and with less than total confidence in the determination of the exact phonemic system for each child), then we can ask how this system changes. The great Russian linguist Roman Jakobson has developed an explicit theory of the development of phonemes (Jakobson, 1968; summarized in Jakobson & Halle, 1956, ch. 4). Jakobson's theory of development is based on another theory of his — the theory of **distinctive features.** A modification of this theory is now widely accepted in linguistics. It is based on the insight that the stock of phonemes of a language is not merely a list but, rather, is organized by a system of contrasts, each **binary** in nature, that is, having two values. For example, the contrast between /p/ and /b/ is the same as the contrast between /t/ and /d/; and this is the same as the contrast between /s/ and /z/. It is the contrast between voiceless and voiced sounds; in the first member of each pair, the vocal cords do not vibrate, in the second, they do. Similarly, the difference between /t/ and /s/ is the same as the difference between /d/ and /z/, and so on. This is the contrast that distinguishes stops from phonemes that do not completely interrupt the flow of air. It is called the **continuant-stop contrast.** The nasal-oral contrast distinguishes /m/ from /b/, /t/ from /n/, and /η/ from /g/. A small number of contrasts, or distinctive features, identify all the phonemes of English. Figure 7.2 partially illustrates how the phonemes fit into a structure of distinctive features. It is customary to label the distinctive feature with the single term, and use "+" and "−" to indicate the two values of the feature. Voiced phonemes are "+voiced" and voiceless phonemes are "−voiced"; nasal phonemes are "+nasal" and oral phonemes are "−nasal," and so on. Notice that not all combinations occur. Jakobson claimed that in every language the phonemes could be efficiently described in this way − that is, that these contrasts are **universal** − and that the total number of distinctive features in the languages of the world was quite small − about fifteen. Each language draws some contrasts from this stock; English uses about a dozen

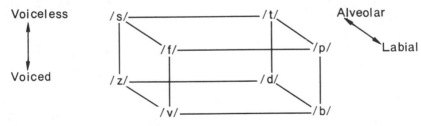

FIGURE 7.2   A portion of the distinctive feature structure of English consonant phonemes.

Jakobson's developmental theory is based on the claim that development consists of the acquisition of distinctive features, that is, **contrasts,** and not the acquisition of phonemes. This is more efficient, since the number of contrasts is less than the number of phonemes. In addition, he stated the order in which the contrasts would be acquired.

The development of a phonemic system, according to Jakobson, is the result of filling in the gap between the two sounds /p/ and /a/, which characteristically make up the first word. These sounds are as different as possible. /p/ is a front consonant, a stop, unvoiced, and represents a nearly total absence of energy. The /a/ sound is a back vowel, a continuant, voiced, and represents a maximum of energy. These are not yet phonemes. Phonemes distinguish meaning in pairs of words, but /p/ and /a/ always appear together. The fundamental utterance is /pa/; with reduplication (very common with young children), /papa/. To establish a system, the space between these two sounds must be differentiated, or **split.**

The first split occurs on the consonant side and, according to Jakobson's observations (here as always based almost entirely on anecdotal evidence), results in a distinction between a labial stop /p/ and a nasal labial /m/. Now there can be two distinct words: /mama/ and /papa/. Velten observed a different distinction emerge at this point in the language of his daughter; the labial-dental contrast led to the two phonemes /p/ and /t/.

Next, according to Jakobson, the consonants divided into labial and dental: /p/ and /m/ versus /t/ and /n/. At this stage, the vowel /a/ merely supports the consonants; it still has no phonemic status. However, it is crucial for it establishes the syllable. Jakobson believed that children always formed consonant-vowel or vowel-consonant syllables in their earliest speech, but this is not so. Chinese children have been observed to produce syllables which consist of vowels only (Weir, 1966). In Chinese, syllabification is measured by vowels alone, while in English and Russian syllables are usually determined by consonant-vowel pairs. And Russian- and English-speaking children produce consonant-vowel syllables. The nature of syllabification appears to be a very early acquisition. Soon the vowels are divided by a contrast. And so the process proceeds.

The second part of Jakobson's developmental theory is a specification of the order in which the contrasts are acquired. Some contrasts are universal; that is, they occur in all languages. For example, the continuant-stop contrast is universal. These contrasts are the first to be developed by the child. After this, development is described by the laws of **irreversible solidarity.** These describe assymmetries in the phonemic systems of the languages of the world. For example, no language has back consonants without having front consonants; however, some languages have front consonants without having back consonants. Back consonants presuppose front consonants, in other words. Therefore, front consonants should precede back consonants in development. And indeed, /p/ and /m/ appear before /k/ or /g/ in child speech. Furthermore, phonemes and contrasts which are rare among the languages of the world, such as the /ae/ phoneme of English, are among the last to be acquired. Such phonemes embody more subtle distinctions than do the more common phonemes. If the acquisition of phonemes is the result of the acquisition of contrasts, then those phonemes that embody such subtle distinctions are naturally acquired after phonemes that embody less subtle, less common distinctions.

It is frequency in the languages of the world, and not how frequent the phoneme is in the particular language the child hears, that is important, according to this theory. The /æ/ phoneme is fairly common in English; it occurs in such common words as *bat, glad, sad,* and *at.* The fact that it is late to be acquired by the child demonstrates that mere frequency of exposure is not the variable that governs acquisition. Instead, there is an underlying connection between acquisition by children and cross-linguistic generalizations. This insight, the foundation of Jakobson's theory, is what Keiler referred to when he wrote (in his preface to the translation of Jakobson's 1941 book):

> ... one finds for the first time, in the Kindersprache [child speech], a formal linking of the problems of linguistic universals and of language acquisition, i.e., the view that any explanation of the latter is to be found in the innate character of the former [Jakobson, 1968, p. 7].

On the basis of these considerations — universality of contrasts, the laws of irreversible solidarity, and frequency in the languages of the world — Jakobson established a universal ordering for the successive differentiation of distinctive features. This ordering is shown in Figure 7.3. No contrast can be acquired before every contrast on the branch leading to it has been acquired. Of course the child learns only the contrasts present in the language about him.

Jakobson's theory is remarkable for its range and its daring. In fact, we do not have nearly enough evidence to draw any firm conclusions. Jakobson's order is clearly too rigid. Velten's study was the first to be conducted under the influence of the theory and he found that the first three contrasts were not oral-nasal, labial-dental, continuant-stop as Jakobson claimed

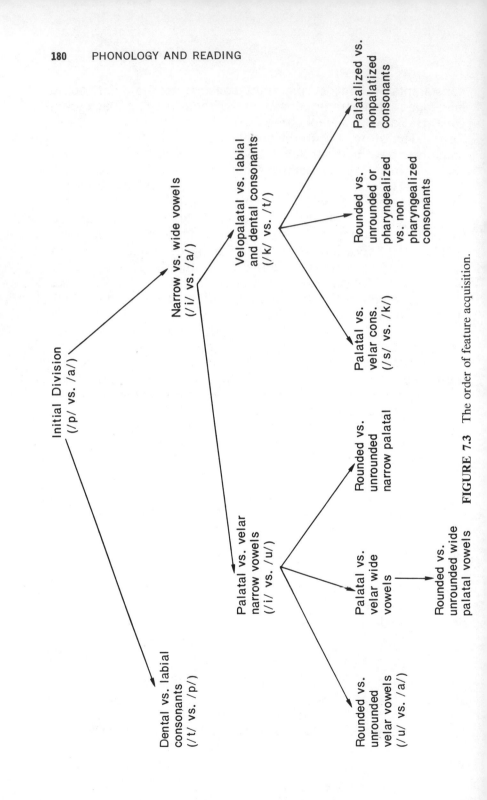

FIGURE 7.3 The order of feature acquisition.

but, rather, labial-dental, continuant-stop, and oral-nasal. Nevertheless, it is remarkable that it is precisely these three features that emerge first. Ervin-Tripp has summarized the little evidence that is available:

> Using a variety of case studies showing contrastive systems [phonemic studies] including some bilinguals before bifurcation of the systems — we can make some tentative generalizations:
>
> (a) The vowel-consonant contrasts are probably the earliest.
> (b) A stop-continuant (/p/ versus /m/ or /f/ contrast is quite early for all children, the continuant being a fricative or a nasal.
> (c) Stops precede fricatives.
> (d) If two consonants are alike in manner of articulation, one will be labial, the other dental or alveolar (e.g., /p/ versus /t/), resulting in the common lack of /k/.
> (e) Contrasts in place of articulation usually precede voicing contrasts.
> (f) Affricates (ch, j) and liquids (1, English r) usually appear later than stops and nasals.
> (g) In Russian and French /l/ precedes a vibrant /r/.
> (h) A contrast between low and high vowels (e.g., /a/ versus /i/ or /y/) precedes a front versus back contrast (e.g., /i/ versus /u/).
> (i) Oral vowels precede nasal vowels, the contrast being acquired late.
> (j) Consonant clusters or blends are usually late.
> (k) Consonant contrasts usually appear earlier in initial position than in medial or final position [1966, pp. 68–69].

These findings are, in general, consistent with Jakobson's predictions, although they can hardly serve to prove or disprove the theory.

The basic claim that phonemic development consists of the acquistion of contrasts must also be evaluated. This is an efficient procedure only if the contrast is acquired in all the appropriate instances at once. If a particular contrast, say, voiced-voiceless, is acquired first for the pair /p/-/b/ and only later is generalized to /t/-/d/ and, still later, to /k/-/g/, it is in no way more efficient than simply adding the three new phonemes /b/, /d/, and /g/. In some cases a contrast is added to the phonemic system in a unified fashion. Burling (1959) found that his son, Stephen, acquired the voiced-voiceless contrast systematically and almost immediately expanded his set of stops from three (/p/, /t/, and /k/) to six (/p/, /b/, /t/, /d/, /k/, and /g/). But in many cases this does not happen; a contrast appears first in just one pair of phonemes and only after a significant interval does the contrast generalize.

In conclusion, it is difficult to evaluate Jakobson's theory at this time. Many of the insights are probably valid, although development is not likely to be as precisely structured and rigid as he suggests. As a theoretical framework for the initiation of research, it is likely to be increasingly fruitful in the future.

Many of the phenomena that occur in the development of syntax have analogues in phonemic development. Just as a grammatical feature may be comprehended before it is produced, a particular sound may be misarticulated even though it is successfully discriminated when spoken by others.

> An example of this was provided in the author's experience by a child who asked if he could come along on a trip to the "mewwy-go-wound." An older child, teasing him, said "David wants to go to the mewwy-go-wound." "No," said David firmly "you don't say it wight [Maccoby & Bee, 1965, p. 67]".[2]

An extreme version of this assymmetry is illustrated by the boy, discussed in Chapter 5, who could not articulate speech at all but whose understanding of English demonstrated successful speech perception and discrimination.

The reverse process, production without discrimination, can also occur. Joan could produce both [p] and [b], but did not phonemically discriminate them. She had a single phoneme which was sometimes pronounced [p], sometimes [b]. Whether she could perceptually discriminate the two sounds (as David could discriminate [w] and [r]), is not known.

The overgeneralization characteristic of syntactic development has an analogue in phonemic development. Velten reports that Joan originally simplified the final consonant cluster /st/ to /s/, for example, pronouncing post as [pus]. When this changed to [pust], many other words ending with [s] (and had been correctly pronounced in this respect) were changed temporarily to end with /st/ also.

Brick is an English word; neither *blik* nor *bnik* is part of our vocabulary. However, *blik* might well become a word someday; perhaps a new laundry detergent or cigarette. *Bnik* doesn't have a chance. Just as there is a fundamental distinction between grammatical and ungrammatical sentences, there is a distinction between sequences of phonemes which are permissible in English and those which are not. When new words are coined, they virtually always follow the permissible patterns of English, which

---

[2]Maccoby and Bee examine several explanations for this lag between perception and production and related phenomena in visual and auditory perception.

are called **morpheme structure rules** (Chomsky & Halle, 1968). Messer (1967) presented pairs of nonsense syllables to three-year-old children, one a permissible sequence, and one not permissible. He found that the children could indicate fairly reliably which one might be a word. Menyuk (1968) found that although four- to eight-year-old children could not reproduce a nonpermissible sequence, there was no difference between permissible and nonpermissible sequences on a memory task that did not require production. The latter result appears inconsistent with Messer's findings.

Underlying and Phonetic Representations

In the discussion of phonology thus far, we have assumed that a morpheme can be represented by a sequence of phonemes. For example, *cat* consists of the three phonemes /kæt/, *glass* consists of four phonemes /glæs/, *sign* consists of four phonemes /sayn/, *critic* consists of six phonemes [krItIk/, and so on. Recent linguistic research in phonology has demonstrated that this is not an adequate description.

In the description of syntactic structure we saw that a description of the surface structure of a sentence does not capture all the important aspects of it, and a distinction needs to be drawn between deep and surface structure. Similarly, the actual pronunciation of a morpheme is only a partial description, and a distinction must be drawn between the **underlying representation** and the **phonetic representation** of the morpheme. Deep structure and surface structure are related by transformations; underlying representations and phonetic representation are related by **phonological rules:**

| Underlying representations | Phonological rules ⟶ | Phonetic representations |

(See Chapter 1 for the interrelationship of phonological, syntactic, and semantic components of a language. The surface structure of a sentence contains, according to the theory of phonology presented here, the underlying representations of morphemes.)

The reasons for the adoption of such a theory in linguistics are similar to the ones which lead to the postulation of deep and surface structure: primarily, that broader and deeper generalizations can be made. Only one kind of evidence will be considered here (Langacker, 1967, ch. 6). Morphemes vary in pronunciation from instance to instance. Consider these plurals: *cats* [kæts], *dogs* [dɔgz], *glasses* [glæsəz]. Here the plural morpheme has three different pronunciations; in other words, three different phonetic representations. It is not difficult to state the cases in which each form is used. After any of the sounds [s z š ž č ĵ], the proper form is [əz]; after any voiceless stop ([p t k]), the proper form is [s]; in all remaining contexts (including the voiced stops and vowels), the proper form is [z].

This description is correct, as far as it goes. But it misses the point that this variation is not an isolated variation. Suppose we assume that the underlying representation of the plural morpheme is always /z/. If we add this to /dog/ we get [dɔgz]; to /bra/ we get [braz], producing the correct phonetic representations. Now for *glasses*. If we add /z/ to /glæs/ we get [glæsz]. This is not the phonetic representation. An [ə] must be inserted between the [s] and [z]; [glæsəz]. This is done by a phonological rule which inserts an [ə] whenever the final consonant of the root is a stop, fricative, or affricate that is produced at the same place in the mouth as the ending being added to the root. The sounds [s z š ž č ĵ] are all produced at approximately the same location as the [z] of the plural morpheme.

This rule is not entirely ad hoc. Consider the past tense in English. It too has three forms: *helped* [hɛlpt], *hugged* (hʌgd], *rotted* [ratəd]. We can assume that the underlying representation of the past tense morpheme is always /d/. This accounts for *hugged*. In *rotted*, [ə] is added. Again, the ending consists of a single fricative, stop, or affricate (in particular, /d/) which is produced at the same location as the final consonant of the root (it is a different location than that for the plural, of course). The rule stated above explains this variation.

The remaining form of the plural is /s/, as in *cats*. The underlying /z/ is changed into [s]. This is the result of a phonological rule that states that if there is more than one consonant in a cluster, they must *all* be either voiced or voiceless. The first consonant in the cluster determines which it will be. Because the final /t/ in *cat* is voiceless, the voiced /z/ must be changed to voiceless [s]. This rule also explains the [t] in the past tense form *helped*. The /p/ is voiceless, and the rule changes /d/ to [t].

The three plural endings, then, all derive from one underlying representation; the variation among them is completely regular and may be explained with just two rules. Both of the rules play an important role in many other places in the description of the phonology of English. As we have seen, they account for the variation in phonetic representation of the past tense morpheme. As another instance, consider the variation in the third person singular morpheme: *pats* [pæts], *stabs* [stæbz], *teaches* [tiyčəz]. Assuming an underlying /z/ for this morpheme, the two rules completely account for the variation.

Just as transformations are ordered, that is, they must be applied in a particular order, so are phonological rules ordered. Consider the underlying representation for *glasses:* /glæsz/. If the rule that changes voicing applied before the rule that inserts [ə], the two rules would produce the phonetic representation [glæsəs]. But if the rule which inserts [ə] applies first, and then the rule that changes voicing, they produce, correctly, [glæsəz].

This variation in phonetic form occurs in roots of words as well as endings. The root *critic* occurs in the words *critical* and *criticize*. The final *c* of the root is pronounced [k] in *critical;* [s] in *criticize*. This alternation is not unique to this pair; it occurs in *medical-medicine, romantic-romanticize,* and in other pairs. In each case, the variation is irrelevant to the meaning of the root morpheme, and it is simplest to assume that the underlying representation has a /k/ and that phonological rule changes the [k] to [s] in certain specified contexts.

Vowels in morphemes also vary in their phonetic representation. It is extremely common in English for unstressed vowels to be **reduced,** that is changed to [ə] where they are unstressed. Consider the vowels in the morpheme *telegraph: telegraph* [téləgræf], *telegraphic* [tɛləgræflk], *telegraphy* [təlɛgrəfiy]. In the first two cases, the second vowel is reduced; in the third case, it is the first and third. This variation is completely predictable on the basis of the stress pattern on these words. They are introduced by the phonological rules; the underlying representation of the morpheme is simply /tɛlɛgraef/. Notice that this is *never* the phonetic representation. Some phonological rule or rules always applies to reduce one or more vowels.

Hardly anything is known about the development of the phonological system as described in this section. Berko's (1958) investigation of morphological development provides some evidence, although it has seldom been analyzed in this way. To test the development of the plural ending, she showed a picture of a strange animal to a child and said: "This is a wug. Now there are two of them. There are two _____." A response of *wugs* demonstrated the mastery of a productive rule for the plural, not simply imitation of observed plural forms.

Phonological rules are basically generalizations across inflectional systems. According to the analysis presented earlier, the plural [s] and the past tense [t] are common instances of a **devoicing rule,** and the plural [z] and past tense [d] are common instances of a rule that inserts [ə]. However, the plural [z] and the past tense [d] do not have anything in common, as they result from the distinct underlying forms to which no rules have applied. Dale (unpublished results) used Berko's tests with all six plural and past tense forms and found that ability to form the plural of *lat* (*lats*) is correlated with the ability to form the past tense of *rick* (*ricked*) and the ability to form the plural of *nizz* (*nizzes*) is correlated with the ability to form the past tense of *mot* (*motted*), but the ability to form the plural of *wug* (*wugs*) is not correlated with the ability to form the past tense of *zib* (*zibbed*). These results suggest that although the underlying representations /z/ and /d/ are acquired independently, the other forms are the result of the acquisition of the two phonological rules. However, R. Baird (personal communication) failed to observe such a pattern of acquisition in a study of the development of the plural and passive endings for nouns and the third person singular ending for verbs. We have only begun to explore the development of the phonological system.

Underlying Representations and Spelling

The writing system, or **orthography,** of English is generally classified as *alphabetic*. In general, each phoneme of spoken English is represented by a characteristic (roman) letter. A purely phonetic orthography would be highly undesirable, because it would indicate many unimportant details, such as the puff of air after the initial /t/ of *tap*, and the lack of this puff after the /t/ of *stop*. Of course, English orthography is far from being a purely alphabetic system, and its deviations from pure "alphabetism" have been much maligned. The discrepancy, however, has many advantages.

If you will look over the examples in the last section, you will see that in most cases the phonetic variations introduced by the phonological rules are ignored by the conventional orthography. Each morpheme is spelled in a uniform fashion, even though it may be pronounced in several ways, that is, have several phonetic representations. The root *critic* is always spelled with a final *c*, *telegraph* is always spelled with two *e*'s and an *a*, and the plural morpheme is spelled *s* or *es*[3] (which is an improvement on three forms).

Linguists have shown that the postulation of **underlying representations** that are strikingly similar to the conventional spelling of the morpheme best accounts for the variation in phonetic representation. This is a surprising finding.

How can a reader correctly pronounce what is printed if this is the case? The orthography does not directly indicate the pronunciation, as would a purely alphabetic, or phonemic system. But it does indicate the pronunciation, because the reader can bring to bear what he knows of the phonology of English, in particular the phonological rules. This procedure is efficient because the variation in pronunciation is generally predictable according to the phonological rules.

One very important advantage of a writing system of this type concerns dialect differences. It appears that many dialect differences stem from changes in phonological rules rather than from differences in underlying representations. Because the conventional orthography reflects underlying representations and ignores phonetic variation, it can serve for both British and American English, and for the range of English dialects throughout the country.

READING AND THE TEACHING OF READING

Reading and the teaching of reading are complex activities, drawing on perceptual, cognitive, educational, and social processes. In this section we will consider only the contribution of linguistics and the study of child language to an understanding of these activities. We will not consider directly what Jeanne Chall (1967) called "the great debate"; the controversy over the relative merits of phonic, look-and-say, and other pedagogical methods of teaching reading.

The first important contribution of linguistics to reading was the concept of the phoneme as the smallest distinctive unit of sound. Just as the speaker of a language learns to make the relevant distinctions between phonemes, he learns to distinguish among the printed symbols of the alphabet; the core of the learning process is the establishment of associations between symbols and phonemes. Leonard Bloomfield (1933), one of the originators

[3]There are many other plural forms, such as *mice*, *children*, and *geese*, These forms are no longer productive in English and must simply be considered exceptions to the patterns discussed above.

of the concept of the phoneme, was among the first to suggest this view of reading, and it was developed more fully by Charles Fries (1963).

Often the learning of reading is described as the establishment of **grapheme-to-phoneme** correspondences. Just as there are many possible pronunciations of a given phoneme, which are functionally equivalent, there are many possible visual configurations for a given letter, which are also functionally equivalent. For example, the three *k*'s discussed earlier can be represented by K, k, κ, and many other versions of the printed symbol. Learning the letters of the alphabet, then, is a matter of learning the relevant discriminations between categories of printed symbols, or **graphemes.**

In practice, such a view emphasizes discrimination training of sounds and letters by the construction of materials which focus the learner's attention on key elements of words, such as teaching a child that the visual difference between *can* and *cat* corresponds to the auditory difference between /kæn/ and /kæt/. To the extent that a language has a purely alphabetic (that is, phonemic) writing system, such an approach is entirely feasible. The writing system of English is only partially alphabetic, however, and this fact has produced varying responses by reading theorists.

The first response has been to utilize only a small subset of the vocabulary of English which does follow a regular grapheme-phoneme correspondence.

> To assist beginning readers in the understanding the relation between the sounds (phoneme) and the letters (graphemes) that stand for the sounds in words, linguists have classified words according to their basic phoneme-grapheme patterns, such as *man*, *fan*, *can* and *cat*, *fat*, *sat*. Through the inductive study of these regular phoneme-grapheme patterns, beginning readers quickly and easily gain insights into these sound-spelling relationships. Through this linguistic approach to beginning tasks, pupils become independent readers from the outset [Rasmussen & Goldberg, 1964, p. 8–9].

Such an approach, if followed rigorously, produces sentences like *Dan can fan the fat cat.* So exclusively is attention paid to the phoneme-grapheme correspondence that other aspects of language are seldom considered. Often the attempt to work into a sentence many words of similar form and spelling results in sentences which are either artificial — "Sam, Ann, Mat, and Tab ate fish and mints [Sullivan, 1966, p. 48]" — or include constructions that are probably not in the children's competence — "Al and the big man began to dig in the big man's pit [Rasmussen & Goldberg, 1964, p. 62]." Reading is more than the identification of words; their meanings must be combined in a way determined by the syntactic structure of the sentence. If the syntactic pattern is unfamiliar to the reader, the sentence will not be understood, no matter how well the sentence may be read aloud.

Although there is little research comparing the oral language patterns of children with their reading ability of various written language patterns, the research of Strickland (1962), Ruddell (1965), and Tatham (1970) strongly suggests that reading, as one type of linguistic performance, draws on the same linguistic competence underlying speaking and listening. Ruddell constructed passages incorporating either high or low frequency constructions in the children's oral language, (*A spacemen could fix the small hole* versus *The leader gave the men short breaks because they needed rest*) and found that the former were better understood, as measured by the *cloze technique*. In the cloze technique, a single word is removed from each sentence, and the subject is asked to fill in the missing word. Effectively, it is a test of the subject's ability to utilize the syntactic and semantic structure of the remainder of the sentence to identify the missing word. Tatham compared the comprehension of single sentences written at two levels of syntactic complexity, measured by correct selection from three alternative illustrations of the meaning of the sentence, and concluded:

> A significant number of second and fourth graders comprehend material written with frequent oral laguage patterns better than material written with infrequent oral language patterns . . . it is logical and in keeping with linguistic knowledge to use children's patterns of language structure in written material to facilitate learning the concept that spoken and written language are related [1970, p. 424].

A second response to the lack of total phoneme-grapheme correspondence has been to look for higher order regularities. It is often possible to identify regular correspondences between pairs of printed symbols and single phonemes or pairs of phonemes; or even longer sequences of graphemes and phonemes. For example, although the letter e has several possible pronunciations, the sequence *el* is almost always pronounced /ɛl/, as in *help*, *bell*, and *belt*. In Reading 7.1, Gibson, Pick, Osser, and Hammond suggest that these higher order invariants may be the basic elements of reading. In this way it is possible to greatly enrich the vocabulary to be used in initial reading, and this will help to avoid some of the problems discussed above. Nevertheless, the stubborn facts of English orthography imply an ultimate limitation to this approach.

The third, and most sweeping, response to the lack of a perfectly regular phoneme-grapheme correspondence (even of sequences of phonemes and graphemes) in the conventional writing system of English is simply to abandon this system. The best-known example of this response is the Initial Teaching Alphabet, (i.t.a.) developed by Sir James Pitman (Pitman & St. John, 1969). The i.t.a. is not perfectly alphabetic (more about this later), but it is much closer to a perfectly alphabetic system than our present writing system. The phoneme /u/, which is spelled in no less than seventeen distinct ways (in *ruby, rule, do, move, fruit, bruise, group, through, moon, wooed, loose, rheumatism, flue, maneuver, grew, canoe,* and *two*), is represented by the single symbol ω in i.t.a. Recognition of printed symbols is facilitated by eliminating capital letters. A larger lower case shape is used rather than a distinct shape, as is common in the conventional orthography. Figure 7.4 illustrates the complete i.t.a.

The i.t.a. is intended only as a temporary alphabet, to facilitate initial reading. After a period of from a few months to two years, the reader is switched to the conventional orthography. Two questions may be raised: first, is initial reading facilitated by the use of i.t.a.? And second, how difficult is it to make the transition from i.t.a. to the conventional orthography?

The evidence currently available (Warburton & Southgate, 1969) supports a positive answer to the first question. Children do learn to read faster using i.t.a. materials. The answer to the second question is still controversial. Very minor and temporary setbacks have been observed in some cases. However, some investigators have claimed that children must essentially start from scratch with the conventional orthography. And about the real question of interest, namely, how do readers who began with i.t.a. and later switch eventually compare with readers who began with conventional orthography, there is hardly any reliable evidence.

The three approaches just discussed — restriction to a subset of English vocabulary, utilization of higher order invariants, and the construction of a more nearly perfect alphabetic writing system — share a common emphasis on phoneme-grapheme correspondences. The phonological theory discussed in the previous two sections leads to a fundamentally new view of the reading process. If the orthography of English indicates the

Character	Name	Example	Traditional
b	bee	bat	bat
c	kee	cut	cut
ḏ	dee	ḏet	debt
f	ef	fit	fit
ɡ	gay	ɡot	got
h	hay	hunt	hunt
j	jay	jest	jest
k	kay	aks	axe
l	ell	lip	lip
m	em	mous	mouse
n	en	nævy	navy
p	pee	pens	pence
r	ray	rist	wrist
ɾ	er	fiɾst	first
s	ess	sord	sword
t	tee	tiet	tight
v	vee	velvet	velvet
w	way	wun	one
z	zed (or zee)	zeebra	zebra
ȿ	zess	horseȿ	horses
ꜩh	chay	ꜩurꜩh	church
ŋ	ing	siŋ	sing
ʃh	ish	ʃhaft	shaft
ꝥh	ith	ꝥhaut	thought
ꝥh	thee	ꝥhis	this
wh	whay	whær	where
ʒ	zhee	meʒuer	measure
y	yay	yot, sity	yacht, city
æ	aid	cæs	case
a	at	caʃh	cash
ɑ	ahd	cɑm	calm
ɑ	ask	cɑsl	castle
e	et	net	net
ɛɛ	eed	nɛɛt	neat
i	it	nit	knit
ie	ide	niet	night
o	ot	not	knot
œ	ode	nœt	note
u	ut	tuf	tough
ue	ued	tuen	tune
ω	oot	tωok	took
ǀω	ood	tωoꝥh	tooth
au	aud	taut	taught
ɷi	oid	tɷi	toy
ɷu	owd	tɷun	town

FIGURE 7.4   A comparison of the initial teaching alphabet and traditional orthography.

SOURCE: Harrison, M. *Instant reading: The story of the initial teaching alphabet.* London: Pitman, 1964. Pp. 110–111. Reprinted by permission.

underlying representation directly and the pronunciation, or phonetic representation, only indirectly via the phonological rules, exclusive emphasis on phoneme-grapheme correspondence may be unwarranted. The purpose of reading is understanding. Understanding means determining the morphemes of the sentence (and also the structure of the sentence). If morphemes have a constant underlying representation, despite varying phonetic representations (and this is really the point of introducing the concept of underlying representations), then a writing system that indicates the underlying representation of the morpheme most directly is most appropriate. If spelling indicates pronunciation, determining the morpheme requires two steps: one to determine the pronunciation, and then one to determine the morpheme:

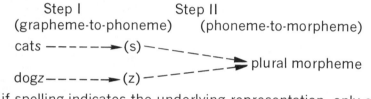

Step I
(grapheme-to-phoneme)

Step II
(phoneme-to-morpheme)

cats ——————→(s)————————————→ plural morpheme

dogz——————→(z)—————————

But if spelling indicates the underlying representation, only one step is necessary:

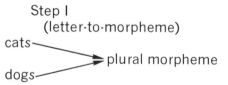

Step I
(letter-to-morpheme)

cats————————————→ plural morpheme

dogs————————

To a surprisingly large degree, this is the kind of spelling system we have in English.[4] What implications might such a system have for reading?

[4]John MacDonald (1970) has pointed to some of the irregularities in the i.t.a. in support of this view. There are a sufficient number of symbols in the i.t.a. to permit a one-phoneme, one-symbol correspondence. However, Pitman does not always depart from the conventional orthography. The phoneme [ĉ], for example, is usually written *ᵮ*, in words such as *which* and *church*. However, in the words *question* and *nature*, the phoneme is written *t*, just as in the conventional orthography. MacDonald comments:

One would normally assume that with just such cases as "question" or "nature" there is need to reflect the phonetic sounds of the words if one is seriously interested in facilitating youngsters' reading practice . . . In actual practice, Pitman appears to apply his alphabet with attention to fine-grained phonetic differentiation in the vowels while leaving the consonant sequences less altered from the conventional orthodox form [1970, p. 320].

Question is related to *quest*, and *nature* to *natal*; in each case there is a *t* in the underlying representation. The i.t.a. unconsciously preserves the underlying representation, because it facilitates the identification of the morphemes. There are many other examples of departures from the consistent application of i.t.a. which preserve part of the underlying representation.

Silent and oral reading are probably more distinct activities than is usually thought. Skillful readers undoubtedly omit a great deal of phonological processing when they read silently. One of the fundamental goals of "speed reading" instruction is to eliminate "silent vocalizing", which suggests that most of us still retain some vestiges of phonological processing in silent reading.

Practice in reading aloud may be useless, or worse, in developing silent reading. For beginning readers there may be no difference, and oral reading may be useful to the teacher. But once past this stage, oral reading may be a hindrance. Reading aloud adds two tasks to the process of reading. Not only is a motor task added (which is probably not important), but much additional mental activity is necessary. Phonological rules must be applied to the underlying representations determined from the printed symbols in order to produce the phonetic representation. This activity is simply unnecessary for silent reading. Oral and silent reading each serve important functions, but it must be realized that practice in oral reading may not facilitate silent reading.

The evidence for a distinction between underlying and phonetic representation derives primarily from Latin-based vocabulary and from complex derivational forms (such as *critical-criticize*). It is very likely that the child of six or seven who is beginning to read has not yet mastered this dual phonological system fully. In most cases, he probably has only the phonetic representations of words. There are two alternative implications for the teaching of reading that can be drawn from this fact. The first is that beginning reading should be taught in the traditional manner, emphasizing phoneme-symbol (grapheme) correspondences and reading aloud. As this process is mastered and the child's vocabulary increases, he will develop a dual phonological system of underlying and phonetic representations "automatically" (as all normal adult speakers of English do), and he will also change "automatically" to a reading process that identifies morphemes directly on the basis of spelling. This approach is essentially how reading is taught currently.

A second possibility is to deliberately enrich the child's vocabulary to include the word groups that will enable him to construct the underlying representations of words; such as *industry-industrial*, *medicine-medical*, *sign-signature*, and so forth. The child's attention should be drawn to the fact that words of similar meaning are spelled alike, even though the pronunciation differs. Carol Chomsky has suggested several exercises which might be useful for this purpose. Some of these are discussed in Reading 7.2.

A combination of these two approaches seems most promising. At the very earliest stages of teaching reading, an attempt to enrich vocabulary in the way just discussed might be confusing. However, once the fundamentals of the reading process have been mastered, the teacher need not wait for the child to increase his own vocabulary. Methods such as those discussed in the previous paragraph can be used.

Summary

Understanding of the sound component of language developed through three stages: first, a set of sound types; second, a set of phonemes; and third, the distinction between underlying and phonetic representations. Research on phonological development has not kept up with these advances. There is much information available on the development of sound types, less on the development of phonemes, and virtually none on the development of underlying representations and phonological rules. It is extremely difficult to analyze phonemically a young child's speech, but the few studies that have been done suggest that early speech is phonemically structured, albeit with gaps and other exceptions. Jakobson's theory (1968) postulates that the basic process of phonemic development is the acquisition of contrasts rather than of features. Much more evidence is needed to evaluate this claim. If the conventional spelling of morphemes indicates most directly the underlying representation, the process of reading may be a more distinct activity than has been recognized. More attention should be devoted to instruction on the relationship between spelling and meaning.

7.1 The Unit of Reading*

What is the critical unit of language for the reading process — the perception of written words? Recommendations for the teaching of

*From Gibson, E. J., Pick, A., Osser, H., & Hammond, M. The role of Grapheme-phoneme correspondence in the perception of words. *American Journal of Psychology*, 1962, **75,** 554–555. Reprinted by permission.

reading have usually depended on the choice and definition of a unit. It was once assumed that the letters of the alphabet were the units, so children began reading instruction by learning their ABC's. The advent of Gestalt psychology (applied in a very simple-minded way) changed all this. Several generations of children, as a result, were taught by the "whole word" method. As Bloomfield points out, such a method loses all the advantages of an alphabetical language. One might as well learn picture-writing. Yet the letters of our alphabet in many cases do not have a one-to-one correlation with phonemic units. Is there, then a proper unit?

    . . . This paper . . . [will] investigate the hypothesis that a unit is constituted by spelling-to-sound correlations. This is a higher order unit formed by grapheme-phoneme correspondences. It is not defined by speech alone, or writing alone, nor is it a morpheme. It is the letter-group which has an invariant relationship with a phonemic pattern. Whole words usually have such a relationship; but often they can be broken into smaller clusters of letters which still have the kind of relationship referred to when they are in a stated position relative to other such clusters. The clusters may be of different sizes and the rules for the grapheme-phoneme correspondence are conditional on what precedes or what follows. The correspondence is not a matter of "sequential probability" but it is to be found in the structure of written English *as it is related to spoken English.*

    The existence of such correspondence has been demonstrated in a study by Charles F. Hockett and a group of coworkers in the Department of Linguistics at Cornell University. This group has classified English graphic monosyllables (1) according to the arrangements of letters in them, and (2) in terms of their pronunciation. The aim of the classification is to discover the rules by which pronunciation can be predicted from spelling. A graphic monosyllable includes a vowel-spelling, an initial-consonant spelling, and a final-consonant spelling. An initial-consonant spelling might be CL; a vowel-spelling, EA; a final consonant spelling, TS. The monosyllable is CLEATS. Rules for pronunciation are formulated conditionally on what precedes and follows as well as in terms of the letter-group as such. Regularities in spelling-to-sound predictability may be termed spelling-to-sound correlations, or grapheme-phoneme correspondences.

    A child who learns to read (well) is forming useful spelling-to-sound habits based on these rules, whether he could tell you so or not.

Even if he is taught by some method which makes it difficult, he must eventually discover the important spelling-to-sound correlations, if he is to be able to generate for himself the way to read new words.

From this starting position, we can proceed to the statement of a psychological hypothesis which has some testable consequences. Reading consists of decoding graphic material to the phonemic patterns of spoken language which have already been mastered when reading is begun. The units to be decoded are not single letters, for these have no invariant acoustic match in our language. The whole word is possible, but is uneconomical as a training unit for it provides no basis for independent decoding of new graphic combinations. The hypothesis advanced is that the reading task is essentially that of discovering higher order invariants, the spelling-to-sound correlations. These are constants which are presumably discovered by exposure to both the graphic and the phonemic stimuli at the same time and in different contexts, so that the invariant combinations can be recognized in many different words. There are not a fixed number of units, such as all the words in the dictionary. There are, rather, all the potential ones which the rules of correspondence generate.

It is assumed that the individual discovers these grapheme-phoneme correspondences as he learns to read, even if he is not specifically taught them. He may not be able to draw up a set of rules but he "has" them, if he is a good reader, just as a young child "has" grammar long before he can formulate rules for it. Once he has them, any letter-combinations which follow the rules are functional units.

7.2 Phonology and Teaching Spelling*

The examples which follow suggest several types of "spelling lessons" that can be constructed to bring out a number of [the meaning-preserving] features of [English spelling]. These samples are

*From Chomsky, C. S., "Reading, Writing, and Phonology," *Harvard Educational Review*, 40, 1970, 305, 307–308. Copyright © 1970 by President and Fellows of Harvard College. Reprinted by permission.

intended primarily to indicate a general approach. In practice, of course, vocabulary would have to be adapted to the abilities of individual classes.

Children could be asked, for example, to fill in the missing reduced vowel in a list such as column (1), and then to justify their choices by thinking of related words which retain vowel quality. They would then produce something like column (2).

(1)	(2)
dem_cratic	democracy
pres_dent	preside
prec_dent	precede
comp_rable	compare, comparison
comp_sition	composer, compose
hist_ry	historical, historian
janit_r	janitorial
manag_r	managerial
maj_r	majority
ill_strate	illustrative
ind_stry	industrial
imm_grate	migrate
cons_lation	console
ab_lition	abolish
comp_tent	compete

Or, simply given column (2), they would be asked to think up other forms of the words, and to characterize the specific ways in which the vowel sounds shift around. Anything that focuses their attention on related words and concomitant pronunciation shifts ought to be good practice for finding specific related words when they need them.

Another helpful exercise involves consonants which are silent in some words but pronounced in others. For example:

(1)	(2)
muscle	muscular
sign, (design)	signature, signal (designate)
bomb	bombard
condemn	condemnation
malign	malignant
soften	soft

Children could be given column (2) and asked to think of related words in which the underlined consonant becomes silent. Or, conversely, they could be given column (1) and asked to think of related words in which the silent consonant is recovered phonetically. Or they could be given the words in column (1) orally and asked to name the silent consonant. For those who can't do it, the column (2) word can be elicited or, if necessary, pointed out as helpful evidence.

Exercises such as these are to be construed as samples of a particular approach which can be extended as the need arises. However, it is perhaps much more to the point for the teacher to develop a way of dealing with spelling errors that the children produce day by day than to equip herself with preselected word lists. Most important is that she transmit to the child the notion that spelling very often is not arbitrary, but rather corresponds to something real that he already knows and can exploit. A good way to handle misspellings that come up in class is to search with the child for a systematic reason why the word should be spelled the way it is, if indeed one can be found. In many cases, such a reason can be found. Often this will mean simply bringing a relation between two familiar words to the child's attention. To use some examples drawn from the spontaneous writing of a group of third and fourth graders, the child who misspells *president* as *presedent* needs to have pointed out that it is related to *preside*. The child who misspells *really* as *relly* needs to think of *reality* to get it right. *Apon* is more likely to be written *upon* if the child realizes that it is a combination of *up* and *on*. *Immagrate* will become *immigrate* if it is connected with *migrate*. *Medisin* will lose the *s* and acquire a *c* if it is connected to *medical*.

Sometimes a related word that could help settle the difficulty for the child is a word he doesn't know. *Illustrative*, for example, may be no part of the vocabulary of the child who writes *illastrate* for *illustrate*. In such cases, it may make better sense to introduce the new word than to have him memorize a seemingly arbitrary spelling for his familiar word.

SELECTED REFERENCES

Berko, J. The child's learning of English morphology. *Word*, 1958, **14**, 150–177.
Berry, M. F. *Language disorders of children*. New York: Appleton-Century-Crofts, 1969.

Bloomfield, L. *Language*. New York: Holt, Rinehart and Winston, 1933.

Burling, R. Language development of a Garo and English speaking child. *Word*, 1959, **15,** 45–68.

Chall, J. *Learning to read: The great debate*. New York: McGraw-Hill, 1967.

Chomsky, C. S. Reading, writing, and phonology. *Harvard Educational Review*, 1970, **40,** 287–309.

Chomsky, N., & Halle, M. *The sound pattern of English*. New York: Harper & Row, 1968.

Eimas, P., Siqueland, E. R., Jusczyk, P., & Vigorito, J. Speech perception in infants. *Science*, 1971, **171,** 303–306.

Ervin-Tripp, S. Language development. In L. W. Hoffman & M. L. Hoffman (Eds.), *Review of child development research*. Vol. 2. New York: Russell Sage Foundation, 1966. Pp. 55–105.

Ferguson, C. A. Baby talk in six languages. *American Anthropologist*, 1964, **66,** 103–114.

Fries, C. C. *Linguistics and reading*. New York: Holt, Rinehart and Winston, 1963.

Francis, W. N. *The structure of American English*. New York: The Ronald Press, 1968.

Gibson, E. J., Pick, A., Osser, H., & Hammond, M. The role of grapheme-phoneme correspondence in the perception of words. *American Journal of Psychology*, 1962, **75,** 554–570.

Halle, M. On the bases of phonology. In J. A. Fodor & J. J. Katz (Eds.), *The structure of language*. Englewood Cliffs, N.J.: Prentice-Hall, 1964.

Irwin, O. C. Infant speech: Variability and the problem of diagnosis. *Journal of Speech and Hearing Disorders*, 1947, **12,** 287–289. (a)

Irwin, O. C. Infant speech: Consonantal sounds according to place of articulation. *Journal of Speech and Hearing Disorders*, 1947, **12,** 397–401. (b)

Irwin, O. C. Infant speech: Consonant sounds according to manner of articulation. *Journal of Speech and Hearing Disorders*, 1947, **12,** 402–404. (c)

Irwin, O. C. Infant speech: Development of vowel sounds. *Journal of Speech and Hearing Disorders*, 1948, **13,** 31–34.

Irwin, O. C., & Chen, H. P. Development of speech during infancy. *Journal of Experimental Psychology*, 1946, **36,** 431–436.

Jakobson, R. *Child language, aphasia, and phonological universals*. Translated by A. Keiler. The Hague: Mouton, 1968.

Jakobson, R., & Halle, M. *Fundamentals of language*. The Hague: Mouton, 1956.

Jesperson, O. *Language*. New York: Holt, Rinehart and Winston, 1925.

Kaplan, E., & Kaplan, G. The prelinguistic child. In J. Elliot (Ed.), *Human development and cognitive processes*. New York: Holt, Rinehart and Winston, 1971. Pp. 359–381.

Langacker, R. *Language and its structure*. New York: Harcourt Brace Javanovich, 1967.

Lenneberg, E. H. *Biological foundations of language*. New York: Wiley, 1967.

Leopold, W. F. Patterning in children's language learning. *Language Learning*, 1953, **5,** 1–14.

Liberman, A. M. The grammars of speech and language. *Cognitive Psychology*, 1970, **1,** 301–323.

Lieberman, P. *Intonation, perception, and language.* Cambridge, Mass.: M.I.T. Press, 1967.

Maccoby, E. E., & Bee, H. L. Some speculations concerning the lag between perceiving and performing. *Child Development*, 1965, **36,** 367–377.

MacDonald, J. W. Review of Sir James Pitman and John St. John, *Alphabets and reading. Harvard Educational Review*, 1970, **40,** 317–325.

Menyuk, P. Children's learning and reproduction of grammatical and nongrammatical phonological sequences. *Child Development*, 1968, **39,** 849–859.

Messer, S. Implicit phonology in children. *Journal of Verbal Learning and Verbal Behavior*, 1967, **6,** 609–613.

Moskowitz, A. I. The two-year-old stage in the acquisition of English phonology. *Language*, 1970, **46,** 426–441.

Muria, J. Speech development of infants: Analysis of speech sounds by sonagraph. *Psychologia*, 1960, **3,** 27–35.

Neisser, U. *Cognitive psychology.* New York: Appleton-Century-Crofts, 1967.

Pitman, Sir J., & St. John, J. *Alphabets and reading.* New York: Pitman, 1969.

Rasmussen, D., & Goldberg, D. *A pig can jig.* Chicago: Science Research Associates, 1964.

Ruddell, R. An investigation of the effect of the similarity of oral and written patterns of language structure on reading comprehension. Unpublished doctoral dissertation, School of Education, University of Indiana, 1965.

Strickland, R. The language of elementary school children. *Indiana University School of Education Bulletin*, 1962, **38,** 1–131.

Sullivan, M. *Storybook 1A.* (Rev. ed.) New York: McGraw-Hill, 1966.

Tatham, S. M. Reading comprehension of materials written with selected oral language patterns: A study at grades two and four. *Reading Research Quarterly*, 1970, **5,** 415–483.

Velten, H. V. The growth of phonemic and lexical patterns in infant language. *Language*, 1943, **19,** 281–292.

Warburton, F. W., & Southgate, V. *i. t. a.: An independent evaluation.* London: John Murray & W. R. Chambers, 1969.

Weir, R. Some questions on the child's learning of phonology. In F. Smith & G. A. Miller (Eds.), *The genesis of language: A psycholinguistic approach.* Cambridge, Mass.: M.I.T. Press, 1966. Pp. 153–168.

Wolff, P. H. The natural history of crying and other vocalizations in early infancy. In B. M. Foss (Ed.), *Determinants of infant behavior.* Vol. IV. London: Methuen, 1966.

FURTHER READING

Chall, J.S. *Learning to read: The great debate*. New York: McGraw-Hill, 1967.

Chomsky, C. Reading, writing, and phonology. *Harvard Educational Review*, 1970, **40,** 287–309.

Chomsky, N. & Halle, M. *The sound pattern of english*. New York: Harper & Row, 1968. Pts I and II.

MacDonald, J. W. Review of Sir James Pitman and John St. John, *Alphabets and reading;* and Warburton, F. W. & Southgate, V. i.t.a.: An independent evaluation. *Harvard Educational Review*, 1970, **40,** 317–325.

Pitman, Sir J., & St. John, J. *Alphabets and reading*. New York: Pitman, 1969.

8

The Functions
of Language

Language is a means of expressing our thoughts. Can we think
without language? Is thought directed or controlled by language?
Language is *the* uniquely human characteristic; how is it related
to man's very considerable powers of reasoning?

   Psychologists have had a love-hate relationship with language. On the one hand, language is often viewed as a controlling, distorting influence on thought. Although this view was
foreshadowed by the German philosophers von Herder and von
Humboldt in the eighteenth century, it was first formulated in
modern times by the American linguist Edward Sapir, who wrote:

> Human beings do not live in the objective world alone, nor alone in the
> world of social activity as ordinarily understood, but are very much at the
> mercy of the particular language which has become the medium of ex-
> pression of their society. It is quite an illusion to imagine that one adjusts
> to reality essentially without the use of language and that language is
> merely an incidental means of solving specific problems of communica-
> tion or reflection. The fact of the matter is that the "real world" is to a
> large extent unconsciously built up on the language habits of the group

... We see and hear and otherwise experience very largely as we do because the language habits of our community predispose certain choices of interpretation [1958, p. 162].

Sapir's student, Benjamin Lee Whorf, argued this position most widely and vividly, and it is often referred to as the Whorf hypothesis (Whorf, 1956).

On the other hand, language is often viewed as a great liberating force for human reasoning, for it frees the mind from total dependence on the immediate appearance of reality in all its detail, allowing generalization and abstraction, as well as consideration of new possibilities. Jerome Bruner, a psychologist, wrote:

In effect, language provides a means, not only for representing experience, but also for transforming it . . . Once the child has succeeded in internalizing language as a cognitive instrument, it becomes possible for him to represent and systematically transform the regularities of experience with far greater flexibility and power than before [1964 p. 4].

Sapir and Bruner, along with most psychologists, are in agreement that language plays a predominant role in thinking. Only one major psychological theorist, Jean Piaget, has opposed this view. He feels

... that a symbolic function exists which is broader than language and encompasses both the system of verbal signs and that of symbols in the strict sense . . . it is permissible to conclude that thought precedes language . . . [that] language is not enough to explain thought, because the structures that characterize thought have their roots in action and in sensori-motor mechanisms that are deeper than linguistics [1967, pp. 91, 98].

There is an alternative formulation of the question of language and thought which may be more fruitful. Human beings use the flexible structure of language for a wide variety of functions: communicating, reasoning ("thinking out loud" about a difficult problem), and memorizing (saying a telephone number over and over to yourself), among others. What is the relationship among these functions of language, and how does the relationship change with development?

The Whorf Hypothesis

Whorf, like many linguists of the early twentieth century, was struck by the differences between languages. He argued that linguists had for too long restricted their attention to the European languages, which are all quite similar. He felt that they could all be lumped together under the heading Standard Average European (SAE), in contrast to the American Indian languages, which are radically different, both from SAE and from each other. These differences led him to propose two hypotheses:

1. All higher levels of thinking are dependent on language. This is **linguistic determinism:** that is, language determines thought.
2. Languages differ drastically; therefore the world is experienced differently by speakers of different languages. This is **linguistic relativity:** the picture of the universe is different for individuals in different linguistic communities.

In Whorf's writings, these two hypotheses are generally found together; in fact, it is not clear that Whorf really distinguished them. Although most research on this issue has concerned itself with the two together, they are actually independent claims. It is possible that one of them might be true and the other false. Suppose language determines thought, but that the languages of the world are all the same, or at least similar insofar as the aspects of language that affect thought are concerned. In this case the linguistic determinism hypothesis would be true and the linguistic relativity hypothesis would be false. On the other hand, it might be the case that speakers of different languages pictured the world differently, but that this is not the result of language but of general culture or environmental differences. In this case, the linguistic determinism hypothesis would be false and the linguistic relativity hypothesis true.

Returning to the Whorf hypothesis as usually stated — linguistic determinism plus linguistic relativity — what kinds of differences between languages led to this extreme position? One important way in which language deals with experience is by **categorizing** it. There are two very important ways in which this is done. Words in general stand for categories, or classes, of objects or actions or properties — not for particular ones. A large category of objects are grouped together under the label "house." A category of colors is grouped together under the heading "green." A category of actions is grouped together under the label "to touch." These are all instances of **lexical categories** (*lex-*, "word").

The second way language represents categories is by means of various grammatical devices. The suffix -*ed* indicates that some aspect of experience is in the category of past-tense-ness; that is, of all possible situations, some of them fall into a category which requires -*ed* for its description. English categorizes *houses, cats, democracy,* and *lightening* together; all are named by *nouns* which are used in certain specific ways in sentences. These are both instances of **grammatical categories.**

Languages differ in how they categorize the world using these devices. One language may simply not have a term equivalent to a term in another language. Many languages do not have a word equivalent to the English word *atom.* English does not have a word equivalent to the German word *Weltanschauung* ("all-encompassing world view"). A more important difference is that languages often differ in providing superordinate terms for classes. For example, English has the word "bird," which covers all birds, while several South American Indian languages do not, although they have words for specific kinds of birds. On the other hand, English does not have a single word which describes both fruits and nuts while Chinese does. There are many such differences between languages.

A third difference, and one that is very useful for experimental investigation, is that languages make different splits in various experimental realms. The color continuum provides the best example of this. Colors vary in hue. All languages do draw distinctions between colors, and they do it in various ways. Gleason (1961) compares the division of hues by speakers of English, Shona, and Bassa:

English

purple	blue	green	yellow	orange	red

Shona

cipsʷuka	citema	cicena	cipsʷuka

Bassa

hui	ziza

Consider a color that we would call "yellowish green"; this falls near the boundary between two English color categories, green and yellow. If such a color were presented to an English-speaker to be named, his response time would be longer than if a pure yellow or pure green were presented (Brown & Lenneberg, 1954). But such yellowish green would probably be a good example of *cicena* to a Shona speaker, and he could give a name for it quickly and easily. Languages not only divide up the color continuum differently; they distinguish colors that are good examples of categories from colors that are more difficult to name in different ways.

The second way in which a language categorizes the world is at the grammatical level. This is more interesting than lexical categorization, because speakers of a language are even less aware of it. Every language embodies a variety of mandatory observations and classifications. These classifications are shown most clearly by comparing different languages. A most vivid example of this comparison was provided by Whorf's teacher, Sapir (1958). As Sapir comments, the natural view is to assume that when we want to communicate an idea, we take an inventory of the elements of the situation and their relations, and that our linguistic task is merely to find the particular words and fit them together according to the rules of the language. Suppose an individual sees a stone falling. If, like ourselves, he is a speaker of English, he will analyze this situation into two parts: the stone, and the act of falling. They are combined by means of English grammar to produce the sentence *The stone falls*. What could be more natural?

A Russian might wonder why it is necessary to specify whether the stone must be conceived of in a definite or indefinite manner — that is, why we must say either *the stone* or *a stone*. *Stone falls* is acceptable Russian, and Latin. A Kwakiutl Indian would agree that definiteness is important, but he might wonder why we do not indicate in some way whether the stone was visible or invisible to the speaker at the time of speaking, as he would do in his description. He would also wonder why we do not indicate something about the position of the stone — is it nearer to the speaker, the listener, or some third party. And he would wonder why we insist on expressing the fact that only one stone fell. A Chinese could describe the situation most economically, with *Stone fall*, where there is no indication of number, visibility, definiteness, and the like. Of course, extra pieces of information can be provided in each language, but we are concerned with what is *required*.

So far the fundamental analysis of the situation into *stone* and *fall* has been unchallenged. But in the Nootka language (spoken on Vancouver Island), the situation is analyzed differently. The two elements in Nootka are, first an element indicating general movement of a stone, and second, an element indicating a downward direction. Imagine that we had in English an intransitive verb *to stone* referring to the movement of a stonelike object. Then the English sentence *The stone falls* would be reassembled by a Nootka speaker into something like *It stones down*. Instead of analyzing the situation into an object and its activity, the two elements are a generalized notion of the movement of a particular class of objects and a direction.

The Whorf hypothesis is a grand and sweeping statement. In an age worried about the use of language to deceive and distort, in propaganda and advertising, it has a certain appeal.[1] We have all had complex ideas or emotions that were impossible to put into words; our language has seemed too rigid and unbending.

But Whorf's arguments have been criticized widely, by linguists and psychologists, especially Eric Lenneberg (Lenneberg & Roberts, 1956). Whorf's reasoning is basically circular. He notices that a language is different from our own, and from this he infers that the speakers of that language think differently. Finally, he concludes that the differences in thinking are due to the differences in language. Actually, differences in language prove only that languages differ. Without an independent measure of the thought patterns themselves, no conclusion can be drawn.

Outside observers, such as Whorf, are usually too sensitive to metaphors that may be completely dead for the speakers of the language. Imagine a Japanese coming to the United States to study the natives and how they think. How quaint of the Americans to think of sleeping as a period of fasting, which we terminate in the morning with *breakfast*. How very food oriented. The word *everybody* must indicate that we always think of people in material terms. Too often, Whorfian analysis takes metaphors such as these, of which speakers of the language are no longer aware, as meaningful and important indicators of the thought of the speakers.

[1]The General Semantics Movement, although of independent origin, is very similar in orientation; see Hayakawa (1964).

And there is another serious objection that can be raised. The German word *Weltanschauung* can be "borrowed" into Engglish; we can talk about fruits and nuts; we can even learn to distinguish between the many kinds of snow for which Eskimos have distinct names. The absence of a single word does not preclude either consideration of the category or naming it. Language is productive, and we can construct English phrases with approximately the same meaning as single words in other languages. Perhaps the difference between languages is simply one of which categories are easily available to speakers of that language: "Languages differ not so much as to what *can* be said in them, but rather as to what it is *relatively easy* to say in them [Hockett, 1954, p. 122]." This more modest version of the hypothesis has come to be known as the *weak* Whorfian position, although Whorf himself never espoused it.

COGNITIVE CONSEQUENCES OF GRAMMATICAL DIFFERENCES

So, despite the persuasiveness of Whorf's writing, his own arguments are not very convincing. Much effort has gone into designing experiments that might give us some information about the hypothesis. The experiments have tried to relate specific aspects of a given language to a specific sort of behavior. They appear rather disappointing in contrast to the grand sweep of the Whorf hypothesis.

Only one study (Carroll & Casagrande, 1958) has been conducted concerning the cognitive consequences of grammatical structure. This is undoubtedly due to the difficulty of devising suitable behavioral measures. In a pair of experiments in the Southwestern United States, the cognitive correlates of both lexical and grammatical categories were examined. English has two verbs, *to spill* and *to pour*, which differ as to whether the action was accidental or intentional. However, either can be used with both liquids and solids. That is, we can say *I spilled the milk* and *I spilled the sugar*. Hopi also has two verbs: *wehekna* "to pour liquid" and *wa:hokna* "to pour sand or other nonliquid loose things." But either verb may be used for both accidental and intential spilling and pouring.

In the experiment, three pictures were presented to the subjects: peaches being poured from a box, coins being spilled from a pocket, and water being spilled from a pitcher. The subjects were asked to decide which two of the three pictures went together. Speakers of English should group the second and third pictures together (*spilling*), whereas speakers of Hopi should group the first two pictures (*wa:hokna*). Carroll and Casagrande devised a number of such items. The subjects were adults, between twenty-four and sixty-six years of age. There were fourteen Hopi adults, all fluent in Hopi, though most also spoke English. There were also twelve rural New England adults of comparable education to the Hopi, and fifteen Harvard graduate students. Table 8-1 presents the results for the twelve sets of stimulus pictures for which there were clear predictions. These data provide some support for the hypothesis, as the Hopi speakers chose the "Hopi choice" more often than English speakers. However, they selected the English choice even more often than the Hopi choice.

TABLE 8-1   *Picture Grouping by Speakers of Hopi and English (percent)*

	Hopi choice	Anglo choice	Other choice
Hopi speakers	34	47.6	18.4
Rural anglo	21.5	59.0	19.5
Harvard grad. std.	18.8	63.9	17.3

SOURCE: From *Readings in Social Psychology*, third edition, edited by Eleanor E. Maccoby, Theodore M. Newcomb and Eugene L. Hartly. Copyright 1947, 1952, © 1958 by Holt, Rinehart and Winston, Inc. Reprinted by permission of Holt, Rinehart and Winston, Inc. P. 26, table 2.

Their second experiment investigated grammatical categories. In Navaho, there is a class of verbs which all have something to do with handling — the verb for carry, for example — and whenever one of these verbs is used, an ending that depends on the shape or some other feature of the object being handled must be added to the verb. To ask a person to hand oneself an object, the word *sanleh* must be used if it is a long flexible object, such as a piece of string; the word *santiih*, if it is a long rigid object, such as a stick; the word *sanilcoos*, if it is a flat flexible material such as a piece of paper; and so on. In this way objects are grouped into categories according to their shape and rigidity. Navaho children are able to use those verbs and endings appropriately by the age of three or four. However, there are no words for these categories in Navaho, nor are the Navaho able to tell why they used a particular form with a given object. Carroll and Casagrande reasoned that since Navaho speakers are required to pay attention to form, they would be more likely to group objects according to form than English speakers would.

The procedure was quite simple. A pair of objects that differed in both color and form, such as a yellow rope and a blue stick, were presented to the child. Then a third object, which had one characteristic in common with each of the two, in this case a blue rope, was presented, and the subject was asked to tell the experimenter which object of the pair went best with this third object.

The subjects were Navaho children between the ages of three and ten. Since most of them were at least slightly bilingual in English and Navaho, the children were divided on the basis of tests into a Navaho-dominant and an English-dominant group. The results are shown in Table 8-2. The data from the Navaho-dominant and English-dominant Navaho children support the hypothesis that speaking Navaho leads to an increased tendency to group on the basis of form. However, there is more data to be reported. As an extra control group, Carroll and Casagrande administered their experiment to a group of white middle-class American children of similar age in the Boston area. Their data is shown in the last column of the table. The Boston children acted more like Navaho speakers than the Navaho speakers. The effect of these data is to render the results of the experiment with the Navaho children completely unclear.

TABLE 8-2 *Object Grouping by Speakers of Navaho and English (percentage)*

Original pair[a]	Third object	Nav. dom.	Eng. dom.	White
(a) Yellow rope	blue rope	70.7	39.5	83.0
(b) Blue stick		29.3	60.5	17.0
(a) Blue rope	yellow rope	70.7	39.5	80.7
(b) Yellow stick		29.3	60.5	19.3
(a) Yellow stick	blue stick	71.2	44.2	76.6
(b) Blue cylinder		28.8	55.8	23.4
(a) Yellow stick	blue stick	72.4	44.2	77.1
(b) Blue oblong block		27.6	55.8	32.9

SOURCE: From *Readings in Social Psychology*, third edition, edited by Eleanor E. Maccoby, Theodore M. Newcomb and Eugene L. Hartley. Copyright 1947, 1952, © 1958 by Holt, Rinehart and Winston, Inc. Reprinted by permission of Holt, Rinehart and Winston, Inc. P. 29, table 3.
[a]The "Navaho" choice is indicated by (a).

There is one possible explanation that does salvage a bit of the experiment and the hypothesis. We know from studies of white children that young children — aged three to six — normally group more on the basis of color than on the basis of form; with increasing age, there is an increasing amount of grouping on the basis of form. It has also been found that children of higher socioeconomic status (SES) make this transition to form-grouping earlier. So the transition to form-grouping seems to be a good indicator of cognitive maturity.

In this experiment, both the Navaho-dominant and the English-dominant children showed an increased tendency to group on the basis of form — to respond with the (a) choice — with age. But the increase began earlier for the Navaho-dominant children. Furthermore, neither of the Navaho groups could really be considered to be "middle class" as were the Boston children. One explanation for these results is that the transition from color grouping to form grouping is natural for all children, and it may be facilitated in several ways. In particular, learning to speak a language like Navaho, which requires the speaker to pay attention to form, facilitates this development. But so does practice with toys of the form-board variety such as middle-class American children are likely to have experience with. Even if this explanation is correct, the role it assigns to language is much less sweeping than that of the Whorf hypothesis.

This experiment illustrates a fundamental problem of cross-cultural experimentation. Language users in two different linguistic communities are separated by more than their languages; many of their attitudes, experiences, and interests are different. But it is just the relation between language and these other factors that we are interested in. Since both groups of variables vary, it is generally impossible to draw any inferences.

COGNITIVE CONSEQUENCES OF LEXICAL DIFFERENCES FOR PERCEPTUAL CONTINUA

One solution to this problem is to restrict experimentation to lexical differences and, in particular, to differences in the division of perceptual continua, such as color. The color space can be specified with three dimensions — hue, brightness, and saturation — and this space is divided into a small number of classes by the given language's set of color names.

Roger Brown and Eric Lenneberg (1954) initiated a series of experiments with color chips to test the Whorf hypothesis. In their study, they investigated how easily colors could be named with several measures, including length of name given to the color, the time to give the name, agreement between subjects on the names, and others. All their measures correlated highly, and they concluded that colors differ in their **codability** in English. Next they asked a second group of subjects to remember colors for varying lengths of time and then recognize them in large array. The more codable colors, that is, those more easily named, were indeed more accurately remembered. This result demonstrates a relation between the set of verbal labels supplied by English and a nonverbal behavior, memory. However, the positive correlation between codability and accuracy of recognition was very low (0.25) when the interval was short (7 seconds) and rose as the task became more difficult (0.49 when four colors had to be recognized after 3 minutes.)

This experiment was repeated with Zuni Indians, with similar results. Although the codability of individual colors in Zuni is quite different from English, those colors that were easily named in Zuni were most accurately remembered by the Zunis.

An even better predictor of memorability for colors is the measure **communication accuracy,** devised by Lantz and Stefflre (1964). They suggested that memory be viewed as a process in which an individual communicates to himself through time, using the brain as a channel. Remembering is similar to communication between separate individuals. If an item can be communicated successfully to another individual, it can be remembered well. Their measure, communication accuracy, was obtained by asking subjects to make up a description of a color that would enable another person to pick it out of an array of colors. Then these descriptions were given to another set of subjects to use in selecting colors. By observing how well the second group of subjects was able to do in selecting the original color on the basis of the descriptions, a measure could be obtained of how well each color could be communicated. Then Lantz and Stefflre performed the recognition experiment with the set of colors used by Brown and Lenneberg and with another very different array. On both arrays, communication accuracy correlated positively (0.32 to 0.86) with recognition accuracy; that is, those colors that could be accurately communicated from one individual to another could be remembered and recognized accurately.

Lantz and Stefflre conclude that their formulation of the relation between language and behavior emphasizes the *productivity* of language — the fact that new descriptions can be formed spontaneously and effectively. *Blue* may be short and conventional, but under many circumstances *light sky blue with a tinge of pink* will communicate more effectively. They argue that the role of dictionary words and grammatical categories is greatly overrated.

Their experiment has been repeated with deaf and hearing adults and with hearing six year olds with similar results (Lantz & Lenneberg, 1966). Although just which colors have the highest and lowest communication accuracy varies from group to group, those colors with high communication accuracy are always recognized most accurately. Communication accuracy appears to be an excellent predictor of recognition accuracy.

As in Brown and Lenneberg's experiment, the correlation between communication accuracy and recognition accuracy was weakest (0.51 and 0.32 for the two arrays) for the easiest task (one color for 5 seconds) and stronger (0.65 to 0.86) for the more difficult tasks (four colors for 5 and 30 seconds). Like the earlier study, this experiment is evidence only for the influence of language on memory.[2]

In recent years, interest in the Whorf hypothesis has generally declined. The disappointing results of the studies just described are one reason; another is the growing interest in language universals. The similarities among languages are now of more interest than the differences. Even in the domain of color names, the focus of Whorf-inspired research, languages do not divide up the color domain in a completely arbitrary fashion. Instead, there are very striking, apparently universal, regularities in color naming (Berlin & Kay, 1969; Heider, 1971).

Language and Memory

The finding, discussed in the previous section, that language plays an important role in memory is not surprising to anyone who has tried to remember a license plate, paint color, or collection of waxed fruit. The most useful strategy in each case is to convert the items to be remembered into a linguistic form. But this encoding is not enough. The use of language for memory requires an active process of **rehearsal** as well. Have a friend show you a telephone number, randomly chosen from a directory. Under normal conditions, it is a trivial task to remember the number for 30 seconds. But if you are also given another three-digit number, say 886, and instructed to count backwards

[2]For the single exception to this trend, see Dale (1969).

by threes for 30 seconds, the task is extraordinarily difficult. Counting backwards interferes with the process of rehearsal of the telephone number.

Young children are not able to use the efficient mnemonic strategy of naming plus rehearsal, even if they know the appropriate names. Kindergartners shown a series of three pictures of familiar objects, neither name the objects nor remember them very well, in contrast to older children, who name the objects and remember them. Children a year or two older can be instructed to name pictures and rehearse the names, which leads to superior recognition. However, when the instructions to rehearse are dropped, they return to their nonrehearsing status, and recognition performance drops (Keeney, Canizzo, & Flavell, 1967). In other words, children of this age have all the component abilities for the use of rehearsal — naming, rehearsal, the use of the rehearsed name for recognition — yet they fail to spontaneously select and integrate these functions. Mastery of the linguistic system is only a first step; an additional measure of cognitive maturity is necessary to use language, here and in other domains.

The use of language for memory is not an unmixed blessing. The word is not reality. Language has evolved to be as flexible and multipurpose as possible; in practice this means that there is seldom an exact fit between reality and language. In consequence, the encoding of reality in verbal form often results in distortion. A classic demonstration of this distortion is an experiment by Carmichael, Hogan, and Walter (1932), later replicated by Herman, Lawless, and Marshall (1957). Ambiguous figures, such as

were presented to adult subjects who were told that they

would later have to reproduce them as accurately as possible. Each figure was named as it was presented. One group was given the label "curtains in a window"; another group, the label "diamond in a rectangle." The subjects tended to distort the figures in their reproductions to conform better to the verbal label. The

example figure was often reproduced as by the first

group, and as by the second group. Though it is easier to

remember verbal labels than these drawings, the result is not always increased accuracy.

If the use of language for memory is a skill that emerges gradually, it would be expected that this kind of distortion in memory should be of less magnitude in children. It is interesting that many psychologists have commented on the keen perceptual skills of children and their ability to remember pictures and perceptual attributes of objects and events.

Even if the influence of language were limited to memory (and this is a considerable oversimplification, as will be seen in the remainder of this chapter), language would play an important role in cognition. Our thinking is seldom based on the here and now; we think about the past and future, our dreams and wishes, what we have been told and what we have told others. Even if cognition is independent of language, the raw material upon which it operates is heavily verbal.

Language and Egocentrism

One of the most seminal investigations of children in this century is Piaget's first published work, *The Language and Thought of the Child* (1955), which first appeared in English in 1926. Piaget was specifically interested in the functions of language. What needs does language serve in the life of a child? In examining the free speech of kindergarten children, he found two major classes of utterances. The first he called *egocentric speech:* speech that, whether uttered in solitude or in the presence of others, can be judged to lack a primary communicative intent. There is no real attempt to take the role of the listener (hence the term "egocentric") or adapt the message to his informational needs. The second class is *socialized speech*, which includes those utterances that do appear to possess a genuine communicative aim.

Piaget distinguished three subclasses of egocentric speech. One he called **repetition,** or **echolalia.** The child repeats, for his own pleasure, his own utterances and those of others. This even occurs in the context of conversation. (All of the following examples are from Piaget, 1955, ch. 1.)

> Jac says to Ez: "Look, Ez, your pants are showing." Pie who is in another part of the room, immediately repeats: "Look, my pants are showing and my shirt, too."

That this is repetition, and not communication, is shown by the fact that Pie's comment is simply not true.

The second subclass is **monologue.** The child talks to himself:

> Lev sits down at this table alone: "I want to do that drawing there . . . I want to draw something, I do. I shall need a big piece of paper to do that."

It is interesting that in Piaget's definition of this type of egocentric speech, he uses the phrase "as though he were thinking aloud." However, he does not follow up this concept, which was to be the central concept of Vygotsky's analysis (1962).

The third subclass, one that is investigated in some detail in Piaget's book, is the **collective monologue.** In such exchanges, children "take turns" talking but without any apparent intention that the other child should hear and respond. Anyone will serve as an audience.

> (The children are busy with their drawings and each one tells the story which his drawing illustrates.)
>
> LEV: "It begins with Goldilocks. I'm writing the story of the three bears. The daddy bear is dead. Only the daddy was too ill."
>
> GEN: "I used to live in Saleve. I lived in a little house, and you had to take the funicular railway to go and buy things."
>
> GEO: "I can't do the bear."
>
> LI: "That's not Goldilocks."
>
> LEV: "I haven't got curls."

This is a conversation in that they are all speaking about the same things, their pictures, but each is talking for himself.

Piaget distinguished five subclasses of socialized speech. The first he called **adapted information.** This is the basis of true dialogues. The primary distinction between this and the collective monologue is that the child actually talks about the topic of the other person's original comment.

> EZ to PIE: "You're going to marry me."
>
> PIE: "No, I won't marry you."
>
> "Oh, yes, you'll marry me."
>
> "No."
>
> "Yes . . . "

There is a clash of wills here, but it is not egocentric speech, as the children realize that there is a difference of opinion about this important question.

Another category is **criticism.** Although "critical" remarks usually assert the superiority of the speaker or depreciate others, as in "I've got a much bigger pencil than you," they are not egocentric in Piaget's nonevaluative sense. There is communication, as arguments and quarrels usually result. Piaget's three remaining categories are self-explanatory: **commands, questions,** and **answers.**

To compute the coefficient of egocentric speech, the category of *answers* must be eliminated, for they are almost always answers to adult questions and, hence, vary in number for extraneous reasons. The coefficient is then the proportion of spontaneous speech (other than answers) which is egocentric. Piaget found it to be about 45 percent. Later investigations have seldom obtained coefficients of egocentrism as high as these. One reason may be the fact that the kindergarten where this study was performed (the Maison des Petites, at the J. J. Rousseau Institute, Geneva, where many of Piaget's studies have been done) was one that placed great emphasis on individual activity and very little on organized group activity.

In another study with children in the early school years (Piaget, 1955, ch. 3), one child was given a body of information by the experimenter and told to relate this information to a second child of the same age. Based on the results, Piaget came to two conclusions. First, children in these age groups do not communicate material very clearly, primarily because, in their egocentrism, they fail to adapt to the role of the listener and his needs. And second, as listeners, they do not understand very well information that is adequately expressed, again because of egocentric factors. Interestingly enough, they almost always have the illusion that they *have been* understood or *have* understood.

The experiment was performed with the transmission of an explanation of a kind of faucet and also with a story. The following is one of several used.

> Once upon a time, there was a lady called Niobe, and she had twelve sons and twelve daughters. She met a fairy who had only one son and no daughter. Then the lady laughed at the fairy because the fairy had only one boy. Then the fairy was very angry and fastened the lady to a rock. The lady cried for 10 years. In the end she turned into a rock, and her tears made a stream which still runs today.

Here is one child's rendition of this story, with Piaget's comments:

> Geo (8 years old) tells the story of Niobe in the role of the explainer: "Once upon a time there was a lady who had twelve sons and twelve girls,

and then a fairy, a boy and a girl. And then Niobe wanted to have some more sons" than the fairy. Gio means by this that Niobe competed with the fairy, as was told in the text. But it will be seen how elliptical is his way of expressing it. "Then she [who?] was angry. She [who?] turned into a rock, and then her tears [whose?] made a stream which is still running today."

Young children typically use gestures and pronouns that convey little information, such as *this, something, there,* the *she* of the above example.

The central concept of Piaget's analysis, which was to become even more important in his later theorizing, is the concept of egocentrism. The young child is the unwitting center of his universe. Only his own point of view can really matter, since he is unaware that there are other points of view. Piaget's later investigations convinced him that egocentrism is a pervasive characteristic of cognition in the preschool years. In one investigation, the child faced a scale model of a landscape and was asked to represent the appearance of the landscape from positions other than by his own by; for example, selecting from a series of photographs the one that depicts what the landscape looks like to a doll sitting on the opposite side. Four and 5-year-old children persistently choose a picture depicting their own viewpoint; children a few years older are able to represent another's perspective.[3]

Two factors might underly egocentrism in communication: lack of **social will** and lack of **cognitive skill** (Kohlberg, Yaeger, & Hjertholm, 1968). Many of the examples of egocentric speech in spontaneous settings seem to reflect a lack of the cognitive skill necessary to communicate complex information. Collective monologues seem to involve both factors. Piaget feels that both factors arise from the young child's inability to differentiate his own perspective from that of others, but he does not consider the distinction closely. It is, however, an important one, because the relation between social will and cognitive skill has strong implications for development. At times Piaget claims that egocentric speech does have a communicative function that the child is unable to realize effectively for cognitive reasons. Thus, with development comes the necessary skill for communication, and egocentric speech drops out in favor of adequate social speech. But at other times Piaget offers a negative characterization of

[3]Ginsburg and Opper (1969) is a particularly clear and readable exposition of Piaget's theory of cognitive development.

egocentric speech, namely, speech without communicative function or intent. This latter formulation in particular has lead to extensive criticism of Piaget's views on the role of such speech, the best-known of which is that of Vygotsky (1962).

Russian Views of Language and Cognition

Since Pavlov, Russian psychologists have generally distinguished the "second-signal system" language — from the "first-signal system" of other physical stimuli (this distinction was introduced at the end of Chapter 2). A recurrent theme in much Russian research with children is the emergence of this second-signal system. This research is often called the development of "verbal control," but it is quite the opposite of the verbal control assumed by the Whorf hypothesis. Language frees the organism from simple, Pavlovian dependence on the immediate events in the environment and allows mental planning and voluntary behavior.

Such a view of the role of language in the development was first elaborated by Lev Vygotsky (1962, original Russian edition, 1934), who summarizes his overall analysis of development as follows:

1. In their ontogenetic development, thought and speech have different roots.
2. In the speech development of the child, we can with certainty establish a preintellectual stage, and in his thought development, a prelinguistic stage.
3. Up to a certain point in time, the two follow different lines, independently of each other.
4. At a certain point these lines meet, whereupon thought becomes verbal and speech rational [p.44].

Vygotsky's major innovation was the concept of **inner speech:** speech for oneself; speech gone underground, unarticulated. Inner speech is not talking to oneself in words and sentences, although this does occur, as when we carefully rehearse a speech silently. Inner speech is the process of thinking in **word meanings:**

Inner speech is not the interior aspect of external speech — it is a function in itself. It still remains speech, i.e., thought connected with words. But while in external speech thought is embodied in words, in inner speech words die as they bring forth thought. Inner speech is to a large extent thinking in pure word meanings. It is a dynamic shifting, unstable thing, fluttering between word and thought, the two more or less stable, more or less firmly delineated components of verbal thought [p.149].

Inner speech has a very different structure from external, or social, speech: it is highly abbreviated and consists primarily of predicates. These characteristics follow from the fact that inner speech serves a totally different function from social speech. In social speech, it is necessary to make one's *topic*, the psychological subject, clear in order to be understood. But in inner speech, the topic is already known. We know what we are thinking *about;* what is of interest is *what* we think about it. Thus it is the *comment*, the psychological predicate, that is novel. In this respect, inner speech resembles social communication between two people on a topic of mutual concern. When two people have been waiting for a long overdue bus, and one of them spies the bus coming, he is unlikely to say *The bus is coming at last;* more likely is a simple *Its coming* or *At last*.

Vygotsky's attempts to understand the development of inner speech led him to differ with Piaget on the nature of egocentric speech. Piaget had observed that egocentric speech gradually declines in frequency with age and finally disappears around the age of six or seven. According to Piaget, egocentric speech simply withers away; one manifestation of the general phenomenon of declining egocentrism in the early school years. The child learns how to communicate; how to take into account points of view other than his own. The order of development according to Piaget, is:

presocial speech → egocentric speech → social speech

Vygotsky claimed that egocentric speech does not indicate a lack of intent to communicate or an egocentric lack of awareness of the listener's perspective. Instead, its failure to communicate is due to the fact that egocentric speech has a different function from that of social speech, namely, *self-guidance*. It is vocalized because the young child cannot direct his actions verbally in covert fashion, as adults do. With development, the vocalization disappears, and egocentric speech goes underground to become inner speech. The order of development according to Vygotsky is:

socialized speech → egocentric speech → inner speech
↘ communicative speech

The language of the child is *overly* socialized at first, not *under-*socialized, as Piaget maintained. Language is primarily social in origin. At first the child does not distinguish between communication with others and communication with the self. Then egocentric speech develops. It is a hybrid form: it has the structure and function of inner speech but is vocalized as social speech. Gradually the child's ability to use egocentric speech for self-guidance increases. The speech becomes increasingly streamlined and effective for this purpose. The end point of such an abbreviation process is the complete internalization of egocentric speech as inner speech.

Vygotsky reports some delightful experiments in support of his views on this question. He argues that Piaget assumes that egocentric speech is a result of insufficient socialization. So by weakening the social constraints, we can cause the incidence of egocentric speech to *increase.* In such situations the possibility for truly socialized speech is diminished, and the proportion of egocentric speech, which is not really intended for communication, should increase. For Vygotsky, the prediction is the reverse. The young child's awareness of the distinction between himself and another as a listener is sufficiently confused that he produces self-guiding speech in a social context. Thus when the social constraints are weakened, for example, when the listener is less like the self or less able to understand the self, the frequency of egocentric speech should *decrease.*

Vygotsky manipulated a number of factors which might affect the nature of the social setting. He placed children with deaf mutes, with children speaking a foreign language, with strangers, at separate tables, and even alone in a room. In every case, the coefficient of egocentric speech dropped considerably. Thus the feeling of being heard and understood — which is an essential condition for social speech — is crucial for egocentric speech also. This finding contradicts Piaget, who claimed that egocentric speech occurs because the child always assumes that he is being understood.

In another experiment, Vygotsky stationed a band just outside the experimental room. On cue it began to play loudly, masking the child's voice and the voices of others. Egocentric speech disappeared. Again, a condition necessary for socialized speech also proved necessary for egocentric speech. However, we might ask if inner speech itself could survive such an onslaught. Imagine trying to think with a brass band blaring at your ears. But if inner speech disappears too, the experiment does not really show a social influence at all, since inner speech is by definition nonsocial.

Interpreting Vygotsky's results is difficult because he does not report either the details of his experiments or the means used to compute the coefficients of egocentric speech. Does egocentric speech alone decrease in his situations, or do all kinds of speech diminish? Which specific types of egocentric and non-egocentric speech are observed? Because of Vygotsky's untimely death at the age of thirty-eighty, we have little more than the hastily collected essays and lecture notes that constitute his posthumously published book.

Vygotsky suggests another source of evidence for his interpretation of egocentric speech. According to Piaget, egocentrism is something that must be eliminated from the language of the well-adjusted adult. Egocentric speech should decrease in quality as well as quantity during this period. That is, the egocentric speech observed should be decreasingly egocentric, just as the overall frequency of egocentric speech is decreasing. Vygotsky observed the opposite trend. Egocentric speech becomes increasingly egocentric, as it becomes better and better adapted to its function. It is least egocentric at age three and most egocentric at age seven, despite the steady decline in frequency. Especially when the child encounters difficulties, highly egocentric speech can be observed. A five-and-a-half-year-old boy was drawing a streetcar when his pencil broke. He tried to continue working, but failed because of the broken point. He muttered to himself *It's broken*, then put aside the pencil, took up watercolors, and began to draw a broken streetcar, continuing to talk to himself from time to time about his picture.

More recently, Kohlberg, Yaeger, and Hjertholm (1968) obtained more evidence supporting many of Vygotsky's conclusions. They have demonstrated clearly a curvilinear relation of egocentric speech (which they prefer to call private speech) to age, and not the monotonically decreasing relation that follows from Piaget's interpretation. The increase in private speech in early childhood reflects the emergence of a new ability in the child; the decrease a few years later reflects the internalization of this function. They also observed an increase in private speech with increasing task difficulty.

Vygotsky's work has been carried on by his student, A. R. Luria, who is also a distinguished neuropsychologist. Luria's work on the **directive function** of language, that is, the ability of language to control motor behavior, has focused on the developing interaction of the two signaling systems: the nonverbal, which is developed first, and the verbal, which arises later. Behavior that is initiated in the verbal system is "voluntary behavior." The verbal component acts as an intention or plan that programs the motor act [Luria, 1959].

Language is a distinctive signaling system that has four functions: a **nominative** role (direct reference); a **semantic** role (conceptual or generalizing); a **communicative** role, and the role of **regulating** (directing or controlling) sequential behavior. When language first appears, it does not have all these functions; instead, it has more of the attributes of the first-signal system — that is, the system of physical stimuli that affect behavior in the classical way. As a signal of objective reality, it is still intimately related to such nonlinguistic factors as the action situation in which it is used and the intonation and the person who uses it. Only gradually does it develop the properties that make it a unique system.

But when language has fully developed, it makes possible a new type of behavior: the production of novel behavioral sequences without prior practice and without a period of trial and error behavior or conditioning. Luria here has borrowed from both Vygotsky and Pavlov. From Vygotsky, Luria adopted the notion of progression from external to internal control. Early in development only the speech of others, particularly adults, can direct a child's behavior; somewhat later, the child's own overt speech becomes a regulator of his behavior; and still later, the child's inner speech assumes this regulatory role. From Pavlov's conception of the two signal systems, Luria derived the hypothesis that speech at first acts like any other physical stimulus, affecting behavior through its physical properties alone, and only later does its semantic side become dominant. To these two derived hypotheses, Luria has added a third, namely, that control over the speech system matures more rapidly than over the general motor system. He maintains that it is easier for the young child to emit vocalization upon command than it is for him to perform some other motor response. This more rapid development of the speech system makes verbal regulation of motor behavior possible for the young child.

Luria has traced the development of these aspects of language, using commands as an experimental paradigm. He found that children younger than two years of age, when asked to give the experimenter one of a number of objects lying on a table, do not always give the one requested. When the experimenter begins to say, "Give me the fish," the child reaches his hand out toward the named object, but then is distracted by nearer or brighter objects on the table, and brings them to the experimenter. The word stimulates him to act, but then other stimuli take over. This suggests that once a child begins to respond, instructions cannot alter his behavior very much, if at all, and this is supported by a number of other studies. In one, a child of two is told to place a ring on a peg, and he complies. However, if this command is repeated several times, the child's activity acquires a momentum of its own, and it is difficult or impossible to stop his activity with a verbal command. In another experiment, a child is given a rubber bulb to hold and instructed to squeeze it whenever a light goes on. Once the child begins to squeeze it, he ignores the light, and it is difficult to get him to stop squeezing the bulb when the light is off. If the instruction, "Don't squeeze" is given by the experimenter when the light is off, it simply stimulates the child to squeeze all the harder.

After about age three, the child can control his motor behavior by producing his own verbal cues. It is apparently easier for him to learn to say "squeeze" every time he sees the light than it is for him to control his squeezing response. But once he has been taught to respond verbally to the light, the verbal response can serve to control the squeezing response. The meaningful, or semantic, aspect of speech does not seem to be relevant here — the child can say "squeeze" or "go" or even nonsense syllables. For this reason, Luria refers to this as the **impulsive** aspect of speech. It is easier for the child to control his speech behavior than his hand behavior, and the speech responses can then control, via the impulsive aspect of speech, the hand responses. This is the simplest example of the directive function of the child's own speech.

The situation is more interesting when the task requires a differentiated response. A child is seated before two lights, and he has a rubber bulb in his hand. He is told to squeeze to a red light and not to a green light. By about three, he can perform appropriately if the experimenter gives him instructions. But if the three year old gives these instructions himself, he squeezes in response to both instructions. When he sees the red light he says "squeeze" and he squeezes. And when he sees the green light he says "don't squeeze" and he squeezes. The act of speaking stimulates him to squeeze. But these children *can* be taught to say "squeeze" to one of the lights and remain silent to the other; and in this way, even three year olds can control their motor behavior verbally in this situation. By the time the children are four or so, they can direct their behavior by saying "squeeze" or "don't squeeze" appropriately; speech no longer appears to be just an impulsive director, it is now also a semantic director. And by age five or six, the initial instructions alone are sufficient; the child can perform appropriately even if he is silent. Luria argues that he has internalized the speech of the experimenter and that he now directs himself by his own inner speech. He points out that five and six year olds will give themselves verbal commands out loud if the task is speeded up or otherwise made more difficult and that such commands do improve their performance.

Similarly, when adults are confronted with a difficult task, such as remembering a three-digit area code plus a seven-digit telephone number or solving a logical problem, they often begin to speak aloud. Just why speaking aloud should be more helpful than speaking to oneself silently needs further investigation. Speaking aloud adds motor and auditory cues to the items to be remembered or manipulated, but the process by which additional cues facilitate memory is not well understood.

Luria does not report the details of his experiment procedure, or the nature of the results, very clearly; and several American psychologists have attempted to replicate his findings under more controlled conditions. Many of these studies are reviewed, in Miller, Shelton, and Flavell (1970), where there also is a particularly comprehensive attempt to replicate Luria. With the exception of their finding that children's performance on all tasks improves with age, they have been remarkably unsuccessful. It is likely that none of them have used precisely the same conditions as Luria. He appears to have administered all tasks to all the children, and probably in the same order. He seems to have given each task just once to each child; in most of the attempts to replicate, each child is given just one task several times. It is reasonable to assume that a child would respond differently to a task like "Squeeze to the red light, but not to the green," on the first trial than on later trials when they occur in rapid succession. Nevertheless, the uniformly unsuccessful attempts to replicate Luria's findings make it difficult to evaluate his theory.

Communication

We use language to talk to one another; communication is the most obvious function of language. Piaget's investigations, however, suggest that language is not a very effective communication system for young children. This is a consequence of the second aspect of egocentrism mentioned earlier: the lack of the cognitive skill necessary to take the perspective of another.

Communication of a specific object, event, or relationship to another is the simplest kind of communication, but it poses serious problems for the speaker. As Roger Brown (1958) has pointed out, referents, whether objects, events, or relationships, do not have a single name (recall the discussion in Chapter 6). A speaker has considerable latitude in the name he selects. His choice must be partially determined by the set of alternatives he must distinguish the intended referent from. A pencil in a box of pebbles may be identified with the label "writing implement"; in a collection of pens, crayons, and so on, the word "pencil" will be adequate; but in a box of pencils which have been used to varying degrees, the phrase "the four-inch pencil" may be required. The difficult cognitive task for the speaker is to consider the set of alternatives from which the listener must select the intended referent and to provide the listener with the appropriate information.

A very simple game situation (Glucksberg, Krauss, & Weisberg, 1966; Glucksberg & Krauss, 1967) can be used to assess the ability of children and adults to communicate a single referent. Two children (or adults) are seated at a table, separated by an opaque screen. Each has a collection of six blocks on the table before him. Each block has a distinctive novel line drawing on it. The drawings are selected so that they are difficult to name, although very easy to distinguish. One subject, the decoder, must select one block at a time from the set of six on the basis of a verbal message provided by the other subject, the encoder.

With the six forms used in this experiment, adult performance is nearly perfect. Children's messages are much less successful. Although preschool children understand the game and can play successfully, provided the referents are easy to encode, such as colors or familiar animals, their selection of blocks with the novel drawings is virtually random. A 50 percent success level is not attained until approximately the seventh grade. Young children's messages are shorter than those of adults, and often are highly idiosyncratic, such as "Mother's dress." The idiosyncratic descriptions are not meaningless; when the children are later given their own descriptions, and asked to serve as decoders, their performance is considerably higher. This is a good example of egocentrism; the child's solution to the problem is quite adequate, *if* the other child knows everything the encoder knows.

When children are given adult messages, their selection is more accurate than the selections of adults who are given children's messages; in other words, children are better decoders than encoders. This may be due to the fact that having an understanding mother, as most children do, does not provide any motivation for less egocentric productions on the part of the child, whereas the child is constantly attempting to understand the messages of others.

A particularly striking difference between children and adults in this task is shown by their respective reaction to feedback from the decoder concerning his understanding. When the decoder requests further information, for example, "I don't understand which one you mean," adult encoders are likely to provide a completely new description or to elaborate on a previous message, whereas children are more likely to simply repeat the description or remain silent.

The most extreme variety of egocentrism is shown by the youngest children, kindergarteners and first graders, who occasionally use pointing, saying "This one" and pointing to one block, despite the presence of the opaque screen, which renders this strategy useless. One equally egocentric decoder replied to such a message by asking "Do you mean that one?", also pointing; he was given the reply "Yes." As Piaget had observed, whether the children are communicating or not, they assume they are understanding or being understood.

Language and Representation in Cognitive Development

A major change occurs in the thinking of the child at the age of six or seven. It is no coincidence that schools around the world begin at this age, for the child is now ready. The change is apparent in many cognitive domains, but one of the most striking is the acquisition of **conservation.** Piaget (Piaget & Szeminska, 1952) first discovered that if children below the age of six are presented with two equal rows of clay pellets:

A   .   .   .   .   .
B   .   .   .   .   .

which they judged to be equal, and if the experimenter then rearranged the pellets (without concealing anything) to:

A   .   .   .   .   .
B   .   .   .   .   .

they now select row A as having more pellets. Similarly, if two beakers of water, equally full, are presented, children judge them to be equal, but if the contents of one beaker are then poured into another, thinner beaker, resulting in a high water level, the taller beaker will be judged to have more.

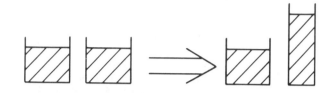

What children of this age (up to about six or seven) lack is the realization that quantity is *invariant*, even though the shape or appearance of the substance can vary. Quantity is conserved, but children do not attain this concept, conservation, until the age of six or seven.

This transition, of which the acquisition of conservation is one of the most striking examples, is a major focus of research on children's thinking. Piaget's own explanation relies on two major advances on the part of the child. The first is the concept of **negation:** The child comes to know that the quantities of liquid in the two beakers, for example, are equal because, as many children express it, "if you were to pour the water back, it would be the same." The second advance is **compensation,** or more generally, **decentration.** The young child can attend to only one dimension at a time, such as length in the pellet experiment, or height in the liquid experiment. With development, he can attend to both dimensions in each situation (decentration), and then realize that a change in one dimension, such as length, is exactly *compensated* by a reverse change in the other dimension, density, so there is no change in quantity.

Bruner (1964) has theorized that the course of cognitive development is basically the history of the evolving use of modes of representation. Representation should be understood literally: How does the mind *re*-present reality to itself in thinking? Children between the ages of two and six are primarily dependent on images for representation. They are more likely to use imagery and the perceptual properties that images are based upon in solving a problem, and their images seem to have greater vividness and detail. Children's performance in classification tasks illustrates well the quality of their thinking. When young children are given a group of pictures to be sorted into categories, they are likely to group on the basis of color or shape or size. Around the age of six or seven, there is a shift from reliance on **perceptual** properties to **symbolic** representations. Older children are more likely to group using a superordinate word, for example, "They are all tools."

Perceptual (or **iconic**) representations are essentially static, and this is their greatest limitation. It is not possible to rearrange or combine the elements of an image. Before the transition from iconic to symbolic representation occurs, the amount of water in a conservation experiment will be judged on the basis of a single, directly observable property — usually the height of the water level. The use of language for representation (and Bruner seldom considers symbols other than linguistic ones) revolutionizes cognition because it is so flexible. "In effect, language provides a means, not only for representing experience, but also for transforming it [1964, p. 4]." Bruner is not entirely clear on the extent to which the term "transforming" is literal or metaphorical, but it is at least some of each. The basic idea is that the linguistic representation of an event, in the form of a phrase or sentence, can be manipulated and various inferences drawn. This gives the child's cognition far greater flexibility and power than it had at the previous iconic stage.

Several kinds of evidence can be offered for this view, including one concerning conservation specifically. This experiment was performed by Francoise Frank at the Center for Cognitive Studies at Harvard. It originated with the hypothesis that if transitional age children, children developing symbolic techniques of representation, could be shielded from the misleading iconic rendering of the situation so that they could represent the situation verbally *before* they see it, their language could serve as a guide.

The children, who were four, five, six, and seven year olds, were all given the standard conservation of liquid quantity test first. Then Frank gave a screened version of the test, in which the actual pouring is concealed by an opaque screen. First the child inspects two partially filled standard beakers and agrees that they contain equal amounts of water. Another beaker, wider but of the same height, is shown to the child. The experimenter pours from one of the standard beakers into the wider beaker, behind the screen. The child who cannot see the water level in either the remaining standard or the new beaker, is asked which has more to drink, or do they have the same amount, the standard or the wider beaker. Figure 8.1 illustrates the results.

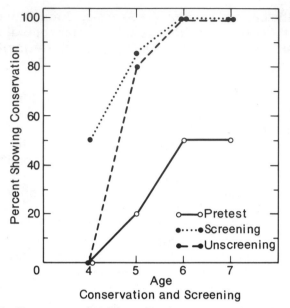

Conservation and Screening

FIGURE 8.1   Percentage of children showing conservation of liquid volume before and during screening and upon unscreening of the displays.

SOURCE: Reprinted from *American Psychologist*, 1964, vol. 19, p. 6, fig. 6, "The Course of Cognitive Growth," Jerome S. Bruner, by permission of the American Psychological Association.

With the screened beakers, there is a striking increase in correct equality judgments. Correct responses jump from 0 to 50 percent among the four year olds; from 20 to 90 percent among the five year olds; and from 50 to 100 percent among the six year olds. When asked to justify their responses, most children reply with something like "It's the same water," or "You only poured it."

Now the screen is removed, and the children are asked again which has more water, or are they the same. All the four year olds change their minds. The perceptual display overwhelms them and they decide that the wide beaker has less water. But almost all the five year olds stick to their original judgment. In fact, they often explicitly mention the difference between appearance and reality: "It looks like more to drink, but it is only the same because it is the same water and it was only poured from there to there," to quote one. And all the six and seven year olds stick with conservation.

A few minutes later, a post test is done with the children. This is the standard unscreened conservation test, but with either a tall thin beaker or several small beakers. Remember that the training test was with a wider beaker, so it was not simply practice for the post test. The four year olds are unaffected by the experimental experience — none of them show conservation in the new task. With the five year olds, 70 percent show conservation, in contrast to the 20 percent on the pretest. With the six and seven year olds, conservation increases from 50 to 90 percent. On the basis of this and other experiments, Bruner argues that the younger children, when freed of what he calls "perceptual seduction," can apply their language to the situation and arrive at correct judgments. If the screen is not present, the impact of perception may be overwhelming (see Figure 8.2).

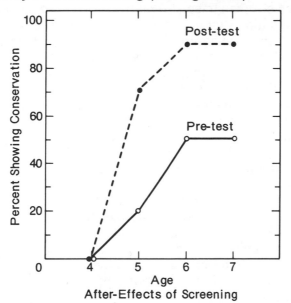

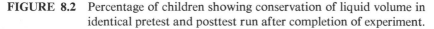

FIGURE 8.2   Percentage of children showing conservation of liquid volume in identical pretest and posttest run after completion of experiment.

SOURCE: Reprinted from *American Psychologist*, 1964, vol. 19, p. 7, fig. 7, "The Course of Cognitive Growth," Jerome S. Bruner, by permission of the American Psychological Association.

Bruner suggests the model of transformational grammar again: a deep structure can be converted to several alternative surface structures. The surface structures are observed, but the deep structure determines the meaning. Similarly, a given amount of liquid may be observed in several different "appearances." The motivating force for the transition between iconic and symbolic representation is conflict; there is a mismatch between the child's current means of organizing experience, the iconic mode, and his emerging linguistic mode of representation. Gradually the child comes to rely on the symbolic encoding, not the direct perception.

Language clearly plays an important developmental role, according to Bruner's theory. Certain properties of cognition are made possible because of language, such as overcoming dependence on perceptual attributes in the conservation task (for others, see Bruner, Oliver, & Greenfield, 1966). However, mere possession of language is not enough; the child must learn to rely on language. Bruner offers the screening-unscreening conservation experiment as evidence that the use of language can bring some children to conservation if they have a chance to deal with the situation first in purely linguistic terms.

In Frank's experiment, the role of language is basically implicit; little can be said about precisely what kinds of language were used or how. A more direct approach to these questions has been taken by Hermina Sinclair-de-Zwart (1969). Bruner pointed out that preconservational and conservational children differ in language they use to describe various stimulus materials. The younger children do not attend to both dimensions at once; they say, "That one is tall and that one is little." But the older children use more sophisticated language. They speak of one glass being "taller, but thinner" than another. Bruner suggested that training children to use language appropriate to the demands of the task would improve their performance on it.

On this point Piaget and his co-workers, including Sinclair-de-Zwart, disagree strongly. According to Piaget, language reflects, rather than determines, cognitive development; therefore special linguistic training will not help children whose level of cognitive development has not yet reached the point where it can comprehend the relevant concepts represented by the words.

Sinclair-de-Zwart tested Bruner's suggestion that non-conserving children could be taught language expressions characteristic of conserving children, and that this would lead to conservation. This required, as a first step, identifying changes in the child's descriptive language which occur with the acquisition of conservation. A number of sets of materials were used for this purpose. In one, two dolls were given equal or unequal amounts of clay or equal or unequal numbers of marbles or pencils that varied in length and thickness. The child was asked to describe these arrangements spontaneously; then the examiner asked the child to arrange the objects according to some verbal instructions, in order to test comprehension. Then all the children were tested to determine if they conserved. Essentially no differences were found between the conservers and non-conservers as to comprehension. But there were three principal differences in spontaneous descriptions produced by the two groups.

Children who conserved used *more relational terms;* they said things like, "One has more than the other" (*a plus que*), or "One has more and the other has less." The other children almost always failed to use these terms; the predominant response was of the type, "one has got a big bit, the other a little bit" (*a beaucoup, un peu*).

Children who conserved used *more highly differentiated* terms. They often used appropriate pairs of terms for specific dimensions, such as "long" and "short" (*long* and *court*) and "fat" and "thin" (*gros* and *mince*). Nonconservers used undifferentiated terms for the two dimensions; "fat" (*gros*) might be used for a long and thick pencil, and "small" (*petit*) for a short and thick one.

Children who conserved produced *coordinated descriptions.* If objects differed in two dimensions, children who did not conserve tended to mention only one of the differences. For example, when one doll had four small marbles and one had two big ones, such a child stated, "one has got a lot of marbles and the other only two." When such a child *did* mention both dimensions, it was usually a four-part uncoordinated description: "This crayon is long, the other is short, this crayon is thin, the other is fat" (*Ce crayon est long, l'autre est court, ce crayon est mince, l'autre est gros*). In contrast, the conservers coordinated the dimensions, saying, "This pencil is longer but thinner, the other is short but thick" (*Ce crayon est plus long mais plus mince, l'autre est court mais gros*).

The descriptive patterns used by a child were a better clue to his conservation or lack thereof than his age. An eight year old who did not conserve used descriptive patterns characteristic of the five year olds, who typically did not conserve.

Next an attempt was made to teach nonconservers the use of the expressions used by the conservers. The training process has not been described in great detail, but it appears to involve the examiner first giving instructions to the child, and then the child instructing the examiner. Easiest to teach was the use of differentiated terms, then the use of relational terms, and finally the use of coordinated descriptions. This is interesting because of the three aspects, the last and most difficult — coordinated descriptions — was most highly correlated with conservations.

Of the children who did learn to use these expressions, very few made the transition to conservation. Children who had given partial conservation answers in the pretest were able to express their arguments more clearly and also more consistently in the posttests. And of those who did not show conservation on the pretest, who indicated that water level indicated quantity, began to spontaneously mention both dimensions — height and width — and even occasionally mention the covariance of the two dimensions. But conservation itself was *not* achieved by these children. One said, "There the water goes up because the glass is thin; the other glass is shorter and wider and there is less to drink there."

These results demonstrate that language training can at best contribute *indirectly* to the acquisition of conservation. Language can lead the child to focus on the relevant dimensions of the task situation. The observed changes in the justifications for the answers given indicate that language can aid in the storage and retrieval of relevant information. But in addition to the selection, storage, and retrieval of relevant cues, a cognitive integration and coordination are necessary for conservation, and language training does not appear to contribute to this directly.

A very different approach to the question of the role of language in cognitive representations and functioning has been taken by Hans Furth (1966; in press), who has compared the performance on various cognitive tasks — concept attainment, memory, conservation, rule learning, and others — of deaf children, who in the vast majority of cases have not mastered English in either its oral or printed forms, with that of hearing children. He has found that in a surprising variety of situations, the performance of the deaf is fully comparable to that of hearing children, supporting his contention (based on the theoretical work of Piaget) that language is not necessary for thought. Furth's results are not conclusive, however. Many deaf children acquire some form of manual communication, either the fully developed American Sign Language or some simplified signing system. Manual communication appears to be a truly linguistic system (Stokoe, 1960) and may well serve deaf children in ways similar to the functions of oral language for hearing children (Kohl, 1966; Spence, 1971).

Summary

The investigations reported in this chapter illustrate clearly the distinction between the structure of language and its functions. Mastering the linguistic system is not the same thing as putting it to work. Language is not used for many functions — memory, classification, inner speech — until a point in development considerably later than the essential mastery of structure. The one function that is present from the beginnings of language — communication — is extremely inefficient in early childhood.

The ability to use language for many purposes seems to emerge simultaneously with the many cognitive advances that occur in middle childhood, around the age of seven. Whether these cognitive advances explain the improvements in using language, or vice versa, remains a mystery. The notion of internalization seems to connect many of the findings. For many functions, the effective use of language begins just before it is internalized. Whether it is the use that permits internalization or the state of readiness for internalization which permits effective use is unknown but basically testable.

A final caution. Psychologists, linguists, philosophers — academics in general — rely heavily on the printed word, and it would not be surprising if we overgeneralize the role of language from our own activities to mental life in general. In *Visual Thinking* (1969), Rudolf Arnheim argues persuasively that all thinking, and not just thinking about art or other visual experiences, is basically perceptual in nature. The relationship between words and images in the mind needs much further investigation.

SELECTED REFERENCES

Arnheim, R. *Visual thinking.* Berkeley: University of California Press, 1969.

Berlin, B., & Kay, P. *Basic color terms.* Berkeley: University of California Press, 1969.

Brown, R. How shall a thing be called? *Psychological Review*, 1958, **65**, 14–21.

Brown, R., & Lenneberg, E. H. A study in language and cognition. *Journal of Abnormal and Social Psychology*, 1954, **49**, 454–462.

Bruner, J. S. The course of cognitive growth. *American Psychologist*, 1964, **19**, 1–15.

Bruner, J. S., Oliver, R., & Greenfield, P. *Studies in cognitive growth.* New York: Wiley, 1966.

Carmichael, L., Hogan, H. P., & Walter, A. A. An experimental study of the effect of language on the representation of visually perceived form. *Journal of Experimental Psychology*, 1932, **15**, 73–86.

Carroll, J. B., & Casagrande, J. B. The function of language classifications in behavior. In E. E. Maccoby, T. M. Newcomb, & E. L. Hartley (Eds.), *Readings in social psychology.* (3rd ed.) New York: Holt, Rinehart and Winston, 1958, Pp. 18–31.

Dale, P. S. Color naming, matching, and recognition by preschoolers. *Child Development*, 1969, **40**, 1135–1144.

Furth, H. *Thinking without language.* New York: The Free Press, 1966.

Furth, H. Linguistic deficiency and thinking: Research with deaf subjects, 1964–69. *Psychological Bulletin,* in press.

Ginsburg, H., & Opper, S. *Piaget's theory of intellectual development: An introduction.* Englewood Cliffs, N.J.: Prentice-Hall, 1969.

Gleason, H. A. *An introduction to descriptive linguistics.* New York: Holt, Rinehart and Winston, 1961.

Glucksberg, S., & Krauss, R. M. What do people say after they have learned to talk? Studies of the development of referential communication. *Merrill-Palmer Quarterly,* 1967, **13,** 309–316.

Glucksberg, S., Krauss, R. M., & Weisberg, R. Referential communication in nursery school children: Method and some preliminary findings. *Journal of Experimental Child Psychology,* 1966, **3,** 333–342.

Hayakawa, S. I. *Language in thought and action.* (2nd ed.) New York: Harcourt Brace Jovanovich, 1964.

Heider, E. R. "Focal" color areas and the development of color names. *Developmental Psychology,* 1971, **4,** 447–455.

Herman, D. T., Lawless, R. H., & Marshall, R. W. Variables in the effect of language on the reproduction of visually perceived forms. *Perceptual and Motor Skills,* 1957, **7,** Monograph Supplement 2, 171–186.

Hockett, C. F. Chinese vs. English: An exploration of the Whorfian thesis. In H. Hoijer (Ed.), *Language in culture.* Chicago: University of Chicago Press, 1954.

Keeney, T. J., Canizzo, S. R., & Flavell, J. H. Spontaneous and induced rehearsal in a recall task. *Child Development,* 1967, **38,** 953–966.

Kohl, H. R. *Language and education of the deaf.* New York: Center for Urban Education, 1966.

Kohlberg, L., Yaeger, J., & Hjertholm, E. Private speech: Four studies and a review of theories. *Child Development,* 1968, **39,** 691–736.

Lantz, D., & Lenneberg, E. H. Verbal communication and color memory in the deaf and hearing. *Child Development,* 1966, **37,** 765–799.

Lantz, D., & Stefflre, V. Language and cognition revisited. *Journal of Abnormal and Social Psychology,* 1964, **69,** 472–481.

Lenneberg, E. H., & Roberts, J. M. *The language of experience.* Memoir 13, Indiana University Publications in Anthropology and Linguistics, 1956.

Luria, A. R. The directive function of speech in development and dissolution. Part I: Development of the directive function of speech in early childhood. *Word,* 1959, **15,** 341–352.

Miller, S. A., Shelton, J., & Flavell, J. H. A test of Luria's hypotheses concerning the development of verbal self-regulation. *Child Development,* 1970, **41,** 651–665.

Piaget, J. *The language and thought of the child.* Translated by M. Gabain. Cleveland: Meridian Books, 1955.

Piaget, J. Language and thought from the genetic point of view. In D. Elkind (Ed.), *Six psychological studies.* Translated by A. Tenzer. New York: Random House, 1967.

Piaget, J., & Szeminska, A. *The child's conception of number*. Translated by C. Gattegno & F. M. Hodgson. London: Routledge & Kegan Paul, 1952.
Sapir, E. Language and environment. In D. G. Mandelbaum (Ed.), *Selected writings of Edward Sapir in language, culture, and personality*. Berkeley: University of California Press, 1958. Pp. 89–103.
Sinclair-de-Zwart, H. Developmental psycholinguistics. In D. Elkind & J. H. Flavell (Eds.), *Studies in cognitive development*. New York: Oxford University Press, 1969. Pp. 315–366.
Spence, C. M. An evaluation of the comparison of hearing and deaf subjects to investigate the language-thought question. Unpublished paper, Department of Psychology, University of Washington, 1971.
Stokoe, W. C. Sign language structure. *Studies in Linguistics*, Occasional Papers, 8. Buffalo: Buffalo University Press, 1960.
Vygotsky, L. S. *Thought and language*. Translated by E. Hanfmann & G. Vakar. Cambridge, Mass.: M.I.T. Press, 1962.
Whorf, B. L. *Language, thought, and reality*. New York: Wiley; and Cambridge, Mass.: M.I.T. Press, 1956.

FURTHER READING

Arnheim, R. *Visual thinking*. Berkeley: University of California Press, 1969.
Brown, R. *Social psychology*. New York: Free Press, 1965. Chap. 7.
Lenneberg, E. H. *Biological foundations of language*. New York: Wiley, 1967. Chap. 8.
Vygotsky, L. S. *Thought and language*. Translated by E. Hanfmann & G. Vakar. Cambridge: M.I.T. Press, 1962.

9

Dialect Differences and Black English

> The Gileadites seized the fords of the Jordan and held them against Ephraim. When any Ephraimite who had escaped begged leave to cross, the men of Gilead asked him, "Are you an Ephraimite?," and if he said "No," they would retort, "Say Shibboleth." He would say "Sibboleth," and because he could not pronounce the word properly, they seized him and killed him at the fords of the Jordan. At that time forty-two thousand men of Ephraim lost their lives (Judges 12:5–6, New English Bible).

All too often language serves as a barrier rather than a flexible and efficient means of communication. We do not all speak the same language. Even within a particular language community, individuals do not speak in exactly the same way. Such variations in language are called **dialects.** Dialect differences are often interpreted as indicators of real or imagined differences in education, religion, morality, social class, race, attitudes, and other aspects of life. Shaw's *Pygmalion* is about a benevolent use of this interpretative tendency: the story from Judges is the other side of the coin.

Geography is not the only source of dialect differences, although it is the first to come to mind. Dialects often arise on the basis of profession. Different occupations have different things to talk about. But they may even use different words for the same things. The words "forecast," "prognosis," and "prediction" all have about the same meaning, but one is associated with the weather, another with medicine, and the third with the sciences.

The so-called generation gap illustrates the role of age in dialect. Two processes lead to age differences in dialect. First, one age group may deliberately coin new words and phrases, such as "uptight," "far out," and so on, and new meanings for existing words and phrases, such as "heavy," "out of sight," and "head." Age differences are preserved by the tendency of speakers to continue using the language they learned when young, although the language as a whole may have changed since then. Old people tend to continue to use words that have been replaced in the general language.

Although profession and age are important sources of dialect differences, there are two other factors that determine far wider dialect differences. One is geography, which was mentioned earlier. Even in the United States, which has a remarkable uniformity of language for a country its size, there are considerable differences that are primarily geographic in nature. The word "greasy" rhymes with "fleecy" in the northern part of the country, while in the South, it rhymes with "easy." In some parts of the East and South, r is not pronounced at the end of words or before a consonant. In such regions, "par" rhymes with "pa," and "startle" with "throttle." In the northeastern part of the country, "stoop" is often used for "porch," and "comforter" for "blanket." The words "hotcakes," "pancakes," and "griddle cakes" are each associated with particular regions. Generally speaking, the greatest differences occur on the East Coast of this country and gradually become weaker as one proceeds inland.

The second major factor determining dialect differences is social class. Dwight Bolinger (1968) has contrasted geography with social class as the horizontal and vertical coordinates of language. These differences are most pronounced when a society is stratified; and in a very real sense, American society is so divided into classes. There is a strong tendency for people to classify other individuals on the basis of their language, and this classification can be strongly evaluative in nature. Differences in speech are often cultivated for just this reason, to influence the opinion of others. Ethnic group differences are usually classified as social class dialects.

Profession, age, geography, and social class are all factors that lead to the use of different dialects by different persons. There is also a factor that leads to the use of different dialects by a single speaker: the particular situation in which a speaker finds himself. Every speaker will modify his speech in a way he feels appropriate for the setting. In most societies, for example, there is a standard formal dialect. In India, formal Hindi has some Sanskrit added to it. In standard formal English, there is much less use of contractions than in informal English — "Let us begin" versus "Let's start." Near synonyms are substituted for each other — *begin* for *start*, and *rise* for *get up*. In standard formal English, adverbs ending with *-ly* are common and may be placed either before or after the verb they modify — *they left quickly* or *they quickly left.* Informal English tends to place the adverb after the verb or change to a different form of modifier, also placed after the verb — *they left quickly*, or *they left right away.*

Sociolinguistics

The study of dialect is a job both for the linguist and for the sociologist. In the past, there has been a division of labor. Linguists have focused on geography, and sociologists, on the role of social class. Each may miss important facts and generalizations that the other would notice, so it is important that both be involved in such studies. Increasingly in recent years there has developed the new discipline of **sociolinguistics,** drawing on the techniques and concepts of both parent disciplines. Foremost among the sociolinguists is William Labov (1970a, 1970b), who has added much to our knowledge of sociolinguistic theory and method and also to our knowledge of the specific dialect of English, "Black English," to be examined later in this chapter.

The study of dialect is particularly challenging because the factors underlying dialect differences are not independent. Suppose that the social class variable and the situational variable — formal-informal — were completely independent. There would be four distinct dialects: a formal standard, an informal standard, a formal nonstandard (say, lower class), and an informal nonstandard. For some purposes it would be very useful if language was arranged in such a manner. For one thing, no matter how casually an educated speaker spoke, we could recognize him as an educated person (education is one of the major factors in the social class distinction in this country).

However, the social class and situational factors are not independent. The same aspects of language which are used in shifting from formal to informal — what Labov calls "style shifting" (see Reading 9.1) — are used to distinguish social levels of English. One such indicator is the pronunciation of *ing* in forms such as *working* and *living*. The [Iŋ] pronunciation is more formal than [In]. In a study of dialect differences in New York, Labov obtained samples of speech under conditions of casual speech, careful speech, and reading style. He calculated the proportion of times *ing* was pronounced [In] in these three situations for four groups of all white speakers: lower class, working class, lower middle class, and upper middle class. Figure 9.1 illustrates the results.

Under each condition, there is social stratification; no matter what the activity, the upper middle-class speakers use [In] least, followed by lower middle-class speakers, and so on. But each group also shows regular style shifting in the same direction. They all use [In] most in the casual condition, followed by the careful condition, followed by the reading condition. Although the social class groups are very different, they are similar in that they all *use* this variable in the same way. If a hearer observes a particular level of this variable in the speech of another person, it is not always possible for him to determine the contributions of social class and situation. The difficulty of judgment is compounded by the fact that most speakers have experience with only one group. Teachers hear the difference between middle- and working-class students in the classroom but do not realize that both groups have changed their speech in the same direction because of the "classroom" situation. A related problem is **categorical perception:** the tendency of human beings, in many cases, to perceive probabilistic phenomena as all-or-nothing. Most people will perceive the speech of another person as being *always* [Iŋ] or always [In], which is erroneous. For example, although few teachers realize it, they themselves occasionally use the same nonstandard forms in their own casual speech.

Labov has found the same patterns of usage for the pronunciation of [d] for *th*, for the absence of *r* in such words as *park* and *car*, and even for some grammatical features, such as the use of *ain't* and double negatives.

Geography and social class are not completely independent, either. Geographic differences become social class differ-

(ing index)

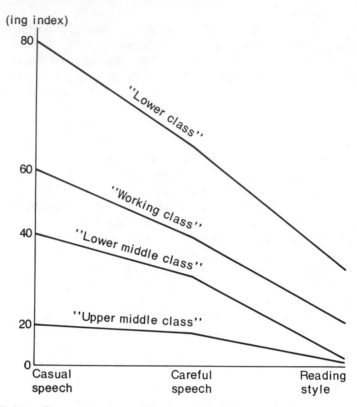

FIGURE 9.1   Class and style stratification of (ing) in *working*, *lining*, and so on, for white New York City adults. From Labov, W. *The study of nonstandard English*. Copyright © 1970 by the National Council of Teachers of English. Reprinted by permission of the publisher and W. Labov. P. 19, fig. 2.

ences whenever a sizeable number of people move into a new setting. This happened in the United States when a regional dialect, Southeastern English, became a lower class social dialect after large numbers of southerners moved north to work in factories in the 1930's and 1940's.

ATTITUDES TOWARD DIALECT DIFFERENCES

A language is a coherent system of rules, and each dialect is also a coherent system of rules. And these systems have a great deal in common with each other. They are not exactly foreign languages, but they confront each other linguistically as equals, as alternative dialects of the same language.

Social class dialects are simply dialects like any other kind of dialect. Unfortunately, they have not always been viewed in this way. There is a strong tendency to see nonstandard[1] dialects as the result of isolated deviations from the standard language, resulting from failure to master the standard dialect. This failure in turn may be blamed on inadequate environment, genetic differences, or other factors.

Social values and attitudes with respect to language are not only strong but also remarkably stable. Even revolutions fail to change them in most cases. In American society, even the most radical and revolutionary figures do not use nonstandard syntax in speaking or in print. Of course it is traditional for politicians to sprinkle a little of the vernacular into their public speeches. But this is almost always in the form of vernacular vocabulary items, seldom in matters of pronunciation and even more rarely in syntax. The same phenomonon appears to be happening in the American black nationalist movement. There is a new trend to use some aspects of the nonstandard dialect, but it is almost always vocabulary items, not sentence construction.

To put this in different words, the entire linguistic community often shares attitudes toward dialects. In Quebec, both English and French are spoken. English-speaking Canadians hearing tapes of individuals speaking French Canadian and English, judge the speakers of English to be more intelligent, more dependable, kinder, more ambitious, better looking, and taller. Given the all too human tendency toward self- and group-glorification, this is not too surprising. The remarkable fact is that French Canadians respond in approximately the same way; that is, they respond more favorably to English speakers than to French Canadian speakers. The negative evaluation of French Canadian is shared by both communities in Quebec (Lambert, 1967). Similarly, although the vowel in *mad*, *bad*, and *glad* is pronounced in many different ways in New York City, there is general agreement that the higher the tongue (pronouncing the vowel closer to that of *beard*), the lower the status of the speaker. These two examples are both instances of a phenomenon that has long been familiar to sociologists: the adoption of majority norms by members of the minority, even when they are highly unfavorable to the minority. It is interesting in this regard that two of the first serious students of the nonstandard dialect spoken by many black Americans were white: William Labov and William Stewart.

[1]"Nonstandard" here refers to any dialect other than the one spoken by the dominant social class under fairly careful conditions. The term is entirely nonevaluative.

These attitudes can, and do change. French-speaking Canadians have become increasingly concerned with preserving their linguistic heritage, and so have many black Americans. But the changes are slow. Often an educated, culturally conscious elite can change its view, but it will have difficulty in affecting the majority of the group.

It is often the case that the people who most strongly condemn a form in the speech of others are among the people who are most likely to use it in their own casual speech. This is undoubtedly due to the fact that they are the ones who are struggling most actively to overcome this trait and are therefore most conscious of it. This situation often leads to what has been called **hypercorrect speech** — adopting the standard form even more strongly than the high prestige group. In studies of the pronunciation of r in such words as *heard*, *guard*, and *car*, lower middle-class speakers sharply increased their pronunciation of r. In reading sentences, their score was almost identical to that of upper middle class speakers; and in reading word lists, it actually exceeded that of upper middle class speakers. This tendency for such speakers to strongly condemn the nonstandard form is particularly important for the educational process, since American school teachers have traditionally been drawn from the lower middle class (although this is increasingly less true).

Of course there is no logical reason or necessity for such unfavorable attitudes. There are many situations in the world which demonstrate that a pluralistic situation can exist successfully. It often happens, for example, that the language used in school is not the native language of the children. Swahili is the school language in continental Tanzania (formerly Tanganyika), although a substantial proportion of the children in this region are not native speakers of Swahili. The Kerman area of Iran is an example of a pluralistic dialect situation. Kermani Persian is the native dialect of the children, while Standard Persian is the dialect of the schools. There is no stigma attached to speaking Kermani when the child is with his family or friends, but Standard Persian is used in school and with people from other areas of Iran.

Black English

In several areas of the United States, nonstandard dialects are associated with ethnic group membership. In the southwestern part of the country, and in parts of New York City, a nonstandard dialect arises as the result of contact between Spanish and English speakers. In many areas, a similar problem exists for American Indians. But the most widespread case is that of the dialect spoken by many black Americans. This is the only such dialect to be considered here, primarily because it is the one case for which there is some reliable, useful sociolinguistic knowledge. Virtually all of this is due to the work of Labov in New York City and William Stewart in Washington, D.C. This dialect is often called "Black English." I am hesitant to use this term because not all black Americans speak it, nor are the features of Black English entirely confined to black speakers. It is a convenient abbreviation and like all convenient abbreviations, somewhat false. However, it is shorter than "Nonstandard Negro English" or "Black Nonstandard English."

From a linguistic point of view, the differences between Black English (BE) and Standard English (STE) are not great. In general, the deep structures of sentences and the underlying representations of lexical items are the same in the two dialects. And so are most of the rules that operate on them: transformations on deep structures and phonological rules on underlying representations. Some rules are different, however; a rule may be present in one dialect but not the other, or the conditions for a rules application may differ. We will consider a few of the most obvious differences; Reading 9.2 contains a carefully annotated sample of BE, with emphasis on syntactic differences.

In STE, the present progressive is marked in two ways; *He is going* contains the auxiliary *be* and the affix *-ing*. In BE, only the second element is necessary: *he goin' home*. In the so-called present perfect, *I have lived here* is the STE form, while either *I have live here* or *I lived here* is permissible in BE. Some possessives do not contain the *'s* marker; *This is John mother* in BE, in contrast to *This is John's mother* in STE. Notice that because of the order of the nouns, the BE form is unambiguous in referring to the mother of John. When the second noun (the object possessed) is deleted, the BE form does mark the possessive with *'s*: *This is John's* is the possessive, whereas *This is John* has a quite different meaning.

In the three constructions just discussed, STE marks a feature twice (*be* + *ing* for the present progressive, *have* + *en* for the present perfect, and *'s* + order for the possessive), whereas BE marks the feature just once. The converse also occurs. Double and triple negatives, as in *Didn't nobody see it*, are common in BE, just as in Russian. *Or either* is sometimes used in BE as just *either* is used in STE. Neither dialect should be viewed as a "simplified" version of the other.

Agreement between subject and verb in person and number is not obligatory in BE; *She have a bike* and *They was going*. Many common irregular verbs are not marked for the simple past tense. For example, the past tense forms of *come* and *see* are *come* and *see*, respectively. This is not to be interpreted as the lack of a past tense or as an indication that the speakers of BE do not have a concept of the past. The two tenses are negated differently: *I don't see it* is the present tense, whereas *I ain't see it* is the past tense form of the negation.

There are some cases where BE makes a grammatical distinction that STE does not make or that can be indicated in STE only by use of a complex construction. The most important of these is the use of the uninflected form of *be* to indicate habitual or general state. *He be workin'* means that he generally works, perhaps that he has a regular job. *He be with us* means that he is generally with us, perhaps that he lives here. In contrast *he workin'* can mean simply that he is working at this moment and *he with us*, that he is here now.

The verb *be* (in its inflected forms) is often not present in constructions which call for *be* in STE. These constructions include sentences with predicate nouns, *he a friend*, predicate adjectives, *he tired*, and the present progressive tense described above, *he workin' with us*. This absence of *be* has been interpreted by some linguists as a difference in deep structure between the two dialects. The simplest explanation for the absence of *be* in the surface structure is the assumption that *be* is not present in the deep structure. However, there is evidence that this interpretation is not correct. The verb *be* does appear in many contexts: as the last word in a sentence — *There he is* (not *There he*) and *I'm smarter* (*than he*); in tag questions and in negatives — *He ain't here, is he?*; in the past tense — *she was here;* and in other contexts. These facts indicate that *be* is present in the deep structure, but that it is deleted, by a transformation or transformations in certain specified contexts in the process of conversion, to the surface structure. The verb *be* is deleted in just those cases where contraction is possible in STE — *He's a friend*, *He's tired*, *He's with us*, but not **There he's* or **I'm smarter than he's*. The absence of *be* may be viewed as a result of contraction to *he's* by the same rule that exists in STE, followed by deletion of a final *s*, which is a very common phenomenon in BE.

David, he say "Here I come" illustrates the common use of a pronoun following the noun subject of a sentence in BE. This is called **pronominal apposition** and does occur infrequently in STE. It serves to focus attention on the "topic" of the sentence.

Labov has asked speakers of BE to repeat the sentence *Ask Albert if he knows how to play basketball*. The most common response is the production of *Ask Albert do he know how to play basketball*. In Chapter 4, the structure of English direct questions was outlined. The declarative *He knows how to play basketball* has a corresponding direct question of the form *Does he know* how to *play basketball?*. But when this is an indirect question, that is, embedded in a sentence, the question is of the form *If he knows how to play basketball*. The question transformation and the transformation which supplies *do* if necessary do not apply in STE. But in BE, these transformations are applied consistently to both direct and indirect questions. Here we have a common kind of difference between dialects; not the present or absence of a transformation in a dialect but, simply, a change in the conditions under which it is applied. A similar difference exists for imperatives. The direct imperative *Don't do that* becomes *I told you not to do that* in STE but retains its form in BE, *I told you don't do that*.

In addition to these and other syntactic differences between STE and BE, there are many phonological differences. It is probably the phonological differences that often make the dialects almost mutually unintelligible. Many of these differences concern consonants at the ends of words. The liquid *r* is dropped before consonants and at the ends of words. As a result, *sore* and *saw* are **homophones** (words pronounced alike), as are *court* and *caught*. Similarly, *l* may be omitted in the same contexts. Thus, *toll* and *toe* are homophones, as are *help* and *hep*.

Consonant clusters at the ends of words are often simplified, especially if the cluster ends with *t*, *d*, *s*, or *z*. *Past* and *passed* are homophones with *pass*; *called* with *call*; *hits* with *hit*, and so on. In many of these cases it is not easy to determine if this is a phonological difference or a syntactic one. Is the final *d* of *called* deleted because of a phonological rule or because the simple past tense is not inflected in BE? Is the *s* of the third person singular form *hits* deleted because of a consonant cluster simplification rule or because number agreement is not obligatory between subject and verb? Both views account for some of the evidence and leave other forms unexplained.

In most cases, there is no distinction between [i] and [ɛ] before nasals and liquids; *pin* and *pen* are homophones, as are *cheer* and *chair*. Often the sounds [ay] and [aw] are changed to the simple vowel [a]. In this case, *find*, *found*, and *fond* are homophones.

The fricative /φ/ in final position is changed to /f/; thus *with* and *bath* are pronounced /wIf/ and /baef/, respectively.

It is still a matter of disagreement whether differences in pronounciation, that is, phonetic representaitons, are due to differences in underlying representation or to differences in the phonological rules that convert underlying representations into phonetic representations. This is a question that has important implications for the teaching of reading, which will be discussed in the final section of this chapter. However, it does seem clear that the majority, even if not all, of the differences are in the rules, and that in these cases the underlying representations are the same in both dialects. An example of such a difference follows.

Many speakers of BE pronounce *risk* as [rIs] and test as [tɛs] From consideration of these forms alone there is no evidence that the final consonant is present in the underlying representations of these words. The most common plural forms for these words are [rIsəz] and [tɛsəz]. Again, it does not appear that the final consonants are present. But suppose a suffix, *-y* or *-ing*, is added. Now the forms are pronounced [rIskiy] and [tɛstIn], in which the final consonants are present. The final consonants sometimes appear even in the root word, when it is followed by a word that begins with a vowel. The conclusion that the consonant is indeed present in the underlying representation appears difficult to reconcil with observed plural forms. However, if the phonological rules are formulated in the proper order, all the observed forms can be explained simply.

Underlying representations: /tɛst/   /tɛst+z/   /tɛst+In/

(1) *consonant-cluster:*   [tɛs/   [tɛsz]   [tɛstIn]

   simplification: [st] → [s]
   if followed by anything
   except a vowel

(2) [ə]-*insertion:*   [tɛs]   [tɛsəz]   [tɛstIn]

the STE rule that inserts the vowel [ə] between two consonants produced at approximately the same location in the mouth; it produces the observed phonetic representations

There are also vocabulary differences between BE and STE. A surprisingly high proportion of slang expressions in STE originate in BE. Probably some words and expressions that occur in both dialects have different meanings, and this contributes to the difficulty of communication. "More research is needed" is a cliche, but nonetheless true for being a cliche.

BLACK CHILDREN AND BLACK ENGLISH

At this point it would be appropriate to look at detailed longitudinal linguistic studies of the development of language by black children, studies of the type done by Brown and Bellugi (1964), Braine (1963), Bloom (1970), and so on. There are none. Labov has worked primarily with black adolescent boys and, to a lesser extent, with black eight and nine year olds. By this age he finds a well-developed linguistic system.

Unfortunately, this lack of knowledge of language development by young black children has not prevented many psychologists, educators, and others from formulating hypotheses or even dogmatic conclusions. There is a widespread belief that the well-documented academic failure of many black children is due to an impoverished or retarded language. The view, often called the **verbal deficit hypothesis,** can be summarized as follows: *Because Negro children from the ghetto hear very little language, much of it ill-formed, they are impoverished in their means of verbal expression. They cannot formulate complete sentences; they speak in "giant words." They do not know the names of common objects, they lack crucial concepts, and they cannot produce or comprehend logical statements. Sometimes they are even reported to have no language at all.*

It is entirely possible that some black children do have difficulties in language development. We know that many aspects of cognitive development are slowed by extreme poverty and other social factors. Nevertheless, the verbal deficit hypothesis, as just stated, is based on shaky assumptions and evidence. First is the implicit assumption that language plays a predominant role in thinking. As we have seen in the previous chapter, this continues to be a controversial claim. Second, the hypothesis does not distinguish between structure and function. Are these children deficient in their mastery of the linguistic system or in their ability to use language in classification, problem-solving, communication, memory, and other cognitive tasks? Third, observed differences between the speech of middle-class white children and that of poor black children confuse race and social class factors. Although the methodological problems are great, due to the overrepresentation of black Americans in the lower social classes, they must be overcome because race and social class are very different variables. A plausible hypothesis is that race is correlated with differing linguistic structure, that is, black and white children master their respective dialects with approximately equal facility, whereas social class is correlated with function, the ability to use language for cognitive tasks. Studies of social class variations in language belong more properly in the next chapter than in this one. And, finally, Labov (1970b) has provided a well-reasoned critical analysis of some "observed differences."

Labov questions the sample of speech from black children available to most investigators. Simply placing a black child in a room with a large, albeit friendly, white adult will produce a defensive withdrawal from the situation, not a fluent sample of speech. Even placing the child in a room with a black adult who is familiar to the child will not draw out the most representative speech from the child. But the situation changed drastically when the procedure was modified:

> . . . in the next interview with Leon, Clarence
>
> (1) brought along a supply of potato chips, changing the "interview" into something more in the nature of a party;
>
> (2) brought along Leon's best friend, 8-year-old Gregory;
>
> (3) reduced the height imbalance (when Clarence got down on the floor of Leon's room, he dropped from 6 ft. 2 in. to 3 ft. 6 in.);
>
> (4) introduced taboo words and taboo topics, and proved to Leon's surprise that one can say anything into our microphone without any fear of retailiation [Labov, 1970b, p. 8].

This procedure led to large quantities of active, argumentative, fluent speech from eight-year-old Leon.

Many of the instances of "illogical" speech from black children are misinterpreted dialect differences. Multiple negations, such as *He doesn't know nothing*, are often pointed to as an example of the lack of logic in the mind of the child. Many languages of the world use multiple negation — Russian and old Anglo-Saxon, a forerunner of Modern English — while others use only single negations — Modern English. BE falls in the former category, STE in the latter. Both types of languages are "logical;" that is, they can be used to convey meaning quite precisely, as long as the listener *knows the rules of the language.*

The verbal deficit hypothesis is contradicted by the observation by many social scientists and others familiar with black culture that there is great emphasis on verbal fluency. There are several stylized types of aggressive verbal behavior, such as "basing" and "sounding" (see the annotations for Reading 9.2); and, in general, superior verbal fluency is a mark of distinction.

This observation is supported by the results of one of the few trustworthy cross-ethnic group comparisons of mental abilities, conducted by Stodolsky and Lesser (1967). They were not so much interested in overall *level* of cognitive abilities — which they knew to be partially a function of socioeconomic status (SES) — but in the *pattern* of these abilities. Are there characteristic patterns of abilities for ethnic groups? To determine the answer, they administered four tests — verbal, reasoning, number, and spatial conceptualization — to four ethnic groups in New York City — Chinese, Jewish, Negro, and Puerto Rican first-graders — of two SES levels. The tests were constructed to be as culture-fair as possible (references to giraffes or xylophones were eliminated in favor of references to fire hydrants, buses, and so on). They were administered in the primary language of the children by an examiner who was of their ethnic group. Stodolsky and Lesser found that there was indeed a characteristic pattern of abilities of each ethnic group. The absolute level, but not the pattern, was a function of SES. The verbal ability of the Negro children, far from being a handicap, was clearly their greatest strength; in fact, only one other group exceeded their average score on verbal ability. A replication study with Chinese and Negro first-graders in Boston produced the same results. It is difficult to reconcile this high assessment of black children's verbal abilities at age six or seven with the low assessment implicit in the verbal deficit hypothesis at age three or four.

Are black children bidialectal, at least to the extent of understanding a second dialect? Black English and Standard English are not foreign languages to each other but distinct dialects of the same language. Black children undoubtedly hear a great deal of STE on television, in the schools, and so forth. We may be overemphasizing the differences by focussing on the speech produced by each group. The two dialects are to a degree mutually intelligible, as would be expected, given the considerable common core of rules. But the small body of evidence available indicates that comprehension of the "nonnative dialect" is inferior to that of the "native dialect," for both black and white children. Osser, Wang, and Zaid (1969) examined the ability of black and white five year olds to imitate and comprehend various constructions in STE. Black children were significantly less able than white children to imitate them, even when translations into corresponding BE constructions were counted as correct; they were also less successful at comprehending STE in a version of the ICP test discussed in Chapter 4. However, these conclusions are weakened by the fact that, as is common in such research, race and social class were confounded. Osser et al. compared white middle-class children with black lower-class children.

Baratz (1969) compared black inner-city third and fifth graders with lower middle-class white children on a sentence repetition task, thus diminishing the influence of the social class factor. Two equivalent taped versions of the test were devised, one in STE and one in BE. In both, the speaker was William Stewart; he was judged by both black and white children to be black when speaking BE, and white when speaking STE. Black children did significantly better on the BE sentences than on the STE ones; conversely, white children did significantly better on the STE sentences than on the BE ones. Taken together, the Osser et al. and Baratz studies demonstrate that neither black nor white children are truly bidialectal. This conclusion emphasizes still further the problems of communication in our society in general and in the educational process in particular.

The Role of Peers

Stewart (1964a) has observed that there is not just one black dialect of English in the Washington, D.C., area but a whole series of them. At one extreme, there is a dialect that is fairly close to the STE in Washington. Stewart calls this dialect "acrolect" (from Greek, *acro* meaning "apex"). At the other extreme is the dialect that is most different from STE, which is called the "basilect" (from Greek, *basi* meaning "bottom"). The features of BE discussed earlier are found most regularly and completely in the basilect. In between basilect and acrolect there is a range of dialect levels, and most Washington Negro speech falls in this middle range. Of course, any individual speaker will shift between levels depending on the situation. However, in addition to the influence of the situation, there is a strong and interesting age pattern.

According to Stewart, the consistent use of the basilect is largely restricted to young children. At about the age of seven or eight, the dialect begins to shift. Many of the features of higher levels of the dialect series begin to appear in speech after this.

Some verbs begin to be marked in the past tense, for example. As a result, the speaker now functions at a dialect level that is higher up in the series than the basilect, although he may still be quite far from the acrolect.

This dialect shift appears to take place quite automatically, in a way independent of formal education. Schooling does not seem to be the cause or to affect it greatly. It is more than coincidental that this shift coincides with a change in the informal social structure of the peer group. At about this age, boys make the transition from "small boy" to "big boy." Both adults and big boys regard the basilect as the natural way for younger children to talk, so that a boy who wants to join the older age group is motivated to change his speech. This rapid dialect shift is much less common among girls, and this may be related to the fact that age-grading into "small" and "big" is much less rigid for them than for boys.

Such an influence of the peer group raises a puzzling and difficult question: from whom do children learn language? Stewart has written:

> It is easy to find cases involving second- or third-generation Washington Negro families in which the parents are speakers of a quite standard variety of English [the acrolect], but where the children's speech is much closer to that of the newer immigrants (from the South) [the basilect or something close to it]. The explanation seems to be that heavy postwar immigration has dialectally swamped much of the younger generation of native Washingtonians. This phenomenon, incidentally, seems to support the theory that children learn more language behavior from members of their own peer group than from their parents, and suggests that educatory concern for the quality of "language in the home" may be misplaced [1964b].

Labov has found similar phenomena for children of both races in the New York area. In many middle class areas of northeastern New Jersey, many parents are from New York City and speak a dialect that drops r's before consonants and at the ends of words. But almost all their children pronounce the r's. It is the local group of the children's peers which determines the new generation's speech patterns.

There is a long-standing split on this question between linguists and psychologists. Linguists, in general, have argued that children speak more like their peers than like their parents. Children of immigrants, raised in a home where one language is spoken, but who play and go to school with children speaking another language, speak the latter. Psychologists, on the other hand, have offered evidence that the speech of first children is generally superior to that of later children, and they have argued that this is due to their greater opportunity for conversation with parents.

This apparent disagreement is probably the result of failure to distinguish between competence and performance. Immigrant children have no difficulty in understanding their parents; in other words, they have linguistic competence in *both* languages. The fact that they speak only one of them is a social fact, not a psycholinguistic one. Furthermore, age may be important in the way that Stewart has suggested: there are specific periods in which peer group influence is especially strong.

It is easy to speculate on the role of parents and peers in the language development of lower class children of either race, given the larger size of families in this setting. In addition, a large proportion of mothers work, leaving the children with even less adult contact. At the present time, however, this can only be speculation. Another unknown is the role of television. In our society, there is a higher proportion of time spent watching television in the lower SES levels. Television provides a supply of verbal stimulation to the child, but this verbal stimulation is not contingent on the child's actions or speech. Does this help or hinder language development?

Dialect and Reading

In the previous chapter, the discussion of reading concerned children only learning to read their native language. Speakers of a nonstandard dialect such as BE face a more difficult task. At least four alternative policies may be conceived.

STANDARD DIALECT

Teach the children to read, using the standard dialect. This is essentially the current policy in most schools, and it is often a failure. It confuses two quite distinct tasks: learning to read and learning a second dialect. It either ignores or stigmatizes as erroneous the child's own dialect. Many black children will read the printed words *I saw it* as "I see it." This is taken to be a reading error. It is difficult to eradicate, and together with many similar errors, leads to anxiety, frustration, and ultimately even poorer reading performance. In fact, since the simple past tense of *see* (which is what the printed word *saw* means) is pronounced "see" in their dialect, they have successfully matched the printed word to the spoken word. There is no reading error at all. They have actually performed a more impressive achievement than their classmate who pronounces "saw," for he has more guidance from the spelling. Many of these children will become even more confused when the teacher attempts to explain that *u* denotes the sound in *sure* while *o* denotes the sound in *shore*, since for them the two words sound exactly alike. It is not difficult to produce dozens of such examples.

FOREIGN-LANGUAGE TECHNIQUES

Teach the children STE, perhaps utilizing foreign-language techniques, such as an oral language, and then teach reading using materials in the standard dialect. This is a straightforward approach to the problem. It assumes that the ability to speak the standard dialect is a useful one, and that reading is learned most efficiently in a dialect the child knows. Nevertheless this is not likely to be an effective policy. The problem is the first step, teaching STE as a second dialect. Elementary school programs to teach foreign languages have become quite popular in recent years, but they have not been notably successful. There are several factors responsible for this lack of success. One is that there is very little psychological or pedagogical research on teaching foreign language to young children. Another is opportunity to practice with the new language or dialect. Many elementary school programs have failed because they provided only 3 to 5 hours a week of instruction, and there was no other opportunity for the children to use the language. The same situation is likely to arise in the teaching of STE as a second dialect. For many of the students, this dialect will simply be left behind when the child leaves school every afternoon.

Motivation is perhaps the most important factor in learning a new language. Foreign languages are learned best by learners who think highly of speakers of that language. For example, those students who admire French and French culture, learn French most successfully. Now young children are likely to have quite neutral feelings about a second language, such as French or Spanish. But young black children are likely to have strong negative feelings about white speakers of STE.

NATIVE DIALECT

Teach the child to read using his own dialect. This approach is currently under active investigation, especially by researchers at the Center for Applied Linguistics (Baratz & Shuy, 1969). Such a policy is a great improvement over the present one, for it simply eliminates an irrelevant task — learning a second dialect — from the context of learning to read.

There is evidence that such a program is entirely practical on psychological and pedagogical grounds. In an experimental program in Chiapas, Mexico, children were introduced to reading in their native Indian languages. When they had mastered their vernacular primars, they were placed in the first grade, where all subsequent instruction was carried out in Spanish. Later reading tests showed that those Indian children who had first been taught to read in their native tongues read Spanish with better understanding than their peers who had been instructed solely in Spanish. Children who were native speakers of Pitean, in Sweden, received an initial ten weeks of reading instruction in Pitean before being switched to literary Swedish; they learned to read more rapidly than the Pitean-speaking children who were taught to read in Swedish from the outset. By the end of the first year, the experimental group had surpassed the control group even in reading standard Swedish.

Despite such successes, some difficulties can be foreseen in extending such an approach to our own society. First, we have assumed that there is only *one* Black English. Unfortunately, very little is known about variations in this dialect, but we would expect to find at least some regional variation. If this is of sufficient magnitude, different sets of beginning reading materials would be necessary. This is made even more likely by the fact that individuals within the black community vary in the exact dialect they use (recall Stewart's findings in Washington, D.C., p. 252). A second possible difficulty is parental attitude. Parents who have succeeded in mastering, or are attempting to master, STE, and wish their children to do the same, are not likely to look with favor on an educational program that appears to reinforce BE. Attitudes toward dialect differences are strong and difficult to change. But they do change at times. A growing acceptance of BE, perhaps in a general acceptance of bidialectism, may in time eliminate this problem. Some critical attention should be paid to the assumption that if the children are at certain times encouraged to use one dialect (BE), their chances of eventually mastering STE are diminished. This is a common assumption among educators but one for which there is really no evidence. The converse is certainly possible: the teacher's acceptance of the child's dialect might serve as a model for the child's later acceptance of STE.

A third objection is that, as stated, this policy avoids the question of whether it is important for all children in our society to be able to read materials in STE. If the answer to this is yes, then additional programs are necessary. Stewart (1969) has suggested a three-stage process. In the first stage, reading materials are in BE syntactic form; *Charles and Michael, they out playing.* At the second stage, the most important syntactic features of STE are introduced, such as the inflected forms of the verb to be: *Charles and Michael, they are out playing.* And in the third stage, sentences are brought into full conformity with STE: *Charles and Michael are out playing.* This reinserts teaching a second dialect into teaching reading, but in a much more controlled way than at present. Like all programs that use techniques or materials for initial reading that are different from those used in later reading (another example is the i.t.a.), the most important question is an empirical one: does it work, or is there a major problem at the transition?

The problem of orthography is also a difficult one. To be consistent with this policy, a writing system reflecting the children's own pronunciation should be used. But this necessitates even greater changes as the reading materials are made more similar to STE. Stewart has suggested a compromise solution, in which BE pronunciations are indicated by minor changes in the conventional writing system of English, with frequent use of the apostrophe as a cue for differences between dialects. Some examples are *ben'* for *bend, bendin'* for *bending, 'bout* for *about,* and *'posed to* for *supposed to.* The apostrophes serve as indicators of points where later instruction will occur.

MATERIAL IN STE READ IN NATIVE DIALECT

Teach the children to read material printed in STE in their own dialect. In fact, this is what many black children spontaneously attempt — to read *I saw it* as *I see it.* It is not so different from the reading process for literate Chinese. Written Chinese is uniform throughout the country, although the spoken language varies considerably. This policy avoids the three difficulties associated with the previous approach. The outcome of such a policy would be children who have access to newspapers, books, and magazines which are overwhelmingly in STE. Two problems are foreseeable. The first is that extraordinarily sensitive and well-trained teachers, capable of great flexibility are required. A teacher's criterion for correct reading must vary with the individual child. A child who normally pronounces the past tense of the verb *see* as "saw" but reads *saw* as "see" must be recognized as having made an error, although a speaker of a dialect that pronounces the past tense of *see* as "see" must be recognized as having read correctly. A related danger is the possibility of confusion to the children due to this situation. In addition to varying her criterion with the individual child, the teacher must discriminate between key indicators of reading ability and the much larger and more salient range of dialect differences. Labov offers this example:

> For the teacher to make this distinction, it is necessary that he know what correct reading sounds like. If a Negro child reads *He always looked for trouble when he read the news* as *He a'way' look' fo' trouble when he read* (rhyming with *bed*) *de news*, the teacher should be able to judge that he is reading correctly. But if he clearly articulates *He always looked for trouble when he read the news*, yet rhymes *read* with *seed*, he is not reading correctly and has to be stopped [1970a, p. 44].

A second problem is that reading might actually be made more difficult for the children in this way because they will have to "translate" the printed word into their own dialect. In fact, children do not seem to have this problem, but this policy has not been attempted on a large enough scale to permit evaluation. Lack of difficulty in reading in this fashion may be evidence for two conclusions stated in this and the previous chapter: that reading is fundamentally a matter of identifying the underlying representations of words or morphemes, and that the underlying representations are nearly identical in BE and STE.

Summary

With the decline of the "melting pot" theory of American society, social scientists have begun to explore and appreciate the diversity of culture and dialect in the country. Recognition of Black English as an autonomous dialect has been delayed by strongly negative attitudes toward it and its speakers. The language of many black children has been seriously underestimated. An educational system should capitalize on the capacities the children bring to school, rather than penalize them. How best to do this, for example, how best to teach reading, will require a combination of imagination and careful research on psychological and pedagogical questions. However, it is hard to resist the conclusion that social factors, especially attitudes, play a dominant role in education, and only a major change in our society can fully resolve the problems.

9.1 Style Shifting*

One of the fundamental principles of sociolinguistic investigation might simply be stated as *There are no single-style speakers.* By this we mean that every speaker will show some variation in phonological and syntactic rules according to the immediate context in which he is speaking. We can demonstrate that such stylistic shifts are determined by (a) the relations of the speaker, addressee, and audience, and particularly the relations of power of solidarity among them; (b) the wider social context or "domain": school, job, home, neighborhood, church; (c) the topic. One must add of course that the stylistic range and competence of the speaker may vary greatly. Children may have a very narrow range in both the choices open to them and the social contexts they respond to. Old men often show a narrow range in that their motivation for style shifting disappears along with their concern for power relationships [for example, old men no longer trying to make it].

We apply the principle stated above in a very concrete way when carrying out research with face-to-face interviews. We do not judge the absolute stylistic level of the speaker by some absolute standard of "casualness." We know that, as long as we are asking questions and receiving answers, the speaker is using a relatively "careful" or "consultative" style, and that he possesses a more "casual" or intimate style with which he argues with his friends or

*From Labov, W. *The study of nonstandard English.* Copyright © 1970 by the National Council of Teachers of English. Reprinted by permission of the publisher and W. Labov. Pp. 19–21.

quarrels with his family. There are techniques for obtaining casual speech in an interview situation, but the soundest approach is to observe the speaker interacting with the peers who control his speech in everyday life when the observer is not there.

Well-developed social variables show a systematic range of style shifting which is correlated to the amount of attention paid to speech. We can easily observe such style shifting in certain long-standing variables which are common to almost all dialects of English. The *th* of *thing* and *that* can appear as a smooth fricative *"th"* sound, the standard variant; as a *"t"*-like sound lightly or strongly articulated; as a combination of these two; or as a zero as in *Gimme' at*. For most Americans, the proportions of these forms are nicely blended and graded for each stylistic level — at different absolute levels for different social groups and different regions. Similarly, the alternation of -ing and -in' in unstressed syllables is a systematic stylistic variable for most Americans — again at different levels for different classes and regions.

At one time, the dialect areas of the eastern United States were sharply divided into r-less and r-pronouncing areas, according to whether consonantal r is pronounced in words like *car* and *card*. But in the last two decades the r-pronounciation of "general American" has become accepted as the standard of broadcast networks and of careful middle class pronunciation almost everywhere. As a result, we find that the new "prestige" pronunication of r in final and pre-consonantal position has become a sociolinguistic variable in the older r-less areas. Almost all younger and middle-aged speakers will show some styles shifting with r, so that in the more formal styles they will use more r and in casual speech practically none at all.

The grammatical variables that show style shifting are quite well-known in general, though we usually lack the exact knowledge of where and when these features are used to signal change of style. Some are well-established stereotypes, like *ain't*. Although dictionaries may vary in the way they label *ain't*, most native speakers are quite clear in their sociolinguistic approach to this word — in their social evaluation of the form. To make the point clear, imagine a community in which *ain't* is the formal style and in which people correct *isn't* to *ain't* when they are careful. Such a community would be very odd indeed — obviously not a part of the same American speech community in which we all live.

The "double negative" or negative concord is an important stylistic marker; it allows nonstandard speakers to express negatives in a particularly emphatic fashion by reduplicating the negative forms (*Nobody don't know about that*) and at the same time register their adherence to the nonstandard form which is stylistically opposed to the standard (*Nobody knows anything about that*).

The passive has two forms in English, which are closely allied but perhaps not equivalent in meaning. If we ask "What happened to him?" the answer can be "He got run over" or "He was run over." The colloquial form is clearly the former; nonstandard dialects depend almost entirely upon this got-passive, to the exclusion of the be-passive. As a result, the be-passive has acquired a standard, rather careful flavor which it would not have if there were no opposing forms.

In all these examples, we can easily demonstrate the meaning of the stylistic alternation by observing the direction of correction in false starts. In almost every interview, one will find speakers making corrections like "Nobody told him noth — anything about it." No matter how rare or how common such corrections may be, we find that they uniformly run in the same direction, since the more formal style is associated with a mental set in which greater attention is paid to speech and the less formal style with a casual and spontaneous use of language in which the minimum attention is given to the speech process.

9.2 An Annotated Transcription of a Sample of Black English[*]

. . . (an) original Black English passage, which is a dramatized enactment of a situation occurring in the ghetto. In this passage we have simply transcribed and edited a section from a phonograph record

[*]From Wolfram, W. A., & Fasold, R. W. Toward reading materials for speakers of Black English: Three linguistically appropriate passages. In J. C. Baratz & R. W. Shuy (Eds.), *Teaching black children to read.* Washington, D.C.: Center for Applied Linguistics, 1969. Pp. 144–147, 152–154. Reprinted by permission.

(Street and Gangland Rhythms, Folkways 5589) and arranged it as a quasi-drama. The record contains the reasonable spontaneous speech of six pre-adolescent Harlem boys. We have made no grammatical changes in the text so that at places it may appear that certain forms are importations from Standard English . . . Our annotations indicate those places where there exist clear-cut contrasts between the grammatical systems of Standard English and Black English. Phonological differences are not annotated except where they affect grammatical form. Differences in the semantic context of lexical items have not generally been noted.

Dumb Boy

(*Scene I*)

CALVIN: One day I was walking. Then I met Lennie. Lennie say,[1,2] "Calvin, what happened to your lip?" I said, "Nothing." And then Lenn came over to me and he say,[1,2] "What you mean by nothing?" Like he always say[2] because he's always interested in me and me and him[5] is[6] good friends. So I told him what happened.[3] "This guy named[3] Pierre, he[7] about fifteen . . ."

LENNIE: Yeah?

CALVIN: He came over to me . . .

LENNIE: Uh huh.

CALVIN: And he hit me in my[8] lip because . . .

LENNIE: Yeah?

CALVIN: I . . .

LENNIE: Done[9] what?

CALVIN: Had done copied[9] off his paper in school.

(*Scene II*)

PIERRE: Uhh, I told you don't do that no more.[10,11]

CALVIN: Come on, please leave me alone, please, please.

PIERRE: Next time I catch you copying off somebody in there, you know what I'll do? I'll strangle you to death! Don't do that no more,[10] hear?

CALVIN: I'm sorry.

(*Scene III*)

LENNIE: What's that guy[12] name?

CALVIN: Pierre.

LENNIE: Where[4] he live at?

CALVIN: Around our block.

LENNIE: How old is he?

CALVIN: About the size of the other guy named Pierre around our block.

LENNIE: Well, tonight it's[13] gonna be a party at 118th Street where I live at. You bring him around there, hear?

CALVIN: I surely will.

LENNIE: Okay.

(Scene IV)

CALVIN: So when I walked in there, everything was silent.

LENNIE: Is that the guy over there?

CALVIN: Yeah.

LENNIE: Hey you, what[4] you hit my little brother for?

PIERRE: Did he tell you what happened,[3] man?

LENNIE: Yeah, he told me what happened.[3]

PIERRE: But you . . . but you should tell your people to teach him to go to school, man. I know I didn't have a right to hit him. But he was copying off me and the teacher said . . . I forgot to tell the teacher.

LENNIE: What[4] you mean you forgot to tell the teacher? What[4] you mean to tell my parents to make him go to school to learn? What[4] you mean by that? What[4] you mean?

PIERRE: Just like I said, man, he can't be dumb, man. I don't be[14] with him all his life.

LENNIE: You basing or you sounding?[15]

PIERRE: I ain't doing neither[10] one.

LENNIE: That's more like it. But we[7] gonna deal tonight.

PIERRE: If you can't face it, don't waste[16] it. If you can't face it, don't waste[16] it.

ANNOTATIONS

1. Some verbs, like "come" and "say", are not marked for past tense in Black English narratives, even when the context is past time.

2. Black English lacks the -*s* suffix which marks the present tense with third person singular subjects in Standard English.

3. When the suffix -*ed* is realized by a stop following a base form which ends in a consonant, the stop is not pronounced (thus, the pronunciation /neym/, for Standard English /neymd/). This reflects a Black English phonological pattern in which syllable final consonant clusters in Standard English correspond to simple consonants in Black English (see note 16). The pattern illustrates how phonological constraints in Black English affect the presence of certain grammatical categories.

4. Sentences which would have a pre-posed verbal auxiliary in Standard English due to the formation of a content question generally have no auxiliary at all in the corresponding Black English sentence. For example, the "do" which would appear in the Standard English equivalent of questions like What do you mean by nothing? is absent for this reason.

5. In coordinate noun phrases, the distinction between objective and subjective forms of the pronoun is often neutralized, so that the "objective" form may function as a grammatical subject.

6. Occasionally (and particularly with coordinate constructions), the singular conjugated forms of "be" ("is," "was") occur with the plural subject in Black English.

7. The present tense form of the copula frequently is not realized in a number of different syntactic environments in Black English. Generally, where the contracted form of the copula may occur in Standard English the stative condition is indicated simply by word order in Black English.

8. In Standard English, sentences like "kiss her on the cheek" and "punch Jack in the stomach" involving a verb of physical contact, a personal nominal reference and body part, the definite article "the" is used with the body part although it belongs to the same person referred to by the personal noun or pronoun. In Black English, the possessive pronoun is used in these constructions instead of the article.

9. The use of "done" plus the past tense of a verb is a construction indicating completed action. Some speakers occasionally include a form of "have" as in "had done copied . . ."

10. In Black English, negation is typically marked not only in the main verb phrase but also in each indefinite determiner or indefinite pronoun in the sentence, as well as in certain adverbs like "hardly" and "never."

11. An embedded imperative may be retained in its original quoted form instead of being realized in an infinitive construction (e.g., "I told you don't do that no more" instead of "I told you not to do that no more.")

12. Black English lacks possessive -*s* so that possession is indicated only by the order of the items.

13. "It," in Black English, can be used as an "expletive" or "resentative" in addition to its function as a pronoun referring to a specific object or participant. In this usage it is equivalent to Standard English "there."

14. The form "be" can be used in Black English as a verb [to] denote(s) iteration or habituation.

15. The expressions "basing" and "sounding" refer to type of aggressive verbal behavior. "Basing" is a kind of back-talk and "sounding" refers to a special type of ritual insult.

16. The items "face" and "waste" have rhyming endings in Black English because the final stop member of a syllable final consonant cluster is frequently absent.

SELECTED REFERENCES

Baratz, J. C. A bi-dialectal task for determining language proficiency in economically disadvantaged Negro children. *Child Development*, 1969, **40,** 889–901.

Baratz, J. C., & Shuy, R. W. (Eds.) *Teaching black children to read.* Washington D.C.: Center for Applied Linguistics, 1969.

Bloom, L. *Language development: Form and function in emerging grammars.* Cambridge, Mass.: M.I.T. Press, 1970.

Bolinger, D. *Aspects of language.* New York: Harcourt Brace Jovanovich, 1968.

Braine, M. D. S. The ontogeny of English phrase structure: The first phase. *Language*, 1963, **39,** 1–13.

Brown, R., & Bellugi, U. Three processes in the child's acquisition of syntax. *Harvard Educational Review*, 1964, **34,** 133–151.

Labov, W. *The study of nonstandard English.* Urbana, Ill.: National Council of Teachers of English, 1970. (a)

Labov, W. The logic of nonstandard English. In J. E. Alatis (Ed.), *20th annual round table.* Washington, D.C.: Georgetown University Press, 1970. Pp. 1–39. (b)

Lambert, W. E. A social psychology of bilingualism. *Journal of Social Issues*, 1967, **23,** 91–109.

New English Bible. Oxford: Oxford University Press, 1970.

Osser, H., Wang, M. D., & Zaid, F. The young child's ability to imitate and comprehend speech: A comparison of two subcultural groups. *Child Development*, 1969, **40,** 1063–1075.

Stewart, W. A. Urban Negro speech: Sociolinguistic factors affecting English teaching. In R. W. Shuy (Ed.), *Social dialects and language learning*. Champaign, Ill.: National Council of Teachers of English, 1964. Pp. 10–18. (a)

Stewart, W. A. (Ed.), *Non-standard speech and the teaching of English*. Washington, D.C.: Center for Applied Linguistics, 1964. (b)

Stewart, W. A. On the use of Negro dialect in the teaching of reading. In J. C. Baratz & R. W. Shuy (Eds.), *Teaching black children to read*. Washington, D.C.: Center for Applied Linguistics, 1969. Pp. 156–219.

Stodolsky, S., & Lesser, G. Learning patterns in the disadvantaged. *Harvard Educational Review*, 1967, **37,** 546–593.

Wolfram, W. A., & Fasold, R. W. Toward reading materials for speakers of black English: Three linguistically appropriate passages. In J. C. Baratz & R. W. Shuy (Eds.), *Teaching black children to read*. Washington, D.C.: Center for Applied Linguistics, 1969. Pp. 138–155.

FURTHER READING

Baratz, J. C., & Shuy, R. W. *Teaching black children to read*. Washington, D.C.: Center for Applied Linguistics, 1969.

Bolinger, D. *Aspects of language*. New York: Harcourt Brace Javanovich, 1968, Chap. 9.

Labov, William. *The study of nonstandard English*. Urbana, Ill.: National Council of Teachers of English, 1970.

Stewart, W. Sociolinguistic factors in the history of American Negro dialects, *Florida FL Reporter*, Spring, 1967, **5;** and Continuity and change in American Negro dialects, *Florida FL Reports*, Spring, 1968, **6.** Both available from the National Council of Teachers of English.

10

Language and Early Education

Measuring Language Development

Any therapeutic discipline, such as medicine, psychotherapy, or education, is highly dependent on its assessment measures and diagnostic techniques. However, this dependence is especially strong for education. We use tests to define the problem for us — "poor children score low on the Stanford-Binet intelligence test" — and also to measure how effective our educational programs are — "Professor X's preschool raises IQ scores by 12 points." Tests are also important for noneducational research. A great deal of research on the effects of various environmental factors on language development can be conducted by comparing language development scores of children of differing social class, native language of parents, birth order, number of siblings, amount of television watched, and so on. How good are the currently available tests of language development?

The three most widely used measures of language development are the Peabody Picture Vocabulary Test, Stanford-Binet

Intelligence Scale, and Illinois Test of Psycholinguistic Abilities. Although the Stanford-Binet is seldom specifically labeled as a language test, it is often used as an evaluation measure by preschool programs that claim to emphasize language development. Most of the research on early education programs to be discussed later in this chapter has used one or more of these devices.

THE PEABODY PICTURE VOCABULARY TEST

The Peabody Picture Vocabulary Test (PPVT) (Dunn, 1965) is well described by its name. The child is presented with four simple line drawings at a time and asked to "Put your finger on the picture of the word I have just said." The words proceed from common to rare. The test is fast to administer, easy to score, and does not require a verbal response, as it is a receptive vocabulary test. Table 10-1 contains a sample of the list and the norms for various ages. As a vocabulary test, the PPVT is carefully designed and well-standardized (although the list appears to be overly loaded with nouns relative to children's vocabulary as a whole). However, it is widely used as a general language assessment tool. The implicit assumption in this use is that vocabulary growth alone reflects language development; there is little or no supporting evidence for such an assumption such as correlations between vocabulary growth and other aspects of language development. The reader should judge for himself the extent to which the PPVT is culture-loaded, that is, assumes a specific cultural background on the part of the child.

TABLE 10-1 *The Peabody Picture Vocabulary Test, Form A*

1. car	13. digging	25. wiener	37. peacock	49. signal
2. cow	14. skirt	26. teacher	38. queen	50. capsule
3. baby	15. catching	27. building	39. coach	60. bronco
4. girl	16. drum	28. arrow	40. whip	70. stunt
5. ball	17. leaf	29. kangeroo	41. net	80. coil
6. clock	18. trying	30. accident	42. freckle	90. submerge
7. clown	19. force	31. nest	43. eagle	100. amphibian
8. key	20. bat	32. caboose	44. twist	110. encumbered
9. can	21. bee	33. envelope	45. shining	120. tartan
10. chicken	22. bush	34. picking	46. dial	130. gauntlet
11. blowing	23. pouring	35. badge	47. yawning	140. raze
12. fan	24. sewing	36. goggles	48. tumble	150. pensile

Norms (no. correct)	Age
20	2;6
25	2;9
30	3;1
35	3;5
40	3;10
45	4;5
50	5;1
60	6;10
70	8;9
80	10;8
90	12;11
100	15;7

SOURCE: Adapted from Dunn, L. *Peabody picture vocabulary test*. Minneapolis: American Guidance Service, 1965.

The PPVT is often used, not only as a measure of general language development, but as a general intelligence test, probably because of the speed and ease of administration. And indeed, PPVT scores correlate quite highly (typically in the 70's) with Stanford-Binet IQ scores, which is the customary validation technique for intelligence measures.

STANFORD-BINET INTELLIGENCE SCALE

Another test used for language assessment is the Stanford-Binet Intelligence Scale (1960). The use of this test for language measurement is perhaps not a bad idea; the test is often attacked for being excessively verbal. Reading 10.1 includes the test items for the 3;6 level. Most of the items require comprehension of complex verbal instructions, and many require a verbal response.

The use of the Stanford-Binet with disadvantaged children is often criticized because of the heavy verbal component. The evidence reviewed in the previous chapter suggests that we should be wary of assuming that disadvantaged children, especially black children, have retarded language development. Dialect differences, such as, *I ask Alvin do he know how to play basketball*, have been misinterpreted as failure to master the structure of English, when in fact they demonstrate mastery of a somewhat different set of rules. When relatively nonverbal intelligence tests, such as the Leiter International Performance Scale (Arthur, 1952) and Raven's Progressive Matrices (Raven, 1966), have been used, disadvantaged children have been found to score even lower than on the highly verbal Stanford-Binet. This finding is support for the use of the Stanford-Binet as an intelligence measure, but it further illustrates the complexity of the relationship between language, cognitive development, and social class.[1]

A common defense of the Stanford-Binet is that IQ scores derived from this test are remarkably good predictors of later school performance. To be sure, interpreting this fact is not easy. Perhaps the only safe conclusion at the present time is that IQ tests and school programs are designed for each other.

The PPVT and the Stanford-Binet make complementary errors in assessing language. The PPVT oversimplifies language by restricting it to vocabulary; whereas the Stanford-Binet overcomplicates language by combining linguistic and cognitive tasks. It is difficult to determine exactly which language abilities are required for successful performance on the Stanford-Binet.

ILLINOIS TEST OF PSYCHOLINGUISTIC ABILITIES

By far the most commonly used assessment device is the Illinois Test of Psycholinguistic Abilities (ITPA) (Kirk, McCarthy, & Kirk, 1968). The ITPA is composed of twelve subtests, which are defined and illustrated in Reading 10.2. The present version of the ITPA is a revision of the experimental edition (McCarthy & Kirk, 1961), which has been widely used. The revision included changes in the names of the subtests, modification of items for easier administration, extension of the age range, and the addition of three subtests — Auditory Closure, Sound Blending, and Visual Closure. The abilities measured by these subtests are assumed to be the basic elements of linguistic behavior. The underlying model of verbal behavior is a modification of a theory originated by Charles Osgood (1957a, 1957b). There is, however, little evidence to support this model of either an experimental nature or derived from factor-analytic studies of the ITPA. (Ideally, any test of language should correlate with one or more of the ITPA subtests, which should in turn *not* be correlated with each other, if the subtests are independent). Several of the subtests appear to have little to do with language at all. It is common for only a subset of the tests to be used — most often, Auditory-Vocal Associa-

[1]Another widely used intelligence test for young children is the Wechsler Intelligence Scale for Children (WISC). It is similar to the Stanford-Binet, but attempts to separate verbal from nonverbal (called "performance") abilities by using separate subtests. See Wechsler (1949).

tion, Verbal Expression (formerly Vocal Encoding), and Grammatic Closure (formerly Auditory-Vocal Automatic). Many aspects of language are not assessed at all, for example, comprehension of various syntactic constructions.

CRITERIA FOR A LANGUAGE ASSESSMENT DEVICE

Rosenberg (1968) has compiled a list of requirements for a satisfactory language assessment device. The available tests fail on most counts.

1. Such a test must be based on knowledge of normal language development. No one would think of publishing a test of motor development without first obtaining a description of the stages of normal motor development. But most of the available tests of language development have not been so based, primarily because of our lack of understanding of normal language development. Although we do not really understand it well now, recent research, [discussed in the first half of this book], does suggest the variety of information that should be sought in such a test.

2. A test must be based on an adequate characterization of what is being developed, namely, adult language. Current tests are concerned with a narrow range of linguistic structure, primarily vocabulary and inflectional morphology. Linguistic research provides a description of language which is much more complex than this. Other aspects of language should not simply be ignored.

3. A test should distinguish between the underlying linguistic competence of the child and his observable linguistic performance. In other words, we should recognize that we want to know what the child *can do*, not what he does in a particular situation, with a particular set of memory and attention constraints, and so forth. For this purpose, it is useful to sample performance of several different kinds, such as imitation and comprehension, as well as production.

4. A test must take into account dialect differences. A test that counts the use of multiple negatives as an error or requires the use of *if* in such contexts as *I ask Alvin if he knows how to play basketball* is simply inappropriate for use in determining how well many black children have acquired the language of the community about them. Of course, they may be useful as tests in teaching a child another dialect, but this is a different matter.

Much research is in progress toward the development of tests of language development that satisfy these requirements (Berry, 1969, ch. 7). Tests under development investigate a much wider range of linguistic behavior, utilizing findings and techniques developed in the study of normal language development. The comprehension test devised by Fraser, Bellugi and Brown, (see Chapter 4 in this book), using pictures that differ in one aspect and corresponding sentences that differ in one linguistic feature, has been generalized and converted into a standardized test by Carrow:

> The form classes and function words tested by the instrument are nouns, verbs, adjectives, adverbs, and prepositions. Morphological constructions tested are those formed by adding *er* and *ist* to free morphs such as nouns, verbs, and adjectives. Grammatical categories that are evaluated involve contrasts of case, number, gender, tense, status, voice, and mood. Syntactic structures of predication, complementation, modification, and coordination are also tested [1968].

Jean Berko's (1958) test of productive use of inflections, such as plural and possessive ending of nouns, third person singular of the verb, the progressive and the past tense, and the comparative and superlative of the adjective has also been adopted in many newly devised tests. In a typical item (Berry & Talbott, 1966), the child is shown a drawing of an imaginary animal and told, *This is a nad.* Then the child is shown a picture of two of the animals and told, *Now there is another one. There are two of them. There are two _____.* The child's task is to supply the missing constructions, *nads*, demonstrating mastery of the morphological rule governing plurals.

An aspect of language that is particularly difficult to assess is meaning. This is not surprising, given the difficulty of defining meaning and observing its development, as discussed in Chapter 6. The cloze technique, requiring the child to fill in a missing word in a sentence, appears to be most fruitful here. A version of the cloze technique is used in the Auditory-Vocal Association subtest of the ITPA in which the child must complete test statements such as *I sit on a chair; I sleep on a _____,* and *An elephant is big; a mouse is _____.* In problems such as this, the child must use his knowledge of meaning, and of the relations between the meanings of the words in a sentence, to correctly identify the missing word.

Memory span tests for sentences may also be useful in the investigation of semantic development. There is much evidence that meaningful material is easier to remember than nonmeaningful material because it forms a coherent whole, not merely a list of independent items. The difference between memory for strings of unrelated words and memory for sentences is a measure of the child's ability to semantically integrate sentences. Syntactic structure must, of course, be carefully controlled, as in the studies of Miller and Isard (1963) and McNeill (1970) discussed in Chapter 6.

Tests of articulation are the best developed of the types of assessment being considered. In a typical test (Templin & Darley, 1960) the child is asked to name pictures of familiar objects which have been carefully selected to include all the sounds of interest. If the child does not know the name of the object, he may be told it by the examiner. Corresponding to tests of productive articulation are tests of auditory discrimination (Templin, 1957). Pairs of pictures of familiar objects whose names are words with similar pronunciation, except for a single sound, such as *string* and *spring*, are shown simultaneously to the child and he is asked to point to the picture named by the word the examiner then presents.

Vocabulary tests are also important in any assessment of language. But just as in the case of articulation, it is necessary to distinguish productive vocabulary from receptive vocabulary. The PPVT measures only the latter. But it is simple to measure the former by pointing to the key item picture on each PPVT card and asking the child to name it. Similar tests are available and have been standardized.

Further progress on the construction of language development tests will require the development of new items (which requires ingenuity as much as anything) and also research on the relationship between the various abilities measured by syntactic, semantic, vocabulary, and articulation items. A test is basically a restricted sampling of behavior. How can the time best be used? Is there a single direction of language development, or are the separate components largely independent? Informal observations suggest that articulation and syntactic development are largely independent of each other. Some children articulate clearly relatively primitive language, while others produce highly developed, complex language in an almost unintelligible manner. It is probably unrealistic to seek a single measure, a "linguistic age" which can represent language development. Most tests are administered by an adult — usually a strange adult — alone in a room with a child. There are many factors that can lead to children not performing as well as they might. It is often found that black children score higher on tests when they are administered by black examiners.[2] Language is as important as race. Children who are bilingual in Spanish and English, such as Puerto Rican children in New York City, score higher when tests are administered in Spanish. Familiarity with the examiner may also affect performance. Several studies have shown that if the examiner spends several sessions with the child, playing and talking with him, the child will eventually score higher on the test (Cazden, 1970, p. 95). And finally, familiarity with the testing situation may be crucial. Testing is, after all, a bizarre sort of activity. At first, it may be intimidating and anxiety producing to the child. This factor is especially important in evaluating training programs, because many experimental programs include a fair amount of testing during the program, and therefore the observed improvement may be due simply to increased "testmanship" on the part of the children. To eliminate misinterpretation of results, control groups should receive the same amount and type of testing experience as the experimental groups who receive the training.

ANALYSIS OF FREE SPEECH

An alternative approach to assessing language development is to abandon the testing situation in favor of the more naturalistic procedure of collecting a sample of the child's free speech for analysis and scoring. Several measures have been proposed for use in this way; the mean length of utterance (MLU), usually in morphemes, is the most common. In Bellugi's (1965) study of the development of questions (discussed in Chapter 4), she found that children at approximately the same MLU produced questions of similar structure, despite their differing ages. Furthermore, Shriner (1969) has found that MLU is highly correlated with psychological scaling judgments of development. He asked 104 students to rate a large number of samples of children's speech (fifty responses per child) on a seven-point scale of development, and compared their rating with several quantitative measures. Although MLU appears to be a very crude measure, it may well be that best single indicator of language development (if a single measure is necessary), at least for children of age five and under.

[2]But not always. For a review of the literature, see Sattler (1970).

The most serious objection to the use of MLU is that it is highly situation dependent. There is little evidence of any reliability of the measure, that is, stability of the measure from one test session to another, unless pains are taken to ensure that the two samples are obtained under identical circumstances. In addition to MLU, various measures of the structure and complexity of utterances collected in the sample have been proposed, but there is little research on the reliability of such measures or on their relation to each other or other language measures.

Assessment based on analysis of free speech cannot be considered fully adequate because they are based entirely on the child's productions. Production by itself reflects a child's competence only imperfectly, for reasons which were discussed in Chapters 2 and 4.

The Social Context of Language Acquisition

SOCIAL CLASS VARIATION

Because social class and race have been confounded in so many investigations, there are very few data on social class variation in language acquisition. Social class itself, of course, can hardly be a direct cause of language development or retardation; presumably some of the many variables which are correlated with social class, such as child rearing practices or the speech heard by the child, may affect language development. But the data available are surprisingly ambiguous.

The cross-ethnic group study of patterns of ability (Stodolsky & Lesser, 1967) discussed in the previous chapter, is a particularly clear demonstration of social class differences. The lower class sample in each of the four ethnic groups scored significantly lower than the middle class sample on the verbal test. This test was essentially a vocabulary test; it included both a productive test, using pictures, and a definition test, using questions of the form *What is a* _____? and *What do we mean when we say* _____? There is much additional evidence for variation in vocabulary development. Stodolsky (1965) found significant differences among groups of black children from welfare, lower, and middle-class families on the PPVT. Templin (1957) found similar variation in vocabulary growth in preschool and school age children.

There is much less evidence for social class differences in the acquisition of syntactic competence. LaCivita, Kean, and Yamamoto (1966) asked lower middle and upper middle class elementary school children to guess the meaning of nonsense words in sentences such as "Ungubily the mittler *gimmled*" and "A twener *baikels* meedily." They hypothesized that, as the task required the child to analyze the nonsense sentence syntactically and produce a word of the same part of speech as the underlined nonsense word (in both examples, a verb), the lower middle-class children would do less well. In fact, the two groups of children performed equally well.

Shriner and Miner (1968) investigated the mastery of morphological rules by middle-class and lower class white preschool children. Both expressive and receptive tests were included. The expressive test was based on Berko's (1958) technique and included plural and possessive inflections for nouns and third person singular, present progressive, and past tense inflections for verbs. The receptive test included noun pluralization only and required a pointing response from the child. No differences were found between the groups on either expressive or receptive items.

Cazden (1970) compared the MLU of black children in a Boston day-care center with the same measure as reported by Brown, Cazden, and Bellugi (1969) in their studies of generally middle-class white children, and concluded that "the lower class Negro children seem to be undergoing grammatical development at a similar rate [p. 82]."

Apparently contradicting these findings, Osser (1966, cited in John & Moskowitz, 1970) observed that lower class black children had a more limited range of syntactic constructions than middle-class white children. Osser analyzed the children's syntax using transformational grammar, and he eliminated dialect differences as an artifact by establishing equivalences between various Standard English and Black English constructions, for example, *If he knows* and *Do he know?* Loban (1965) observed much less use of subordinate clauses, that is, embedding, in lower class school children.

The lack of clear-cut substantial differences in syntactic development is consistent with the rationalist position, discussed in Chapter 3, which places great emphasis on the common biological endowment of human beings for language acquisition. Vocabulary development, which does manifest considerable social class variation, is very different from syntactic development; it can be considered a problem in concept formation (see Chapter 6). Cazden has proposed that "the acquisition of grammar and the acquisition of vocabulary required different kinds of environmental assistance [1968, p. 12]."

A similar conclusion is suggested by a training study conducted by Ammon and Ammon (in press) with black disadvantaged preschool children. One group of children received vocabulary training; a second group received sentence training. Both groups received twice-a-week, 20 minute training sessions for a period of six weeks. A control group received no special training. Receptive and productive vocabulary and syntactic development, using a sentence imitation test, were measured before and after the training. The sentence imitation test and the sentence training focused on features that occur in both STE and BE; sentences containing prenominal adjectives, possessive nouns, locative prepositional phrases, relative clauses, and adverbial clauses were used. Vocabulary training led to increased recognition and production of the words taught, but there was no transfer to sentence imitation. Sentence training has no significant effect. The authors conclude that "time devoted to early language training . . . is better spent on vocabulary than on sentence construction."

Differences in language function may be more significant than differences in structure. Heider (1969) tested the communication abilities of middle-class and lower class ten year olds in a task similar to that of Glucksberg and Krauss (1967), discussed in Chapter 8. Consistent differences in encoding style were found: middle-class children tended to describe one part of the stimulus at a time, and in purely descriptive terms — *It has an opening at the top.* Lower class children described the entire stimulus at once, in ways they went beyond the actual stimulus — *It looks like a hat; He looks like someone hit him.* The middle-class children were superior encoders, as measured by giving encoded messages from both groups to other decoders, and superior decoders, as measured by giving the same messages to both groups.

A related study by Heider, Cazden, and Brown (1968) suggests that the difference between social classes may not be one of ability but of motivation. In this experiment, the decoder could ask the encoder for more information. Decoders made nearly twice as many requests to the lower class encoders as to the middle class encoders. Eventually they were virtually as successful at identifying the stimulus picture with the lower class encoders as with the middle-class ones. Thus the performance of the lower class children was far superior to their performance in a standardized situation, with the amount of "probing" controlled or eliminated.

Studies of communication effectiveness, such as these, are global; information about specific aspects of language in communication is needed. The use of nouns and pronouns appears to be important for communication. In a study of the free speech of five year olds, Hawkins (1969) found that middle-class children tended to use nouns whereas lower class children made much more use of pronouns. Nouns are easily and flexibly modified — *These two very long railroad trains*. Modification of pronouns is extremely limited. The ability to add further information by means of modification is very useful for communication. Hawkins also found differences in the use of pronouns. Lower class children, in describing a picture, tended to use pronouns that referred directly to the situation — *They're playing and he kicks it*. The speaker seems to assume that the listener can see the picture (another example of egocentrism). In contrast to these **exophoric pronouns, anaphoric pronouns,** referring to previously mentioned nouns, were used by middle-class children — *The boy kicked the ball, and it broke the window*.

There is little evidence on social class differences in other functions of language. The use of language for memory and for self-guiding would seem to be particularly important. "Discussions of the goals of education, like analyses of child language, too often focus on language form when they should be concerned with language use [Cazden, 1970, p. 97]."

THE SITUATION

Research on child language has generally ignored situational effects on language and language development. Nevertheless, situational differences may be even more important than social class differences; important for assessment, for theories of development, and for educational programs. Situational effects are important for assessment, because we are interested in the child's competence — the best he *can* do — as well as in performance — how well he actually *does* in particular settings. They are important for theories of development because the answer to the question Where is the child using his most advanced language? is also a clue to where language is being acquired. And, finally, situational effects are important for the design of educational programs because they suggest how we can facilitate the child's talking and his talking in his most advanced language.

Cazden (1970) has argued forcefully for the importance of the situation in understanding language development, and she has surveyed the small amount of evidence available. Three of the most important situational variables are the *topic*, the *task*, and the *listener*. Four and five year olds talk more about a toy or a silent film of the toy than about a still photograph of the toy (Strandberg, 1969). Elementary school children given ten colored magazine covers to talk about, consistently have more to say about some pictures than about others (Cowan, Weber, Hoddinott, & Klein, 1967). Kindergarten and elementary school children given stories and pictures and invited to ask questions about them, ask more questions about stories and pictures that are novel or surprising (Berlyne & Frommer, 1966).

The nature of the task influences the language produced by children. Preschool children given pictures and asked to tell stories about them, produce longer stories, which are better integrated logically, when the pictures are removed before the telling of the story (Brent & Katz, 1967). Integration of the story into a conceptual unit requires the child to go beyond the discrete sequence of distinct pictures and form a continuous story. Kindergarten children recorded in a variety of activities, produce more speech, and more advanced speech, in housekeeping play and group discussion than in play with blocks, dance, and woodworking (Cowe, 1967). Both physical factors, such as noise and the presence of something concrete to talk about, and social factors, such as adult participation and the presence of other children, are important.

Finally, the listener has an influence on the speaker. Smith (1935) found that preschool age children produced longer sentences at home than when playing with other children. The age of the listener is very important. One three year old spoke her longest sentences to her mother, her shortest sentences to her younger sister, and intermediate sentences to herself (unpublished results, cited by Cazden, 1970). On the other hand, Frederick (1971) observed a two-and-a-half year old who spoke more to his mother at home but used longer and more advanced sentences at a preschool facility. This child had a relatively overprotective mother who administered to his needs almost before they were expressed. The disparity between the two children illustrates the importance of the nature of the relationship between the speaker and the listener.

Language Training Programs

Many experimental early educational programs for disadvantaged children emphasize language. Some focus specifically on structure (Bereiter & Engelmann, 1966) and some on function (Blank & Solomon, 1968), but most do not draw a clear distinction between the two aspects of language. The justifications for emphasis on language are varied. Some, such as an assumption of a causal link between language and thought or the belief that the language of black children in particular is deficient, are questionable. A more defensible position holds that, while language is not necessary for thinking, it is required for communication of what has been thought, from teacher to child and from child to teacher. Teachers assume an adequate command of language by most children, as the following excerpts from teacher's manuals illustrate:

> Lead the group in a discussion about relative size by asking questions such as "Are the two big cars the same size? Are the two little cars the same size? Is the first car in the row bigger than the second? Look at the last two cars. Which is bigger? [Carillo & Zumwalt, 1965, cited in Osborn, 1968]."

> "Put your finger on the spoon. What is at the top of the spoon row? Draw a line under the same at the bottom of the spoon row. You were right if you underlined the last picture [McNeill, 1966, cited in Osborn, 1968]."

Entering first-grade pupils are expected to understand terms such as "two," "big," "same," "bigger," "row," "last," and "bottom." If they lack such understanding, they will be greatly handicapped.

Even if language is not given a central role in either thought or instruction, it may still be the most efficient focus of activity. We cannot influence a child's cognitive functioning directly. All that can be done is to present stimuli with which the child can interact and learn. These stimuli may be most efficiently presented through language.

EXPERIMENTAL EDUCATIONAL PROGRAMS

Evaluating experimental educational programs is extremely difficult. Experimental preschools are different from standard preschools. Standard preschools do not usually have three experienced and highly trained teachers for every fifteen children; special materials, often including expensive audio-visual equipment; and a strong committment to promoting language. We know that virtually any innovation, if accepted enthusiastically by teachers, is likely to lead to some improvement on the part of the children. This may be a global and beneficial instance of the Rosenthal effect, or "experimenter bias." Rosenthal and Jacobson (1968) informed elementary school teachers that several children in their classes had been diagnosed as "potential academic spurters." Over the course of the following year, these spurters made remarkable advances in their IQ scores: 22 percent for the first graders and 16 percent for the second graders, in contrast to gains of 12 percent and 7 percent, respectively, for the other children in the classes. The spurters were, in fact, randomly chosen from the classes. The expectancies teachers have of the children in their classes may well be "self-fulfilling prophecies."

The "Hawthorne effect" also plays a role in education. Children are likely to realize that they are in special programs and therefore may be highly motivated. The difference between the Rosenthal effect and the Hawthorne effect is that the former begins in the mind of the teacher and the latter, in the mind of the child. Both may be effective under certain conditions.

Related to the Hawthorne effect is the problem of selection of pupils and use of control groups. Typically, children in experimental groups have been volunteered by their parents. Control groups are often randomly selected from the population of interest. It is very plausible that parents who volunteer their children are different from those who do not in ways that affect the children and their performance in school.

Experimental programs are not designed as a careful sequence of research studies, with each variable identified and manipulated in a factorial design. Each program is constructed as a whole. They are not, therefore, directly comparable to each other; and strong inferences cannot be drawn about the effect of specific elements of the program on the results. The situation is comparable to the problem encountered in medical research on new drugs or treatments; there is a conflict between the researcher (medical or psychological) who seeks increased theoretical understanding and therefore needs controlled experimental results, and the practitioner (physician or educator) who seeks to help and therefore includes everything that might be useful.

A final difficulty of evaluating experimental programs stems from the generally unsatisfactory language tests currently available, as discussed earlier in this chapter.

STRUCTURE OF EXPERIMENTAL PROGRAMS

One dimension along which experimental preschool language programs vary is that of structure. A program is structured to the extent that it attempts to directly teach specific skills, such as language. Typical middle-class nursery schools of the kind that have existed in this country for decades are relatively unstructured. Emphasis is usually on social development, encouragement of communication between children, "widening the horizons" of the children through field trips, and the like. It is a fairly reliable finding that the scores of disadvantaged children are not significantly increased by these unstructured programs. This does not mean that they are not of value for the children for whom they were designed. Different children have different needs, and it is very unlikely that there is a "best" program for all children.

Early Training Project and Perry Preschool Project

Semistructured programs lie somewhere in the middle on this dimension. Two of the best known examples are the Early Training Project (Klaus & Gray, 1968) and the Perry Preschool Project (Weikart, 1967). The Perry project combines preschool experience with home visits by other staff members to involve other members of the family in the educational process. The program uses many of the traditional preschool activities, such as story telling, music, playing with blocks, and so forth; but it emphasizes language much more than is customary. The teacher is constantly commenting on the situation and asking the child questions. Weikart has described this activity as "verbal bombardment." The child need not answer; the goal is to make him aware of the various uses of language. After two years of this program, children made significant IQ gains on a wide variety of measures, such as the Stanford-Binet, the PPVT, the ITPA, and others, relative to the performance of a matched group of control children who did not attend a preschool. By the end of the kindergarten year in the public schools, however, this progress had vanished. This is a common finding, and a discouraging one.

These results may be misleadingly pessimistic. The goal of a preschool program, after all, is not to increase Stanford-Binet scores but, rather, to improve learning performance. Training may build a foundation for future learning, but it may take time for measurable results to emerge. The first group of children who participated in the Perry Preschool Project were watched closely for the following four years, and it was found that although IQ differences between experimental and control groups gradually diminished to zero, achievement test results and teacher ratings of academic motivation for the two groups continued to diverge, even after three years in the public schools. In fact, the differences in achievement test scores did not become significant until the very end of the first grade. This is a very encouraging finding. Unfortunately, this pattern was not found in the follow-up data of Klaus and Gray.

Bereiter-Englemann Program

The program developed by Bereiter and Engelmann (1966) is the most highly structured of current programs. It is based on the belief that the disadvantaged child is lacking language that is crucial for thinking and for school learning, and that the remedy for this is direct language teaching. The school day lasts two-and-a-half hours per day and includes several teacher-directed group activities: music, story telling, and so forth. But the heart of the program lies in three 20 minute sessions, one each for language, arithmetic, and reading. During these periods, a group of five or six children work with one teacher. Drill and pattern practice are the most important activities. Each new pattern is introduced for the children to imitate in unison, then each child produces it alone, and finally the children learn to use the pattern in appropriate contexts, such as answering questions.

The program begins with patterns with one content word: *This is a cup. This is not a cup. These are cups.* Next, patterns with two content words are introduced: *This cup is big. This cup is not big. This cup is (on, over, under,) the table. This cup is white. This cup is striped. This animal is a zebra.* In later stages of the program, category terms, such as *animal, clothing,* and *vehicle* and also verb tenses, conjugations, and the personal pronouns are presented.

The pace of the program is very rapid; at almost any moment either the teacher or the children are speaking. There is a strong emphasis on instant feedback, and the teachers do not hesitate to correct (or even interrupt) incorrect responses. The authors of this program find this is necessary because they feel that "the child should not practice an incorrect response, and the other children in the group should not hear wrong responses [Osborne, 1968, p. 46]."

The Bereiter-Engelmann program has produced some of the largest increases in Stanford-Binet scores obtained in experimental programs (see Table 10-2). In addition, reading performance in kindergarten and first grade is well above the expected level.

TABLE 10-2 *Stanford-Binet Test Results for Four-Year-Old Children Participating in the Bereiter-Engelmann Program*

Year entering	Pretest	After one year	After two years
1964[a]	97.6	104.2	106.9
1965	97.0	111.5	120.4
1966	91.1	102.9	
1965 control[b]	94.5	102.6	99.6

SOURCE: Adapted from Osborn, J. Teaching a teaching language to disadvantaged children. In M. A. Brottman (Ed.), *Language remediation for the disadvantaged preschool child.* Monographs of the Society for Research in Child Development, 1968, **33** (Serial No. 124), table 1, p.47.

[a]The pretests for the 1964 group only were given after the children had been in the program for three months. Many studies are showing that most disadvantaged children gain about five to seven points their first few months in any program. It is likely that the 1964 group gain would have been greater had the children been tested before entering school.

[b]Children in the control group spent one year in an enriched, but basically traditional, preschool program. After one year, they entered a public kindergarten. The final score recorded repesents the mean Stanford-Binet after this year in kindergarten.

Critics of this program point to the omission of planning for the children's social and emotional needs. There are no toys, except those materials directly used in teaching, and no free time. This criticism is countered with the argument that cognitive development must receive the highest priority and that time is limited. Children do participate in this program with enthusiasm, as can be seen in a film of the program in action.[3] There are no data on the effects of such a program on the social or personality development of the children participating. Curiously, evaluations of educational programs never include asking the children if they like school.

[3]"Language," available from the B'nai Brith Anti-Defamation League.

The Bereiter-Engelmann program relies heavily on imitation and reinforcement in language learning; two processes whose role in normal language acquisition was questioned in Chapter 5. However, the fact that imitation and reinforcement may not be important in normal acquisition does not mean that they cannot be useful in an intervention setting. Reinforcement is usually valued for its *motivating* effect, but it also serves as a vital source of *information* for the child. It is clear to a child, in an immediate reinforcement situation, just what is required of him. This may be especially important for disadvantaged children, for whom the school setting is likely to be unfamiliar and anxiety provoking.

STRUCTURED VERSUS LESS STRUCTURED PROGRAMS

Other structured programs have been based on Piagetian concepts, programmed instruction, Montessori materials, and other theoretical approaches. There is a general feeling that the relatively structured programs are more effective, at least in the short run. Although this generalization is widely accepted, and is supported by comparison of the results of each program in its initial setting, the few comparative studies that have been performed have not produced results that consistently support such a conclusion.

Dickie (1968) randomly assigned sixty-eight Negro children to three different programs: a Bereiter-Engelmann program, a programmed language training program (Gotkin, 1968), and a "traditional enrichment" program. Dickie described the traditional enrichment program as seeking

> to arrange an environment that will stimulate perception and expression and then to have the teacher available to encourage and amplify when the child expresses interest in some aspect of this environment [p. 63].

Such a program lies near the "unstructured" end of the dimension; Gotkin's program lies somewhere between "semistructured" and "highly structured"; and the Bereiter-Engelmann program is "highly structured."

The children, who were randomly selected from a public housing project, were matched using an Expressive Vocabulary Inventory, in which questions were asked about pictures, and a test of auditory discrimination. After five months of the program, the Auditory-Vocal Association subtest and the Vocal Encoding subtest of the ITPA were administered. At the end of the school year, the Stanford-Binet and a test of color naming were administered. The results are shown in Table 10-3. Because of the small sample size, the scores of the two structured programs are combined in this table. The programs were all about equally effective, and clearly superior to a control (no preschool) group. The only statistically significant difference between the programs was an interaction: the highly structured programs were more effective than the unstructured one for children whose initial performance was low, whereas the traditional program was more effective for the children whose initial performance was high.

TABLE 10-3 *A Comparison of Several Methods of Language Training*

Test	Structured	Unstructured	Control
Stanford-Binet			
IQ	101.8	97.3	85.5
ITPA[a]	55.6	51.9	37.0
Vocal Encoding			
Auditory-Vocal Association	54.7[b]		37.5
Color Naming[c]	6.3	5.7	2.4

SOURCE: Adapted from Dickie, J. P. Effectiveness of structured and unstructured (traditional) methods of language training. In M. A. Bottman (Ed.), *Language remediation for the disadvantaged preschool child.* Monographs of the Society for Research in Child Development, 1968, **33** (Serial No. 124), tables 2 and 3, pp. 67 and 68.

[a]Scores reported in Mental Age in months
[b]Score for all experimental groups combined
[c]Units for Color Naming Test not specified

Many factors may be implicated in the lack of differentiation between the structured and unstructured programs. All three programs were similar in several important details. In each, there was a 20-minute period each day in which the class was divided into small groups of five or six and a teacher. The emphasis during this period was on language, although the actual activities varied considerably. During the remainder of the two-and-a-quarter hour day, the three programs were identical. In addition, the explicit emphasis on language, and knowledge of an eventual evaluation of the children's language, undoubtedly motivated the teachers to emphasize language more than the other preschool activities. Although staff observers monitored each teacher's procedures, the teachers knew each other and of course talked about their classes together. As a result, the three methods did not remain "pure." The three programs were probably not as distinct as was hoped and, therefore, produced similar results.

Although the test scores did not differentiate clearly among the groups, observers reported very different general impressions of the programs. It usually appeared that much more was being accomplished in the structured groups. In contrast, the teachers in the unstructured groups spent far more time handling disciplinary problems.

Parental attitudes toward the programs varied greatly. Parents of children in the structured programs viewed the programs as teaching the child something useful. They made comments like "They are really learning something." They may have given more praise and encouragement to their children and have tried harder to get the children to school regularly. In contrast, many parents of children in the traditional program were openly hostile to the permissiveness of the program. They were concerned that their children would have difficulty in the public schools. One common explanation for the deterioration of the disadvantaged child's performance in the first and second grades is the considerable change in what is expected of the child between kindergarten and the first grade. The transition may be too abrupt for many children. Of course, this leaves open the question of which should be changed. Structured programs are similar to conventional schools and help children to succeed in that setting; but an alternative worth exploration is changing the nature of classroom organization in elementary schools.

One of the most comprehensive comparison studies of preschool programs for disadvantaged children both in number of children and number of programs, is in progress at the University of Illinois, under the direction of Merle Karnes (Karnes, Teska, & Hodgins, 1970). Ninety-two children were assigned to four training programs. Each group was approximately 2:1 Negro: Caucasian; 1:1 male: female: and 1:1:1 Stanford-Binet level (70-89: 90-99:100+). In order to compare the relative effectiveness of the programs for children of varying ability, a wide range of IQ levels was desired. As a result, the mean IQ (about 95) of the children in the four programs was higher than that of the population from which they were drawn.

The programs were all approximately two hours and fifteen minutes daily and extended over about eight months. There were four programs.

1. *The Traditional Program*   "Teachers were instructed to capitalize on opportunities for incidental and informal learning, to encourage the children to talk and to ask questions, and to stimulate their interest in the world around them [Karnes, Teska, & Hodgins, 1970, p. 60]," Activities included music, story telling, art, indoor and outdoor play, and show and tell. The pupil-teacher ratio was 5:1.

2. *The Community-Integrated Program*   The sixteen disadvantaged children assigned to this program were divided into groups of two to four and simply integrated into four neighborhood nursery schools in the area. These were nursery schools for predominantly upper and middle-class white children and were similar in activities to the traditional program (No. 1). This program was included to test the hypothesis that presentation of advantaged peers as models might facilitate the language development of the disadvantaged children. The pupil-teacher ratio in these nursery schools ranged from 6:1 to 10:1.

3. *The Montessori Program*   The local Montessori organization conducted a special program for this research project. The heart of the Montessori program consists of specially designed materials, such as templates and stylus, cylinder blocks, dressing frames, touch boards, and counting devices. The children spontaneously select the materials they wish to play with, but each material must be used in a specified fashion. In addition, there are conversation, singing, and exercise activities. The Montessori program is highly structured, but there is relatively little teacher-child, or child-child interaction. The pupil-teacher ratio was 8:1.

4. *The Experimental Program*   This highly structured program included three 20-minute periods per day of small group instruction. "Content to be learned was presented in a game format which employed manipulative materials but was structured by the teacher to require concurrent verbal responses (Karnes, Teska, & Hodgins, 1970, p. 61)." While not identical to the Bereiter-Engelmann program, this is closer to it than to any other. Emphasis was placed on immediate correction of incorrect responses and reinforcement of appropriate responses. Language was emphasized in all aspects of the program, although there was only one specific language period. The language arts period included reading readiness. The teacher read to the children while each of them held his own copy of the book. The story telling setting was used for development of sequencing of events, elaborating on vocabulary, development of memory, and for making inferences. In the science and social studies period, one of the

units was "kitchen science." Vocabulary such as *melt*, *boil*, *freeze*, *hot*, *dissolve*, and *sweet* was introduced. Other units focussed on seeds and plant growth, the weather, and so on. The mathematics period was least linguistic in nature. Instruction on number concepts, geometric shapes, and beginning addition and subtraction was included, along with the development of a useful vocabulary for these concepts.

Pre- and postevaluations of the children in all four groups were obtained on three measures: the Stanford-Binet, the ITPA, and the PPVT. The results are shown in Table 10-4. The largest gains on the Stanford-Binet were made by the children in the Experimental Program. Even more striking is the fact that *every* child scored a gain of at least four points on this test. In other groups, some children gained and some lost. In the Community-Integrated Program, over half of the children either lost points or made only a minimal gain (one to four points). Only three children made large gains (twenty to twenty-nine points), and they were essentially responsible for the mean gain of the entire group.[4] Observers reported that most of the disadvantaged children in this program did not fully participate in the activities of the nursery schools. They often sat on the edges of groups and did not attend closely. Neither the teachers nor the advantaged children appeared to be rejecting the disadvantaged children. It is possible that because most of the children were doing so well the silence of the disadvantaged children was not noticed as strongly by the teachers as it might have been.

The scores on the most linguistic of the ITPA subtests (Auditory-Vocal Association, Vocal Encoding, and Auditory-Vocal Automatic), and on the test as a whole, show the same pattern as those on the Stanford-Binet. The Experimental Program was the most effective, followed by the Traditional Program, followed by the other two programs, which had little or no effect. The strikingly poor performance of the children in the Montessori program is corroborated by the reports of observers that the children actively played with the materials for considerable periods of time but with little or no speech. The lack of successful integration of the children in the Community-Integrated Program,

---

[4]Karnes, Teska, and Hodgins (1970) comment, "No obvious characteristic of these three children or their group placement seems to have been related to their high gains. A particular community preschool did not account for these gains, since each of the three attended a different preschool. Their racial distribution was the same as that of their intervention unit, two Negro and one Caucasian. There were two females and one male, and there was one child from each of the three intelligence strata."

TABLE 10-4 A Comparison of Four Educational Programs for Disadvantaged Four Year Olds

Group	Stanford-Binet			ITPA[b]				PPVT			
	Pretest	Posttest	Difference	Test 3	Test 5	Test 7	Total	Pretest	Posttest	Difference	N
Traditional	94.5	102.6	8.1	1.9	10.0	3.9	4.3	80.2	92.6	12.4	28
Community-Integrated	93.3	98.4	5.1	1.5	−4.7	−1.0	1.1	81.4	85.6	4.2	16
Montessori	94.1	99.6	5.5	.4	−2.2	−10.2	−1.4	83.3	87.3	4.0	16
Experimental	96.0	110.3	14.3	6.7	11.2	10.7	6.2	85.8	96.1	10.3	27
N[c]											87

SOURCE: Adapted from Karnes, M. B., Teska, J. A., & Hodgins, A. S. The effects of four programs of classroom intervention on intellectual and language development of 4-year-old disadvantaged children. American Journal of Orthopsychiatry, 1970, **40**, tables 1, 3, 6, and 7, pp. 65, 69, 72, and 73.

[a]Stanford-Binet and Peabody scores are reported as IQ; that is, Mental Age divided by Chronological Age.

[b]ITPA scores on the subtests and total are reported as changes in ITPA Mental Age in months minus the eight months elapsed between pretest and posttest. An ITPA score of 1.0 indicates an advance of 9 months as measured by the test.

[c]The traditional and experimental groups and an initial number (N) of thirty children each. Five children withdrew from the program before the posttest battery and no data for these children is included.

discussed above, reduced their opportunities for verbal inter-action with the advantaged children.

The PPVT results show a similar pattern. The performance of the Experimental group is not quite as outstanding as on the previous tests.

The results of this study do not support the conclusion that structure is the key dimension in preschool programs. The Experimental Program is highest in structure, followed by the Montessori Program, followed by the Traditional and Community-Integrated Programs. But the pattern of results is, in general, Ex-perimental, Traditional, Community-Integrated, and Montessori. What conclusions can be drawn from these results?

Pupil-teacher ratio may be one of the most important single variables in determining effectiveness of intervention pro-grams. The two most effective programs, Experimental and Tradi-tional, had ratios of 5:1 each. The two least effective programs, Montessori and Community-Integrated, had ratios of approxi-mately 8:1 each.

Pupil-teacher ratio is one determinant of the quantity of interaction between child and adult. Another is the nature of the program. The Montessori program is designed to promote in-dependent activity on the part of the child. There is little or no emphasis on the interaction of the child with the teacher. The child need not make appropriate comments on his activities, as he would if he were in the Experimental Program. Nor does the teacher provide verbal models for him.

The results of this study may unfairly disparage the Montes-sori program. Maria Montessori developed her program for chil-dren younger than the four year olds who participated in this study and also for retarded children. It can be argued that this program provides a sensorimotor base for later development and that long-term follow-up data of children who participate in such a program will show them to have been helped by it. Furthermore, the selection of tests is inherently biased against the Montessori program, which does not seek to advance language development. Administration of a fine motor coordination task, such as peg-board play, or a pursuit rotor task to all the groups of children might well show that the Montessori program is superior, as might tests of attention and perseverence. Montessori teachers demonstrate, rather than explain; perhaps children in such a pro-gram develop superior imitative skills.

The disappointing results of the Community-Integrated Program indicate that simply moving small numbers of disadvantaged children into classes of upper and middle-class children will not, by itself, be effective. This does not prove that socioeconomic integration is of no value for disadvantaged children, only that such integration at four years of age, for a relatively short period of time, and with no further activities undertaken to facilitate true participation is not effective.

Perhaps the most striking result is the superior performance of the children in the Traditional Program. Remember that only the Traditional and Experimental Programs were actually administered by the investigators. It is appropriate to ask just how "traditional" was the Traditional Program. It is very likely that, as in the Dickie comparison study, the two programs were quite similar. Only a careful monitoring of the classrooms can answer this question, and this is seldom done, as it is time consuming and expensive. Nevertheless, it is essential, because designing a program of a particular type is not the same thing as doing it.

A TUTORIAL PROGRAM

A tutorial program developed by Blank and Solomon (1968) combines individual instruction with explicit emphasis on the use of language for cognitive tasks. Blank and Solomon feel that group instruction allows the child to passively imitate; individual tutorial sessions can challenge the child to independent abstract thinking. They use a variety of techniques to help the child begin to use language in new ways. To develop the ability to produce and use language internally, the child is asked to look at a picture, say the name to himself, and after the picture is removed, give the name to the teacher. To develop the ability to use language to represent and transform reality, the child is asked to think through the results of possible, but not actually present, actions. For example, he may be asked *Where would the doll be if it fell from the table?* To increase the child's conscious awareness of language and its power, he is asked to give the teacher commands. This program has resulted in increased IQ scores for the very limited number of children who have participated. More important, Blank and Solomon report that these techniques substantially altered the linguistic performance of the children. Given the lack of assessment measures for mastery of the functions of language, this is difficult to quantify, but such measures may well be the most appropriate ones for educational programs.

NEW TRENDS

Currently two new trends in early education are emerging. The first is the development of programs for infants and toddlers. Social class differences in cognitive functioning do not appear to emerge before the age of three or so (Golden, Birns, Bridger, & Moss, 1971). Working with infants younger than that may prevent a deficit from developing, eliminating the need for remediation programs later. For practical reasons, such programs often must be conducted in the home; and many of these programs work with mothers, training them to play with their children in specific ways (for a relatively successful example, see Karnes, Teska, Hodgins, & Badger, 1971).

A second trend is the development of programs for various nonwhite groups, especially blacks and Indians, based on the experiences and cultures of the minority groups themselves, in contrast to the programs discussed above, which have virtually all been developed by white academic researchers. These efforts toward community control are just beginning, and there is little information available on either the programs or their results. But this trend is likely to become increasingly important in the future.

Summary

No other chapter in this book can have as tentative, unconfident a summary as this one. Until we have better measures of language development — measures based on knowledge of normal language development of children from a broad spectrum of social classes and ethnic groups which sample the full range of language in the child's own dialect — we cannot really state the problem. It is not even certain that language is properly the focus of early educational programs for disadvantaged children. In particular, the distinction between structure and function of language must be kept in mind in attempting to define the problem.

The problems of educational research are great, and it is difficult to draw any firm conclusions at this time. However, the relatively few comparative studies that have been performed suggest that programs are most likely to be effective in raising test scores if they (1) have a high ratio of teachers to children; (2) have highly motivated teachers who expect to improve their pupil's linguistic and intellectual performance; and (3) center around small group activities that induce the children to participate verbally.

10.1 Items for the Three-Year, Six-Month Level from the Stanford Binet*

1. *Comparison of Balls*

   Material: Card with large and small sphere.

   Procedure: Show and card and ask, "Which ball is bigger? Put your finger on the big one." Give 3 trials alternating the relative positions of the large and small balls. In case one of the first three trials is failed, give 3 additional trials, continuing to alternate the positions of the balls.

2. *Patience: Pictures*

   Material: Two cards with pictures cut in two vertically.

   Procedure: Place the two halves of the card before the child so that the cut edges are toward the outside . . .

   (a) Say, "Put these two pieces together and make a ball."
   (b) Place the two halves of the other card before him and say, "Put these two pieces together and make a pig."

3. *Discrimination of Animal Pictures*

   Material: Two cards with pictures of animals.

   Procedure: Superimpose Card A over Card B, arranged so that the rabbit in the lower left corner is framed by the rectangular slit in Card A. Say, "See all of these animals? Find me another one just like this up here," pointing to the rabbit in the frame.

   Correct an error on the rabbit by saying, "No, find me one just like this," again pointing to the rabbit. If S still fails, show him the rabbit. S is not given credit for finding the rabbit after correction. Proceed from left to right in order. R to L for the middle row, and L to R for the top row. Say, "Find me another one just like this one," for each animal. Since the items of this test have not been arranged in the order of their difficulty, it is not safe to assume that failure on the first few items indicates inability to pass the test.

4. *Response to Pictures: Level 1*

   Material: Three pictures, Grandmother's Story, Birthday Party, Wash Day.

---

*From Terman, L. M., & Merrill, M. A. *Stanford-Binet intelligence scale.* Boston: Houghton Mifflin, 1960. Pp. 74–75. Reprinted by permission.

Procedure: Present the pictures in the following order: Grand-mother's Story, Birthday Party, Wash Day. Say, "Look at this picture and tell be all about it." If there is no response, repeat the request, "Tell me all about it," If the child names one or two things in a picture and then stops, urge him on by saying, "Tell me more about it." Only one question of this type, however, is permissible in a trial. Do not remove the picture until it is clear that no further response is forth-coming.

5. *Sorting Buttons*
Material: Twenty half-inch buttons, 10 black and 10 white. Small box.
Procedure: Empty the button box onto the table in front of the child and place the box cover beside the box ready for sorting the buttons. Take a button of each color from the mixed pile in front of the boxes, saying, as you illustrate: "See, the black buttons go in this box, and the white buttons go in that box. Now you put all the black buttons in that box and all the white buttons in this box." Time limit, 2 minutes.

6. *Comprehension I*
Procedure: Ask:

(a) "What must you do when you are thirsty?"
(b) "Why do we have stoves?"

If there is no response, repeat the question.

10.2 Subtests of the Illinois Test of Psycholinguistic Abilities*

Functions Tested at the Representational Level

A. The Receptive Process (Decoding).

There are two tests at this level which assess the child's ability to comprehend visual and auditory symbols.

*From Kirk, S. A., McCarthy, J. J., & Kirk, W. D. *Examiner's manual: Illinois test of psycholinguistic abilities.* (Rev. ed.) Urbana, Ill.: University of Illinois Press, 1968. Reprinted by permission.

Auditory Reception (Auditory Decoding). This is a test to assess the ability of a child to derive meaning from verbally presented material. Since the receptive rather than the expressive process is being sampled, the response throughout is kept at the simple level of a "yes" or "no" or even a nod or shake of the head . . . The test contains fifty short, direct questions printed in the *Manual.* Typical items are: "Do dogs eat?" "Do dials yawn?" "Do carpenters kneel?" "Do wingless birds soar?"

Visual Reception (Visual Decoding). It is a measure of the child's ability to gain meaning from visual symbols. In this test there are forty picture items, each consisting of a stimulus picture on one page and four response pictures on a second page. The child is shown the stimulus picture for three seconds with the directions, "See this?" Then the page of response pictures is presented with the directions, "Find one here." The credited choice is the object or situation which is conceptually similar to the stimulus. The other choices include pictures with varying degrees of structural (rather than functional) similarity or pictures which are associated with the stimulus or with the acceptable choice.

B. The Organizing Process (Association)

At the representational level this process is represented by the ability to relate, organize, and manipulate visual or auditory symbols in a meaningful way.

Auditory-Vocal Association. This test taps the child's ability to relate concepts presented orally . . . A sentence completion technique is used, presenting one statement followed by an incomplete analogous statement, and allowing the child to complete the second statement appropriately. There are forty two orally presented analogies, such as, "I cut with a saw; I pound with a＿＿＿＿." "A dog has hair; a fish has＿＿＿＿."

Visual-Motor Association. The organizing process in this channel is tapped by a picture association test with which to assess the child's ability to relate concepts presented visually. The child is presented with a single stimulus picture surrounded by four optional pictures, one of which is associated with the stimulus picture. The child is asked, "What goes with this?" (pointing to the stimulus picture). "Which one of these?" (pointing to the four optional pictures). The child is to choose the one picture which is most closely related to the stimulus picture, such as a sock belonging with a shoe, or a hammer with a nail.

C. *The Expressive Process* (*Encoding*).

This process at the representational level involves the child's ability to use verbal or manual symbols to transmit an idea. There are two subtests, one requiring vocal and the other manual responses.

Verbal Expression (Vocal Encoding).   This test taps the child's ability to express ideas manually . . . In this test fifteen pictures of common objects are shown to the child one at a time and he is asked to, "Show me what we do with a_____." The child is required to pantomime the appropriate action, such as dialing a telephone or playing a guitar.

Functions Tested at the Automatic Level

. . . no effort has been made to measure purely receptive or purely expressive processes at this level. The following subtests are basically "whole level" tests which measure the child's ability to perform automatic, nonsymbolic tasks.

A. *Closure*.

The following tests assess the child's ability to fill in the missing parts in an incomplete picture or verbal expression (or the ability to integrate discrete units into a whole).

Grammatic Closure.   This test assesses the child's ability to make use of the redundancies of oral language in acquiring automatic habits for handling syntax and grammatic inflections. In this test the conceptual difficulty is low, but the task elicits the child's ability to respond automatically to often repeated verbal expressions of standard American speech . . . The test measures the form rather than the content of the missing word, since the content is provided by the examiner.

There are thirty-three orally presented items accompanied by pictures which portray the content of the verbal expressions . . . Each verbal item consists of a complete statement followed by an incomplete statement to be finished by the child. The examiner points to the appropriate picture as he reads the given statements, for example: "Here is a dog; here are two_____." "This dog likes to bark; here he is_____."

Supplementary Test 1: Auditory Closure.   This is basically a test of the organizing process at the automatic level. It assesses the child's ability to fill in missing parts which were deleted in auditory presentation and to produce a complete word . . . In this test the child is asked, "What am I talking about: bo – – le? tele – – one"? There are thirty items ranging in difficulty from easy words such as "airpla – –" to more difficult ones such as "ta – le – – oon" and "– ype – – iter."

Supplementary Test 2: Sounding Blending.   This test provides another means of assessing the organizing process at the automatic level in the auditory-vocal channel. The sounds of a word are spoken singly at half-second intervals, and the child is asked to tell what the word is. Thus he has to synthesize the separate parts of the word and produce an integrated whole . . .

Visual Closure.   This test assesses the child's ability to identify a common object from an incomplete visual presentation. There are four scenes, presented separately, each containing fourteen or fifteen examples of a specified object. The objects are seen in varying degrees of concealment. The child is asked to see how quickly he can point to all examples of a particular object within the time limit of thirty seconds for each scene.

B. Sequential Memory

The two following tests assess the child's ability to reproduce a sequence of auditory or visual stimuli. They are tests of short-term sequential memory.

Auditory Sequential Memory   This test assesses the child's ability to reproduce from memory sequences of digits increasing in length from two to eight digits . . .

Visual Sequential Memory   This test assesses the child's ability to reproduce sequences of nonmeaningful figures from memory. The child is shown each sequence of figures for five seconds and then is asked to put corresponding chips of figures in the same order.

SELECTED REFERENCES

Ammon, P. R., & Ammon, M. S. Effects of training black preschool children in vocabulary vs. sentence construction. *Journal of Educational Psychology*, in press.

Arthur, G. *The Arthur adaptation of the Leiter international performance scale.* Washington, D.C.: Psychological Service Center, 1952.

Bellugi, U. The development of interrogative structures in children's speech. In K. Riegel (Ed.), *The development of language functions.* University of Michigan Language Development Program, Report No. 8, 1965. Pp. 103–138.

Bereiter, C., & Englemann, S. *Teaching disadvantaged children in the preschool.* Englewod Cliffs, N.J.: Prentice-Hall, 1966.

Berko, J. The child's learning of English morphology. *Word*, 1958, **14**, 150–177.

Berlyne, D. E., & Frommer, F. D. Some determinants of the incidence and content of children's questions. *Child Development*, 1966, **37**, 177–189.

Berry, M. F. *Language disorders of children: The bases and diagnoses.* New York: Appleton-Century-Crofts, 1969.

Berry, M. F., & Talbott, R. *Exploratory test of grammar.* Rockford, Ill.: Author, 1966.

Blank, M., & Solomon, F. A tutorial language program to develop abstract thinking in socially disadvantaged children. *Child Development*, 1968, **39**, 379–390.

Brent, S. B., & Katz, E. W. A study of language deviations and cognitive processes. Progress Report No. 3, Office of Economic Opportunity Job Corps Contract 1209, Wayne State University, 1967.

Brown, R., Cazden, C. B., & Bellugi, U. The child's grammar from I to III. In J. P. Hill (Ed.), *Minnesota symposium on child psychology.* Vol. 2. Minneapolis: University of Minnesota Press, 1969. Pp. 28–73.

Carillo, L. W., & Zumwalt, E. N. *Teacher's guide for "Let's Look," "Words to Read," and "Pictures to Read."* San Francisco: Chandler, 1965.

Carrow, M. W. The development of auditory comprehension of language structure in children. *Journal of Speech and Hearing Disorders*, 1968, **33**, 99–111.

Cazden, C. B. Some implications of research on language development for preschool education. In R. D. Hess & R. M. Bear (Eds.), *Early education.* Chicago: Aldine, 1968.

Cazden, C. B. The neglected situation in child language research and education. In F. Williams (Ed.), *Language and poverty.* Chicago: Markham Publishing Company, 1970. Pp. 81–101.

Cowan, P. A., Weber, J., Hoddinott, B. A., & Klein, J. Mean length of spoken response as a function of stimulus, experimenter, and subject. *Child Development*, 1967, **38**, 191–203.

Cowe, E. G. A study of kindergarten activities for language development. Unpublished doctoral dissertation, School of Education, Columbia University, 1967.

Dickie, J. P. Effectiveness of structured and unstructured (traditional) methods of language training. In M. A. Brottman (Ed.), *Language remediation for the disadvantaged preschool child.* Monographs of the Society for Research in Child Development, 1968, **33** (Serial No. 124), 62–79.

Dunn, L. *Peabody picture vocabulary test*. Minneapolis: American Guidance Service, 1965.

Frederick, L. The social situation as a determiner of language usage. Unpublished paper, Department of Psychology, University of Washington, 1971.

Glucksburg, S., & Krauss, R. M. What do people say after they have learned to talk? Studies of the development of referential communication. *Merrill-Palmer Quarterly*, 1967, **13**, 309–316.

Golden, M., Birns, B., Bridger, W., & Moss, A. Social-class differentiation in cognitive development among black preschool children. *Child Development*, 1971, **42**, 37–45.

Gotkin, L. G. Programmed instruction as a strategy for developing curricula for disadvantaged children. In M. A. Brottman (Ed.), *Language remediation for the disadvantaged preschool child*. Monographs of the Society for Research in Child Development, 1968, **33** (Serial No. 124), 19–35.

Hawkins, P. R. Social class, the nominal group and reference. *Language and Speech*, 1969, **12**, 125–135.

Heider, E. R. Style and effectiveness of children's verbal communications within and between social classes. Unpublished doctoral dissertation, Department of Social Psychology, Harvard University, 1969.

Heider, E. R., Cazden, C. B., & Brown, R. Social class differences in the effectiveness and style of children's coding ability. Project Literacy Reports, No. 9. Ithaca, N.Y.: Cornell University Press, 1968.

John, V. P., & Moskovitz, S. Language acquisition and development in early childhood. In A. H. Marckwardt (Ed.), *Linguistics in school programs*. Chicago: National Society for the Study of Education, 1970, Pp. 167–214.

Karnes, M. B., Teska, J. A., & Hodgins, A. S. The effects of four programs of classroom intervention on the intellectual and language development of 4-year-old disadvantaged children. *American Journal of Orthopsychiatry*, 1970, **40**, 58–76.

Karnes, M. B., Teska, J. A., Hodgins, A. S., & Badger, E. D. Educational intervention at home by mothers of disadvantaged infants. *Child Development*, 1970, **41**, 925–935.

Kirk, S. A., McCarthy, J. J., & Kirk, W. D. *Examiner's manual: Illinois test of psycholinguistic abilities*. (Rev. ed.) Urbana, Ill.: University of Illinois Press, 1968.

Klaus, R. A., & Gray, S. W. *The early training project for disadvantaged children: A report after five years*. Monographs of the Society for Research in Child Development, 1968, **33** (Serial No. 120).

LaCivita, A., Kean, J. M., & Yamamoto, K. Socio-economic status of children and acquisition of grammar. *Journal of Educational Research*, 1966, **60**, 71–74.

Loban, W. Language proficiency and school learning. In J. D. Krumboltz (Ed.), *Learning and the educational process*. Chicago: Rand McNally, 1965. Pp. 113–131.

McCarthy, J., & Kirk, S. *Examiner's manual: Illinois test of psycholinguistic abilities* (experimental edition). Champaign, Ill.: University of Illinois Press, 1961.

McNeil, J. D. *The ABC learning activity: Language of instruction.* New York: American Book, 1966.

McNeill, D. The development of language. In P. H. Mussen (Ed.), *Manual of child psychology*, Vol. 1. (3rd. ed.) New York: Wiley, 1970. Pp. 1061–1161.

Miller, G. A., & Isard, S. Some perceptual consequences of linguistic rules. *Journal of Verbal Learning and Verbal Behavior*, 1963, **2**, 217–228.

Osborn, J. Teaching a teaching language to disadvantaged children. In M. A. Brottman (Ed.), *Language remediation for the disadvantaged preschool child.* Monographs of the Society for Research in Child Development, 1968, **33** (Serial No. 124), 36–48.

Osgood, C. E. Motivational dynamics of language behavior. In M. R. Jones (Ed.), *Nebraska symposium on motivation.* Lincoln: University of Nebraska Press, 1957. Pp. 348–424. (a)

Osgood, C. E. A behavioristic analysis. In *Contemporary approaches to cognition.* Cambridge, Mass.: Harvard University Press, 1957. (b)

Osser, H. The syntactic structures of five-year-old culturally deprived children. Paper presented at Eastern Psychological Association Annual Meeting, New York, 1966.

Raven, J. C. *Psychological principles appropriate to social and clinical problems.* London: H. K. Lewis, 1966.

Rosenberg, S. Problems of language development in the retarded. Paper presented at the Peabody-NIH Conference on Social-Cultural Aspects of Mental Retardation, Nashville, Tennessee, 1968.

Rosenthal, R., & Jacobson, L. Teacher expectations for the disadvantaged. *Scientific American*, 1968, **218**, 19–23.

Sattler, J. M. Racial experimenter effects in experimentation, testing, and psychotherapy. *Psychological Bulletin*, 1970, **73**, 137–160.

Shriner, T. H. A review of mean length of response as a measure of expressive language development in children. *Journal of Speech and Hearing Disorders*, 1969, **34**, 61–68.

Shriner, T. H., & Miner, L. Morphological structures in the language of disadvantaged and advantaged children. *Journal of Speech and Hearing Research*, 1968, **11**, 605–610.

Smith, M. E. A study of some factors influencing the development of the sentence in preschool children. *Journal of Genetic Psychology*, 1935, **46**, 182–212.

Stodolsky, S. Maternal behavior and language and concept formation in Negro preschool children: An inquiry into process. Unpublished doctoral dissertation, Department of Psychology, University of Chicago, 1965.

Stodolsky, S., & Lesser, G. Learning patterns in the disadvantaged. *Harvard Educational Review*, 1967, **37**, 546–593.

Strandberg, T. E. An evaluation of three stimulus media for evoking verbalizations from preschool children. Unpublished master's thesis, Eastern Illinois University, 1969.

Templin, M. C. *Certain language skills in children: Their development and interrelationships.* Minneapolis: University of Minnesota Press, 1957.

Templin, M. C., & Darley, F. *The Templin-Darley tests of articulation.* Iowa, City: Bureau of Educational Research, State University of Iowa, 1960.

Terman, L. M., & Merrill, M. A. *Stanford-Binet intelligence scale.* Boston: Houghton Mifflin, 1960.

Wechsler, D. *WISC manual.* New York: The Psychological Corporation, 1949.

Weikhart, D. P. *Preschool intervention: A preliminary report of the Perry preschool project.* Ann Arbor, Mich.: Campus Publishers, 1967.

FURTHER READING

Brottman, M. A. (Ed.) *Language remediation for the disadvantaged preschool child.* Monographs of the Society for Research in Child Development, 1968, **33** (Serial No. 124).

Marckwardt, A. H. (Ed.) *Linguistics in school programs.* Chicago: National Society for the Study of Education, 1970.

Rist, R. C. Student social class and teacher expectations: The self-fulfilling prophecy in ghetto education. *Harvard Educational Review,* 1970, **40,** 411–451.

Williams, F. *Language and poverty.* Chicago: Markham Publishing Company, 1970.

APPENDIX
Exploring the Language of Children

Young children are not the docile experimental subjects that rats and college students are. This is part of their charm. Long, tedious, rigid experimental procedures are simply not feasible. As a result, many of the experiments discussed in this book are easy to repeat. Such replication is valuable for two reasons: first, because many of the findings are surprising in themselves, either because the child is more capable than might have been thought — Berko's study (see Chapter 7, this book) of the productive use of morphological endings, for example — or because the child is less capable — Carol Chomsky's finding (see Chapter 4, this book) that the sentences of the form *The doll is easy to see* are systematically misinterpreted, for example. Second, because there are remarkable similarities that hold among children in many cases, especially similarities of sequence.

Projects that I have asked students to undertake fall into two categories: experimental investigations, in which each student tests one child, and naturalistic observation and analysis of the child's speech. The following general instructions are given (with thanks to Helen Bee, Ken Kaye, and other colleagues) for each project:

> These projects are designed to give you an opportunity to work with individual children and to gain some understanding of the way children operate in simple situations. In addition, they are designed to give you a chance, collectively, to "check" the results of some of the studies discussed earlier. Effectively, we will be doing replications of studies in the area of language development.

GENERAL TESTING INSTRUCTIONS

> Once you have obtained permission, you should arrange a time (or two times if necessary) when it is possible for you and your subject to be more or less alone in some room. It is much better if the parents or siblings are not present. Tell the child you want him to play some games with you and that you want him to try as hard as he can. Often, if you introduce yourself as a student and tell the child you are doing this for school work, you can get excellent cooperation. Follow the instructions given as closely as possible. If you feel you *must* deviate in some way, do so, but indicate this in your report and indicate how and why you changed

the procedure. If the child's attention seems to be wandering, you may of course stop the testing and chat or play with the child for a period of time. If necessary (and this is particularly likely with the younger children), break the testing into two sessions, to be given on different days. Do *not* force the child to do anything he does not want to do. You may urge and encourage if he is resistant, but do not force him. The subject should always have the right to terminate the testing if he does not want to continue.

Afterward, show the parents the child's answers and tell them that as far as you know the responses were typical of children his age. You might suggest that they try asking the child some of the same questions in a year or two and note the differences. If the parents seem surprised at the fact, for example, that their four-year-old child cannot identify someone else's left and right hands, you might mention that adults often overestimate how much children of this age know. Do not attempt to diagnose the child as an individual, and do not say anything that an anxious parent might construe as a judgment of the relative intelligence of the child.

PARENTAL PERMISSION

You *must* get the signature of one of the child's parents *before* you question the child. The reason for this is an ethical one: you are invading the family's privacy. Even though what you are doing cannot harm the child or the parents, they might think that it can, and the harm will have been done.

Children are not laboratory animals, they are people, and you have a responsibility to act maturely, as a professional. Each child has the right to refuse to participate, and his parents have the right to refuse to let you question him, at *any* point in the interview. If you do not complete the procedure with a particular child, indicate why in your report, make a copy of the blank data sheet, and find another subject.

You should explain to the parent that you are a student taking a course about children. Assure him that the project is for your own training, that the results will not be used for any other purpose, and that you are not studying individual children or comparing one child with another but, rather, are trying to learn about the things that are true of all children. Then let him (or her) read the signature form and sign it.

Parental permission form.

_____ has my permission to ask questions of my child _____ as part of a class project at the University of _____. I understand that the results of this observation will be used only for the purpose of training students to become good observers and interviewers of children, and that my child is not being compared with other children on an individual basis. The student has adequately explained the nature of the questions to be asked.

(signed) _____

(date)   _____

"Mini Experiments"

Only a handful of experiments for replication are suggested below. New experiments are constantly appearing in the literature, and the instructor should keep an eye out for techniques suitable for class projects. As a general rule, sheets should be prepared and duplicated for each student which indicate explicitly what is to be said and shown to the child and on which the child's responses may be recorded.

1. MORPHOLOGICAL DEVELOPMENT

This experiment is suitable for children in the three- to eight-year-old range. The experimenter attempts to elicit a correct plural or past tense form from the child using pictures. Nonsense words are used, to insure that successful production represents the functioning of a productive rule rather than repetition of a previously heard form. There is one item for each of the three primary plural forms (the s of *cats*, the z of *dogs*, and the *ez* of *glasses*) and one item for each of the three primary past tense forms (the t of *walked*, the d of *hugged*, and the *ed* of *wedded*).

The pictures to be used in the examples for plural should have the following form:

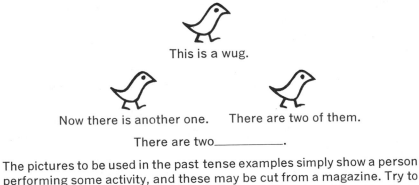

This is a wug.

Now there is another one.   There are two of them.

There are two_____.

The pictures to be used in the past tense examples simply show a person performing some activity, and these may be cut from a magazine. Try to find pictures of people doing things that the children would not be likely to have a name for. Swinging objects, doing exercises, and operating machinery are some ideas. Put the pictures and drawings on 4-by-6 inch cards or other conveniently sized card. In the drawings to be done for the plurals, pictures of animals can be used if the child does not already know the word, or any kind of fanciful creature can be drawn. One creature can be on one side of a card and the two creatures on the other, or both can be on the same side, or whatever seems most convenient.

Before the experiment proper, there will be two practice items with similar words. Prepare cards for one past tense and one plural item in the same way as described above but make sure the activity and the object are things the child would know (and that they have *regular* past tense and plural forms).

Procedure: Give the trials in the following order, using the verbal presentation given below as an example.

Practice Trials

A. Plural. One object, and then two. "This is a ____ (appropriate name). Now there are two of them. (Point to picture of two objects.) There are two _____ (wait for response).

B. Past tense. "This is a man who knows how to _____ (appropriate verb). He is _____ing. He did the same thing yesterday. What did he do yesterday? Yesterday he _____ (wait for response).

Experimental Trials

1. Plural (z). "This is a wug. Now there is another one. There are two of them. There are two _____."

2. Past tense (t). "This is a man who knows how to rick. He is ricking. He did the same thing yesterday. What did he do yesterday? Yesterday he _____."

3. Plural (ez). "This is a gutch. Now there is another one. There are two of them. There are two _____."

4. Past tense (d). "This is a man who knows how to gling. He is glinging. He did the same thing yesterday. What did he do yesterday? Yesterday he _____."

5. Plural (s) "This is a zat. Now there is another one. There are two of them. There are two _____."

6. Past tense (ed). "This is a man who knows how to mot. He is motting. He did the same thing yesterday. What did he do yesterday? Yesterday he _____."

Scoring: Listen carefully to what the child says in each case, and classify it as one of the following:

Incorrect: no sound added (for example, giving the plural the same as the singular).

Incorrect: something added, but not the right sound.
Correct: correct plural or past tense.

2. THE MEANING OF "LEFT" AND "RIGHT"

This experiment is suitable for children between four and seven. Ask the child to show you his left hand and then his right hand. Next, while facing the child, ask him to point to *your* left hand and then *your* right hand.

3. COMPREHENSION OF SYNTACTIC FORMS

One of the best ways to explore the child's comprehension is to ask him to demonstrate the action described in a sentence with dolls or other toys. Bellugi-Klima (in press) has suggested a variety of such comprehension tests, and undoubtedly more can be constructed. Many of these tests may be attempted with children as young as two and a half. The general procedure is to place the objects on the table before the child, identify them, and demonstrate the action. This is done so that the only contribution the child must make is the translation of syntactic form into action. The simplest test is of active sentences. Place a toy cat and a toy dog on the table and ask the child to show "the dog chases the cat" and conversely (though not necessarily consecutively).

Before the possessive inflection appears in children's speech, they appear to produce possessive constructions — for example, *mommy dress*. Comprehension of the possessive may be tested by showing the child a small boy doll and a larger man doll (identifying the former as the son and the latter as the father) and asking him to point to "the boy's daddy" and then "the daddy's boy."

Understanding of singular and plural endings on nouns and verbs may be tested by showing the child two girl dolls lying down and asking the child to show "the girl walks" and "the girls walk."

Reflexive pronouns, as in *He hurt himself*, do not appear in children's speech until a late period. Comprehension of reflexives may be tested by showing the child two dolls and a washcloth, demonstrating the action of washing, and asking the child to show "John washed him" and "John washed himself."

Passive sentences are not only late in appearing in the child's speech, they seem not to be comprehended before age four or so. They may be tested by the same method used for active sentences: ask the child to show "the cat is chased by the dog" and "the dog is chased by the cat."

Other test items may be obtained from Bellugi-Klima (in press), Fraser, Bellugi, and Brown (1963), and Carrow (1968).

4. THE "EASY TO SEE" CONSTRUCTION

This experiment is suitable for children between four and eight. Place a blindfolded doll on the table in front of the child. Ask, "Is this doll easy to see or hard to see?" If the child responds, "Easy to see," ask "Would you make her hard to see?" (End of experiment). If the child responds "Hard to see," ask "Would you make her easy to see?" Then ask, "Why was she hard to see in the beginning? What did you do to make her easier to see?"

Analysis of Spontaneous Speech

Despite the problems of drawing inferences about children's linguistic competence from studies of their productions (discussed in Chapters 2, 4, and 5), one of the most enlightening exercises that can be undertaken is the observation and analysis of a child's free speech. It is difficult to specify a suitable age. The child should be producing at least a moderate quantity of multiword utterances, sufficiently clearly that the observer (perhaps with the help of the child's mother) can identify the words. However, the child should not be too advanced, or the analysis will be impossible with a small corpus. Three and a half to four is probably the upper limit, although two to three is the optimum range.

At least one hundred utterances should be collected, preferably more. Single-word utterances should be excluded, unless they are of particular interest for some other reason. The number of morphemes in each utterance should be counted, and a mean length of utterance (MLU) computed. Counting morphemes in child speech is easier than in adult speech, since many complexities of morphology do not appear, but difficulties do arise. The most serious is the problem of contractions, such as *that's* and *can't*. These consist of two morphemes in adult English. However, if a child does not produce both *can* and *can't* or does not produce both *that* and *that's*, there is little evidence for assuming that the compound actually consists of two morphemes. Ideally, the observer should look over the entire corpus and decide if two independent units are being combined or if the word is a single morpheme. However, no serious error will be introduced if such words are analyzed as if they are two morphemes in every case. The MLU resulting will be a slight overestimate of the true MLU.

If the MLU is not over about 2.0, it is feasible to attempt to describe the linguistic system as a whole. If the MLU is longer, the system is likely to be too complex for this task; instead, specific subsystems such as negations, questions, or noun phrases may be analyzed. The formalism used for this purpose is not important; the goal is to describe the kinds of combinations of words that can occur and the constraints on the order of words in such combinations. The first task is to describe the surface structure of the child's sentences. For those children who have advanced to the point where a distinction between deep and surface structure is appropriate (for example, the later stages in the development of questions), an attempt can be made to specify the transformations and the deep structures on which they operate. Specific linguistic features can be scored — for example, use of *be* as an auxiliary, use of *do* as an auxiliary, inversion of auxiliary and subject in questions, and so on — and a "scalogram" analysis performed to identify the sequence development through which the children appear to be moving. A scalogram analysis amounts to asking, for each pair of linguistic features A and B, "Does one always appear before the other"; that is, "Are there children who have achieved A but not B, but not children who have achieved B but not A?" In addition, correlations can be computed between MLU and the appearance of each linguistic feature (point biserial coefficients, described in Edwards, 1969, are appropriate). To the extent that such correlations are high, MLU is a good single indicator of linguistic maturity.

An interesting extension of this investigation is to compare the child's imitations with his spontaneous speech, which is a partial replication of Ervin's (1964) research. For any half dozen or so features of interest, one or more sentences should be prepared in advance. After the spontaneous speech has been collected, ask the child to "Say what I say." For example, *I see John's ball* tests the possessive and *The boy can see a cow* tests the use of *can*, a model auxiliary. Almost any linguistic feature can be tested in this way, although it is extremely difficult to get a child to imitate a question. The tendency to simply answer the question is almost irresistible. For each feature, the child should be scored as having or not having mastery in the spontaneous speech (this judgment should be based on the corpus as a whole, and not simply on the question "Does the child *ever* produce the form") and as having imitated it or not. The chi-square statistic (Edwards, 1969) can be used to measure the agreement between the two kinds of performance.

SELECTED REFERENCES

Bellugi-Klima, U. Some language comprehension tests. In C. Lavatelli (Ed.), *Language training in early childhood education.* Champaign, Ill.: University of Illinois Press, 1971.

Carrow, M. A. The development of auditory comprehension of language structure in children. *Journal of Speech and Hearing Disorders*, 1968, **33,** 99–111.

Edwards, A. L. *Statistical Analysis.* (3rd ed.) New York: Holt, Rinehart and Winston, 1969.

Ervin, S. Imitation and structural change in children's language. In E. H. Lenneberg (Ed.), *New directions in the study of language.* Cambridge, Mass.: M.I.T. Press, 1964.

Fraser, C., Bellugi, U., & Brown, R. Control of grammar in imitation, comprehension, and production. *Journal of Verbal Learning and Verbal Behavior*, 1963, **2,** 121–135.

Indexes

Subject Index

Author Index